CAREER MOVIES

CAREER

American

Business and

the Success

Mystique

MOVIES

JACK BOOZER

 UNIVERSITY OF TEXAS PRESS, AUSTIN

This book is dedicated to my father Jack Sr. — who was an outstanding university teacher and leader, a progressive moral activist, and a minister to the community — as well as to my mother Ruth — who has brought a love of life and the arts of dance and music to me and thousands of others.

Requests for permission to reproduce material from this work should be sent to Permissions, University of Texas Press, P.O. Box 7819, Austin, TX 78713-7819.

∞ The paper used in this book meets the minimum requirements of ANSI/NISO Z39.48-1992 (R1997) (Permanence of Paper).

LIBRARY OF CONGRESS CATALOGING-IN-PUBLICATION DATA

Boozer, Jack, 1944–
    Career movies : American business and the success mystique / by Jack Boozer.
        p.   cm.
Includes bibliographical references and index.
    ISBN 0-292-70911-0 (alk. paper) — ISBN 0-292-70912-9 (pbk. : alk. paper)
    1. Business in motion pictures.   2. Motion pictures—United States.   I. Title.
PN1995.9.B87 B66   2002
791.43'655—dc21

                                                    2002002336

CONTENTS

ACKNOWLEDGMENTS

This project was supported by a book initiation grant from Georgia State University and by three summer grants from the Department of Communication at Georgia State. I am also indebted to my wife Pamela, who not only put up with my book-related schedule over the last few years, but was kind enough to read over the manuscript, give useful advice, and proofread.

I was further aided over time by the wise counsel of my friend and former colleague Frank Tomasulo. Graduate assistants at Georgia have also been helpful, including particularly Timothy Burchfield. Other grad assistants who have made contributions include Miglena Sandmeier, Jeremy Wilson, and Redelia Shaw. Editor Jim Burr and the staff at the University of Texas Press also deserve high praise for their patience and many contributions along the way to bring this book to fruition.

CAREER MOVIES

At least I don't measure a man's success by the size of his wallet.

—CARL FOX TO SON BUD IN *Wall Street*

Now you're not naive enough to think we're living in a democracy are you, buddy? It's a free market and you're part of it.

—GORDON GEKKO TO BUD FOX IN *Wall Street*

INTRODUCTION

The two clips of dialogue above, which are taken from director/co-writer Oliver Stone's 1987 film, suggest issues that are critical to American career ideology as it has functioned under a capitalist system. In *Wall Street*, college graduate Bud Fox (Charlie Sheen) must choose between the opposing economic viewpoints and character of two paternal figures: his father, Carl (Martin Sheen), who represents a tradition of lifetime corporate service; and his chosen hero Gordon Gekko (Michael Douglas), who represents the Reaganomics decade of deregulation, greed, and profiteering scams. Bud's dilemma for his time also highlights a prime concern of this book, which addresses the way characters in Hollywood business films define themselves and their career success in light of their given social and ideological contexts. Business career life has been central to American experience, and Hollywood has produced so many significant films on the subject that they deserve special consideration in their own right. Looking back, business films can be seen to reflect great shifts in economic and technological conditions, and thus attitudes toward career. Following the Great Depression in the 1930s, and the World War II era of personal sacrifice and industrial expansion in the 1940s, America gave birth to a new age of corporate culture based in mediated promotionalism and mass consumerism. This study concerns those American corporate and entrepreneurial business films released between 1945 and 2001 that focus on culturally significant middle-class careers and their relationship to personal and national growth and meaning.

Historically, this important body of films represents the way business has provided individuals with opportunities and challenges, but has also at times left them in distress, disillusionment, and alienation. The ever-present American Dream of increased affluence through hard work is obviously not guaranteed, any more than business career advancement and monetary success is necessarily indicative of personal fulfillment. Because of often conflicting public and private views of success, one can find fulfillment in a career or calling that may appear to society as financially unrewarding, or be financially successful in a career that leaves one indifferent, unhappy, ethically compromised, or like Bud Fox, legally culpable. On the individual level, work fulfillment can be seen to require first of all opportunity, but also commitment to the correct career choice, to the correct career approach in a given setting, and to the ability to find satisfaction in one's accomplishments. Bud Fox chooses Gordon Gekko as his mentor and boss despite his awareness of the man's legal transgressions. Bud bathes in the financial power and celebrity of Gekko's public notoriety right up to the point that the young man is arrested on felony charges by the Securities and Exchange Commission. Bud's rapid career rise under Gekko is short-lived simply because he just happens to get caught for overstepping a thin line between legal and criminal business activity. This also makes Bud's legal come-uppance less than reassuring, even though he manages to provide state's evidence against Gekko. Oliver Stone's morality tale is finally less concerned with legal retribution than with the troubling reality of a widely accepted model of success that is increasingly characterized by predatory attitudes and behavior. Through Gekko, the film evokes the enduring appeal of audaciously ego-centered money power. The seductiveness of this personal empowerment myth represented by Gekko captivates Bud and, by association, American youth generally, further distancing individual career success from links with family and community.

Bud's two fatherly career models in *Wall Street* also represent a 1980s version of a conflict that has always existed in American business That conflict is between *laissez-faire* enterprise entirely free of government oversight, and business that is sufficiently regulated by government to actively prevent the kinds of financial and social abuses that are demonstrated by Gekko here. President Reagan's fiscal policy in the 1980s preached the indirect, "trickle-down" benefits of private, Darwinian

11 *Wall Street* (1987).
Bud Fox (Charlie Sheen) listens to the advice of wealthy and powerful corporate raider Gordon Gekko (Michael Douglas, bottom) rather than to his father (Martin Sheen), the lifetime corporate employee.

business success in a "deregulated" marketplace. His policy showed little interest in the fate of employees, patrons, and even the economic health of the government, which was rapidly finding itself awash in debt at a time of growing unemployment. A primary issue in Stone's film is that Bud's commercial urban milieu has already taught him to be awed by publicly recognized financial power figures such as Gekko, rather than by less visible but no less dedicated salaried workers like his father. Bud's father is strong, but he is already overmatched by the me-diated consumer images Bud is heir to. Bud's experience with private enterprise suggests that societies which reify narrow business values inevitably run the risk of breeding a cynical youth for their work force.[1]

From Gekko, the audacious corporate raider, Bud gets the self-centered, no-holds-barred fever of business as war,[2] while Bud's father, Carl, empitomizes success through long-term allegiance to his col-leagues and his company in relation to the quality of their public ser-vice. But Carl's devoted role as an airline technical manager and labor rep, for whom the issues of company working conditions, salary, and pension are primary, already appears to his son to be outdated and class-bound. Carl also admonishes Bud to consider the quieter satisfactions of building a business on his own, which could provide a service and make a contribution rather than simply feeding off the work and problems of others. But this too falls on deaf ears. What captivates Bud is Gekko's flashy style in hostile corporate takeovers, which grab headlines and boost his authority image in direct correlation with his profit margins. Gekko trains Bud in his methods, which include the kinds of securi-ties manipulation and bogus investment schemes that were hitting front page news at the time. This film's timeliness was proven by an event immediately prior to its public release date—the Black Friday stock market disaster in October of 1987. This crash occurred in an atmo-sphere of junk bond supported corporate buyouts, insider trading, and poor investment and lending practices, particularly at underregulated Savings and Loan institutions across the country.

Major Hollywood studio directors prior to Oliver Stone have been especially aware of the central role American business plays in everyday life and in the nation's political economic ideology. This role is promi-nently featured in classical-era films beginning in the 1940s such as Orson Welles's *Citizen Kane* (1941) and *The Magnificent Ambersons* (1942), Frank Capra's *Meet John Doe* (1941) and *It's a Wonderful Life* (1946), How-ard Hawks's *His Girl Friday* (1940) and *Red River* (1948), and Douglas Sirk's *All That Heaven Allows* (1955) and *Written on the Wind* (1957). Many other important studio-era directors including Billy Wilder, Martin Ritt, Elia Kazan, and Alfred Hitchcock also feature business concerns in a sizable proportion of their film output. In Bordwell, Staiger and Thompson's study of classical Hollywood films, they go so far as to recognize "in the goal-oriented protagonist a reflection of an ideology of American individualism and enterprise," which lends itself to "a rigorous chain of cause and effect."[3] Social advancement through individualist enterprise, therefore, may be recognized as an impulse that is aligned with the very definition of film character identity and plot structure in the age of Hollywood studio cinema and in American film generally. But it is the business career film that most directly represents the nature and practice of American economic ambition as it most frequently and significantly exists in commercial and mercantile activity.

Since the 1950s and the close of the classical era in film, America has seen an accelerated pace of economic and technological change, and middle-class business experience and attitudes have changed along with it. Business films of the transitional Hollywood cinema period, which begins in the 1960s and runs through the 1970s, reflected a national trend of conscious, resistant attitudes toward racism, misogyny, the Vietnam War, and "the establishment" of big business as well as big government. These films often have narratives involving personal and institutional failure or collapse whether they are focused on entrepreneurial (*The Apprenticeship of Duddy Kravitz*, 1974, *Save The Tiger*, 1977), or corporate endeavors (*Network*, 1976, *The China Syndrome*, 1979). Business films of the 1980s and 1990s further suggest that the affluent consumer society based in the notion of endless corporate expansion and conglomeration was not eliminating serious social problems, but showing a tendency rather to constantly create them. This appears due in part to the raised expectations created by promotional consumerism, where each generation has been encouraged to exceed the material expectations of the preceding one. In *Wall Street*, Bud initially explains to his father why the maintenance of his expected lifestyle image now makes it impossible for him to live off only $50,000 a year. Bud Fox is hence the creation of a promotional culture that encourages the kinds of quick fix business ambitions and immediate gratification that can create a growing debt against the future. *Wall Street* is predicative first of later film homages to aggressive business cynicism in films such as *Boiler Room* (2000), and secondly of very current realities such as the late-2001 auditing scandal and bankruptcy of the giant Enron Corporation discussed at the conclusion of this book.

The sheer variety and cultural relevance of business films in the 1980s and 1990s are further testimony to their significance. Colin Higgins's broad comedy *Nine to Five* (1980) dramatizes the assertion of new women's issues in the corporate office setting; John Landis's comedy *Trading Places* (1983) wryly comments on big speculative capitalism in relation to homeless poverty and race; Francis Ford Coppola's *Tucker: The Man and His Dream* (1988) looks back to show the fate of an inventive and safety-conscious postwar entrepreneur forced to take on the entire Detroit auto industry; Barry Levinson's *Disclosure* (1994) considers the vulnerability of the individual business manager in an environment of political (gender) correctness and litigation, global labor markets, and high-tech company mergers; Cameron Crowe's *Jerry Maguire* (1996) demonstrates the hard road of an individual sports agent vying against big corporate competition; and Michael Mann's *The Insider* (1999) traces the difficult role of a corporate executive who becomes a whistle-blower against Big Tobacco. In all of these comedic or dramatic narratives, a struggling entrepreneur or corporate worker stands against superior business odds and wins some concessions but little or no significant power. For ultimately what these recent examples convey is the possibility of somehow holding the most exploitative elements of corporate capitalism at bay while trying to preserve one's personal integrity and a meaningful career life at the same time. This is the primary dilemma in most of the business career films to be discussed here. Other than through the psychosocial dynamics of family life, but also closely related to them, it is through gainful employment that the protagonist's career desires and ethics, as well as America's potent success myth, are most realistically tested.

FROM AMERICAN DREAM TO SUCCESS MYSTIQUE

The nation's entrepreneurial and corporate success ethic has been understood to act in tandem with a democratic idealism, although the realities of American democracy have not always meant equal opportunity for all of its peoples. More specifically, the nation's almost religious devotion to individual self-initiative in work as a ticket to upward mobility has been an unrealistic expectation for certain disenfranchised groups, including those trapped in restrictive cycles of poverty, racism, and/or gender and ethnic discrimination. But for the greater middle class since the end of World War II, the belief in economic mobility through devotion to business careers has nevertheless continued to define mainstream American ideology. A simple formula for career success (cs) would see it as equal to career attainment (ca), which is defined largely by society, over career fulfillment (cf), which is defined largely by the individual, or cs = ca/cf. This equation assumes, of course, that career attainment may in some cases be qualified by the degree of self-fulfillment in any final determination of career success. The difficulty of balancing society's dominant economic view of career attainment with one's personal sense of career fulfillment remains a common theme in the business career film.

This is the case in Arthur Miller's revealing Pulitzer Prize–winning play, *Death of a Salesman,* in 1949, which, explicitly addresses career problems with the American Dream. The play had long and successful runs in and outside the United States, and was adapted twice to film, first by Laslo Benedek in 1951, and then by Volker Schlörndorff in 1985. This drama is certainly America's most well known cultural investigation into the mythic force of the traditional success dream for its time. Benedek's earlier film version, with Fredric March as traveling salesman Willy Loman, conveys, like the play, the personal anguish that can result from an overdependence on a public success image. Willy lives the hail-fellow-well-met style of success in his mind, increasingly overlooking the discontinuities and contradictions that separate him ever further from honest personal fulfillment. Willy is ironically seduced by that very promissory status world that he solicits as a regional salesman. Willy's response to personal job failure along the way is *not* to live closer to reality and to readjust his views of himself, his family, and his career, but rather to persist more vigorously in his *rhetorical* affirmation of his personal and career performance and ideology. The schism between Willy's inflated perceptions of success and his work and family reality thus becomes a chasm. Increasingly, his career failures belie his inflated self-image. The mainstream success dream becomes a self-defeating phantom precisely because Willy allows the image rather than the essence of self-fulfillment to drive him. The significance of this is not so much that Willy is a failure as an individual because he has permitted himself to be misled, but that the seductive power of the Dream invites failure because the social pressures to at least *appear* successful are so great. Defending the intent of his work in the introduction to his *Collected Plays* in 1957, Miller writes that "Willy Loman has broken a law . . . which says that a failure in society and business has no right to live." Willy becomes trapped in the success image because there is no alternative measure of esteem, no recognized optional course of dignity to help in times of economic failure.

The American success dream is shown to be most destructive where it is most fully embraced as the image-obsessed consumer ideal that it has largely been allowed to become. In these terms, Benedek's film, following closely the theme of Miller's play, poses an American middle-class tragedy based on an increasingly warped version of that personal initiative that America has so long celebrated. As if caught up in the Dale Carnegie view of success offered in his 1936 best-seller, *How to Win Friends and Influence People*—a boosterist methodology for "getting ahead"—Willy Loman, who is past 60 years of age, believes that being well liked equates with being financially sound. But his other-directedness also separates him from his own particular strengths and talents. It is only when he is no longer supported by his employer of 34 years that he first begins to recognize that he never "accomplished something" worthy beyond his own mythical self-promotion. Just prior to Willy's final act of suicide, his oldest son Biff stands before their help-less family and pleads with his oblivious father: "Dad, will you take the phony dream and burn it before something happens?"

By the mid-1950s, the entrenched model of the white middle-class family with the father at work and the mother overseeing the home was under assault on a variety of fronts. And Hollywood's trend in "social problem" films made this amply apparent at the time. (See, for example, Martin Ritt's *No Down Payment* [1957].) The traditional family that had restricted the woman to domestic affairs was going to be tested by single women already devoted to their own businesses (*The Revolt of Mamie Stover,* 1956). Additionally, the demands of racial and ethnic minorities for equal rights in work and society were also being fore-grounded in major films (see *Imitation of Life* [1959] and *Giant* [1956]). In the new corporate environment of professional management, too, the trend toward bureaucratization was increasingly perplexing if not counterproductive (*The Solid Gold Cadillac,* 1956). In all these arenas, a shared definition of the American Dream was becoming harder to define.

Materially speaking, the success dream was realized for great num-bers of middle-class whites in the affluent 1950s, but it also proved un-stable and fleeting. In the three decades that followed World War II, from 1945 to 1965, America's economy became more privatized and bent on the notion of individual success and consumer status. The idea of the American career success dream—a fantasy of wealth and happiness through personal advancement and material attainment— also became increasingly externalized into consumer image terms. It grew more self-conscious, competitively isolating, and contentious— a dream that was growing more fragmented and less attached to a common purpose. The externalized and splintered new version of the American success dream could thus henceforth more accurately be described as a "success mystique." A growing promotional industry was beginning to displace the ownership of personal goals with its own promises and dream images. In the process, the individual's search for the most appropriate career path seems to have become yet more troubled (*The Arrangement,* 1969). The new success mystique concerns wealth and attainment just like the old dream, but as the business career film now began to imply, the mystique also involves an added awareness of the ecstacy and defeat of highly individualized consumer competition, and of certain business and government attitudes and practices that were actually causing a decline in the overall quality of life (*China-town,* 1974).

In its unique focus on the working details of commercial enterprise and individual career identity, therefore, the history of this film form offers useful insights into important changes in the individual workplace experience, and its association with subtle changes in the larger success ideology. That so many major Hollywood films fall into the business career category reflects significantly on America's devotion to commercial interests as they have come increasingly to dominate individual, family, and political life.

DEFINING THE GENRE AND OTHER THEORETICAL APPROACHES

It is largely because of the enduring prevalence of business career cinema and its direct links with economic and increasingly technological changes and political ideology that it deserves historical consideration as a genre. Genre study is informed by a strong interest in the practical cultural contexts of films, and it is aided here in particular by sociological, psychoanalytic, and progressive postmodernist considerations. These concerns will necessarily include, then, where appropriate, specific issues that touch on class desire, gender roles, racial/ethnic positioning, and the increasing role of communications media. In addition to film genre scholars, the social, psychoanalytic, and ideological theorists to be included here range from C. Wright Mills and Peter Biskind in the Hollywood classical era, through Raymond Williams, Nancy Chodorow, and Christopher Lasch, to the recent practical sociological theory of Paul du Gay. Current scholarly perspectives such as those of Doug Kellner are also included that look to Postmodernism and the metatheory of Jean Baudrillard and further address issues of subjectivity reception, and agency in today's media technocracy.

Any proposal for recognition of generic status requires its categorical identification by several means: through a grouping of representative texts and their basic, distinguishing genre characteristics; through an historical overview of a genre's longevity and variations over time; and through considerations of already available theoretical and critical methods for recognizing film genre as a body of texts operating within a cultural field of production, exhibition, and reception. I will briefly address each of these genre concerns here.

While it is obvious that the drive for career success also plays a significant role in movies about labor or the professions, much of what I say here might apply to them, I believe the business genre is the dominant career category in its overall cultural and ideological significance. The other career areas which I have had to exclude in the process of tracing the business genre's parameters might therefore be considered important subcategories in relation to the larger business career domain. I have left out labor films and their preoccupation with labor and management issues, not because they are unimportant, but because they have been previously addressed by other scholars and generally do not demonstrate the same issues found in white-collar business films. I have also excluded films involving the professions, because they too have their own immediate categories of concerns which tend to take precedence over, or at least alter in special ways, the problems that are typical of strictly commercial pursuits. Hence, films involving the practice of medicine, psychiatry, law, journalism, and education, among others, all reflect a body of considerations that are unique to those areas and hence beyond the scope of business issues treated here. In films about the professions, issues of conformity or resistance to particular professional standards tend to predominate. This also applies to police/detective and artist/performer texts. Artist/performer films, for example (*All About Eve,* or the three versions of *A Star is Born*), typically offer very direct accounts of career experience, but their public performance and celebrity aspects are removed from the everyday world of most insider business practice. It is the direct and fully dominant profit orientation of private enterprise—and again its lack of universally defined professional career guidelines—that sets it apart.

A diachronic overview of genre also remains essential as a way to trace genealogical variations and transformations, as well as periods of cultural indifference. The prevalence of specialized film clusters and recurring cycles within a genre's unfolding history can provide important indicators of genre validity and significance, as well as useful signs of genre flexibility and sensitivity to specific cultural trends. Primary among these for the business career film is the basic textual distinction that must be made between entrepreneurial and corporate endeavor, since different expectations and structures of experience apply to each one. This is also true for gender issues in commercial enterprise. These two kinds of categorical distinctions remain salient concerns throughout this study.

Business career cinema also satisfies the defining characteristics of most other genres which are recognized at least in part by their protagonists' occupations, as well as by their settings, iconography, and narrative focus.[4] The typical small business entrepreneur or white collar corporate figure considered here usually has managerial status and spends considerable time in offices or serendipitous business locations. This central character is also typically dressed for the job and organized around a relevant work etiquette and schedule. It is the protagonist's endeavor predominantly in the business workplace that most often provides this genre's defining characteristic. The struggle for upward job mobility further provides a common plot formula focused largely on issues of economic status. Business films are all about the basic ambitions, methods, and ethics of an individual's career quest, in relation both to a particular company of employ and to America's larger success myth.

The business career genre also demonstrates a comfortable fit with theory and criticism that has sought to define how genres are constituted relative to their individual texts as well as to their wider cultural recognition as a category. Writing in *Genre,* Steven Neale sees film genres as not simply groupings of similar texts but as "systems of orientations, expectations and conventions that circulate between industry, text and subject."[5] American cinema viewers have generally been so thoroughly acquainted with business life that it is often taken for granted in the promotional and consumer discourse that surrounds these films. References to business career struggles are not uncommon in Hollywood's film advertising or in critical journalistic and academic reviews. The centrality of business enterprise to America's version of success ideology, however, has not been widely investigated, particularly as an historical generic category. Borrowing from the vocabulary of semiotics, Rick Altman has noted that genres are a familiar "field of language/image paradigms that exist in a syntax of particular myths and rituals."[6] The business career film has special resonance here because it is formulated as a narrative of career pursuit (the story content or "semantic" field), where the individual is ritualistically tested against the particular demands of a business institution and/or marketplace for the right to advancement and mythical success (the cultural "syntax").

For Thomas Schatz, genre films are further loaded with "value-laden narrative conventions." Schatz elaborates on the genre film's ritual, mythic function: "In its ritualistic capacity, a film genre transforms certain fundamental contradictions and conflicts into a unique conceptual structure that is familiar and accessible to the mass audience."[7] Here too, the American business film sets up the career plot as a quest for a largely economic success ideal, which typically leads to "fundamental contradictions and conflicts" resulting from the mix of personal career goals with commercial institutional demands. The particularized career struggle thus creates a "unique conceptual structure," but one that is also quite "familiar and accessible to the mass audience."

The career struggle not only poses the central conflict in the business drama, but it also tends to have one of two outcomes in the protagonist's search for success. The first involves a negative business outcome despite real commitment to the mainstream success dream (*Death of a Salesman, Tucker*). This is the most common business drama plot and it is most typical of the entrepreneur film. The second outcome is career success, but a success that fails to bring the expected fulfillment (*The Man in the Gray Flannel Suit* [1957], *Wall Street*). This outcome is particularly common to the corporate drama. Even business comedies that provide positive romantic and/or business closure usually go to great lengths to demonstrate just how conformist and ludicrous the world of business can be (*How to Succeed in Business Without Really Trying* [1967]), or how tenuous the relationship between advancement, wealth, and happiness (*Will Success Spoil Rock Hunter?* [1957]). Excessive measures to attain career success are problematic in drama but mainly funny in comedy. In one comedy vehicle for Jerry Lewis, *Who's Minding the Store?* (1963), the bumbling Norman Pfeifer (Lewis) is told by his boss, "You have to make your choice: honesty or wealth!"

In Hollywood films, the business protagonist may realize personal growth through the refinement of job focus and improved skills, although career success is seldom sufficient without the complementary presence of romantic and/or family interests, which are often the primary motivation for the career quest in the first place. These private interests are also at times represented as a fallback alternative when a job or career choice becomes a dead end. Director and cowriter Billy Wilder's film *The Apartment* (1960), for example, can be broadly categorized as a dark romantic comedy, although the prevailing tone and meaning of the film comes from the workplace setting and career struggle of the main character Bud (Jack Lemmon), making it more precisely a dark romantic comedy of (rather than "within") the business career genre. Bud allows his ambition in the corporate pecking order to invade and nearly overwhelm his domestic and romantic space. The price for his final lack of cooperation with his unethical superior's demands is job termination, which is less important to him than that he gets the girl and retains his sense of personal values. Because corporate leaders are so frequently shown to be unethical or narrowly obsessive in the postclassical business film, the rising protagonist typically represents a healthy call for change. But closer observation usually reveals also that it is the business ethics of the individual hero rather than those of the corporate institution and its market and political milieu that provide hope for business reform.

Like most genre cinema, the business career film does not point to social solutions so much as it reflects on certain contradictions within the larger rituals and myths of success. In this regard, recent theoretical discussions of genre have drawn distinctions between the usefulness of text based, structuralist cultural ritual approaches, as opposed to genre approaches based on the extratextual practices of industries and audiences (see the "inter-textual relay" in note 5). Both of these approaches also tend to oppose what has been called the ideological approach, which has been too narrowly defined as a kind of Marxist ideology of capitalism's imperial political economic mandates on culture and genre production, where genre is necessarily read as simply reinforcing the status quo. But this reductive definition of a dominant ideology ruling genre doesn't do justice to the pervasive importance of central myths and ideology in genre conception, production, and reception. The centrality of economic and hence political ideology in American genre—and its obvious place in the ritual and mythic dimensions of the business career texts that are under study here—necessitates a constant and open consideration of ideology's function in both textual and extra-textual approaches to genre.

ORGANIZATIONAL STRUCTURE

An historical overview of the business career film from one decade to the next reveals many alterations in business circumstance and thematic focus. The several special subcategories and cycles of business texts over time also require a closer look. In addition to the distinctions between corporate and entrepreneurial business, and between male and female employee issues, it is the cycles of particular business film types that make up the chapter and division headings of this book. Chapter 1 is devoted to the basic prototype of big business career cinema prominent in the 1950s: the classical corporate executive film. This particular movie type grew from a wide cultural interest in the new corporate life, including particularly the development of a new kind of managerial executive class attuned to new forms of corporate bureaucracies.

Chapter 2 takes an overview of the struggles of business and career women in cinema. It begins with those films featuring women's rapid migration into the paid workforce during World War II, which continued after a brief lull into the decades that followed and made a huge impact on gender role and workplace issues. But the emergent career woman since the early 1970s has been presented as a very mixed success story on the screen. Whether an institutional employee or entrepreneurial character, she faces the same issues women have always faced in society, only more so owing to the expansion of her duties to include career responsibilities. Women's business identity in film as in life has centered around their often divergent domestic and career goals, particularly for the single working mother. She is a central figure in the representation of the cultural dichotomy between nurture and economic competitiveness.

Chapter 3 is devoted to the small business entrepreneur. Since 1944, the all-important small business film appears only about one-third as frequently as those concerned with the corporate world, which has of course dominated the American economy. And while the entrepreneur film may not suggest as much economic and political relevance nationally as does the corporate business film, it does provide the primary test for the controversial but still fundamental belief in the success that will surely follow self-initiative and determination. Entrepreneur comedies (of which there are only a few) typically support the ideal of complete success through small-business enterprise; entrepreneur dramas, on the other hand, usually contradict that ideal.

Entrepreneur films that reflect immigrant, racial, and ethnic perspectives are also central to America's promise of economic opportunity. White prejudice against racial and ethnic minorities in the business landscape often creates additional conflict within and between these minority groups, which has largely predictable consequences for career identity and success. This section looks at five films involving immigrant and African American entrepreneurs, whose identity and business ethics bring new challenges to the dominant American business community, resulting either in various forms of assimilation or in counterstrategies for survival. The outcomes of all five of these immigrant and interracial small-business films are ultimately tested against the controversial "assimilation" model.

In every decade since the war, small business has been represented fairly equally on celluloid by male and by female protagonists, although this does not suggest gender parity in work. A closer look at women in start-up business films also reveals a special subcategory of texts dealing with entrepreneurial females who use sex to get ahead in the marketplace. Most of these characters are variations of the femme fatale, who display much the same basic kinds of initial business ambitions and long-term goals as do legitimate women entrepreneurs. This category of sexually active women "entrepreneurs" convey a great deal about the nature of commodification and exchange in contemporary society. Most primary entrepreneurial women characters in film have played a part in challenging or redefining family, workplace, and in some cases the political economic landscape, and have thus given new meaning in reality and in film to Freud's old question, "What do women want?"

The two closing chapters consider the two most important influences on contemporary consumer culture and career economics. Chapter 4 addresses the surprisingly large number of films about advertising and public relations. These narratives reveal the internal workings of promotional activity, a media branch of business that has become increasingly central to all business endeavor. The escalating energy and expenditure devoted to promotionalism has played a massive, immeasurable role in the economy and culture of the United States that would seem to justify the many fiction films that are based upon it. (The huge promotional budgets for contemporary Hollywood films are also part of this phenomenon.) The issue of productive work and identity in advertising also insinuates a consciousness of the possible absence of meaning that develops in the endless round of promoting and consuming. Hence, these texts are considered with an eye to the way this industry has partly defined business, government, and success ideologies in general.

Chapter 5 considers the other major influence in contemporary business and career life: the revolution in televisual experience and advanced digital communications. Communications systems are having an increasing impact on the economy and job market, but they also play a role in enlarging consumer expectations and the overall speed of the production/consumption cycle, adding to the further collapse of culture into pure commerce. The new convergence of advanced media systems promise instantaneous outreach and interactivity. Increasingly installed across the nation in businesses and private homes, these startling information resources carried by fiber-optic, microwave, and cyber technology have also, however, decreased privacy and exacerbated the pressure on the individual to keep up and be a full participant in the information revolution, with all the demands for new learning and consumer trendiness that is implied. This speeded up and intensified data environment can be daunting, turning workspace into mediated fishbowls of accomplishment or failure. The new technoculture workplace has become the critical testing ground for social self-worth in a society that insists upon the images of economic success for identity confirmation. One political commentator from India recently observed about America: "There is a terrible emphasis on success. It is not a country that has much patience with failure."[8]

Because of the new technology, old distinctions between business and domestic environments have crumbled, and electronic screens have become a constant presence of commercially determined reality that opens up the world at the same time that it changes that world and brings it closer together. In the latest employment and lifestyle scene, as recent business films suggest, the old questions of subjectivity and subjective vulnerability remain central. The films included in Chapter 5 suggest how workplace and success ideology increasingly exist within a televirtual space, a total field that saturates and collapses the private into the public dimensions of experience.

What *Career Movies* finally provides, then, is a historical genre mapping of changes in Hollywood's view of the world of business career identity and success. It considers American cinema's exploration of individual career trajectories as they relate to cultural constructions of productivity, consumption, and meaning. Because genres such as this one are so closely aligned with their historical moment, there is good reason to weight the interpretation of these films toward their actual narrative content and time-specific tensions. The genre protagonist's difficulty in identifying and pursuing career fulfillment reveals the most important intersection of the personal and cultural at the most critical point of value exchange. The consistency of this genre in the latter half of the twentieth century provides informative reflections on and projections of the changing world of career experience in its social, mythic, and existential dimensions. The question Who am I? remains bound to the career related question What is my purpose and goal in life? In sum, from the postwar era to the postmodern millennium, business career films represent an important generic history. They reflect not only changes in the business world and in personal career life, but also changes in the way Hollywood has come to see and evaluate the increasingly technocratic consumer economy's impact upon the individual's business experience and success ideology.

The new chief executives are "not the owners of the corporate properties, and yet they run the corporate show. . . . Have not these chief executives carried through a silent revolution, a managerial revolution from the top, and has not their revolution transformed the very meaning of property?"

—C. WRIGHT MILLS, *The Power Elite* [1]

CHAPTER 1
THE CLASSICAL CORPORATE EXECUTIVE FILM

The classical corporate executive film is central to business career cinema. It was born in the decade following World War II, and its era ended by 1958. These films were a reflection of new socioeconomic conditions after the war, particularly as these conditions were filtered through popular fiction and drama about big business. Hollywood cinema of the 1930s and early 1940s often punctured images of elitist business power and wealth, as in several films directed by Frank Capra, including *Mr. Deeds Goes to Town* (1936), *You Can't Take It with You* (1938), *Mr. Smith Goes to Washington* (1939), and *Meet John Doe* (1941). In the latter three, the heavyset visage of the calculating fat-cat businessman or politician (Edward Arnold) stands out as a negative image of traditional capitalist authority. The generally populist attitudes in these films toward big business and its leaders did not continue through World War II, however, when attention shifted to the campaign for military victory. Very different economic circumstances and cultural perspectives began to prevail in the postwar era. Big industry rapidly converted its production to private consumer goods, which were suddenly in high demand. As the economy began to boom, big business also began to look more like a hierarchy of opportunity, an arena where one could make a contribution to society as well as develop a lucrative, long-term career. Novels and plays and films began to appear that for the most part glorified the new business hierarchies and their leaders. It is those films about corporate executives and corporate successorship that were released in the mid-1950s that provide the main focus of this chapter. This important film cycle includes *Executive Suite, Woman's World, Patterns,* and *The Man in the Gray Flannel Suit.*

Before turning to these big business texts, it is useful to sketch a bit more of the corporate business circumstances of the time. The manufacturing boom during the war years that lifted America out of the economic doldrums of the Depression was driven by massive government buying and capitalization that helped large industries convert and continue to expand right through the 1950s. Fueled further by the postwar explosion in consumer demand, America's big corporations grew in size and complexity, leading to the increased departmentalization and bureaucratization of their vertical organizational structures, often along the lines of military chains of command. Increased compartmentalization and specialization within the larger corporate structure was considered essential to the efficient operation of big companies. Most mature corporations had already buried their often dictatorial founding fathers and were steadily replacing them with image-conscious company presidents surrounded by professionally trained senior executives and their managers. The influx of this new breed of formally educated and carefully groomed corporate executives, who were already familiar with the monopolistic and bureaucratic marketplace setting, created what came to be called a "managerial revolution."

Members of the new managerial elite differed in several ways from the robust entrepreneurial dynasty builders who had long been the figureheads of Western capitalism, and of the films that helped to mythologize their experience. Generally positive examples of this dynamo figure played by a Clark Gable or John Wayne are still evident in films of the early 1940s such as *Boom Town, The Spoilers,* and *Pittsburgh.* These texts represent an already nostalgic, conservative/centrist American ideal of business opportunity and success through risk taking and toughness. But change is already signaled in King Vidor's *An American Romance* (1944), in which an immigrant steelworker, Stephan Dangos (Brian Donlevy), works his way to the top only to find that he is increasingly forced to listen to his vice presidents and department managers, who advise him on subjects such as labor relations and government regulatory policy. They gradually move him away from the freewheeling audacity of the sweat-equity speculator or elitist robber barons of yore.

The alternative rags-to-riches business mogul typical of more-liberal films differs from the centrist type in that the rise to success is followed by rapid decline, as in the prototype rise-and-fall narrative, *The Power and the Glory* (1933), later followed by *Citizen Kane* (1941). In the former film, Preston Sturges's script is loosely based on the life of C. W. Post, just as Orson Welles's film is loosely based on the life of William Randolph Hearst. The business protagonists in both texts become more intractable as they grow older, wealthier, and more powerful. These two films are also models for the postwar business rise-and-fall narratives that look to the past. These include the historical drama of a tobacco magnate, *Bright Leaf* (1950), and the Hollywood producer story, *The Bad and the Beautiful* (1952). In all four of these tales of the downfall of a business executive released between 1933 and 1952, the power lust that creates dynasties also leads to their demise. But these moralistic stories of overambition and greed further place the burden of business success and failure on the egocentric magnate and his personal life,[2] and pay less attention to systemic problems in monopoly capitalism that begin to appear more frequently in popular big business films by the late 1950s.

While ownership in most large firms of the mid-1950s resided with majority public shareholders represented by boards of directors, senior managers (sometimes with little ownership stake) increasingly assumed control of company operations. They often put departments for professional standards of behavior and measurement into place in an effort to offset administration purely by personal whim. But in the process, authority and responsibility for decisions was also diluted and "passing the buck" became commonplace. Writing in 1953, C. Wright Mills describes the new senior managers as fetishists of the corporate bureaucracy, where "the forms of power that are wielded, all up and down the line, shift from explicit authority to manipulation."[3] Writing in 1956, Mills describes how "some corporations, in fact, at times seem less like businesses than vast schools for future executives," who must learn "usefulness to those above, to those in control of one's advancement."[4] Senior executives, because of the similarity of their corporate leadership duties, also gained increased mobility from one firm to the next.[5] These powerful but little understood upper-level managers and their families became the new, self-sustaining executive class,[6] which furthermore became the focus of an awed public curiosity. It was in this environment that the modern corporate executive film was born. The heroes of these mid-1950s big business films tend to be sophisticated tacticians who question the domineering methods of their aging company leaders. They sound out the office politics and look to build supportive alliances in their career climbs to leadership positions.

All four of the films given primary consideration in this chapter are

also derived from popular literary or TV drama sources, which pre-
sume to offer realistic boardroom and bedroom revelations of those in
the mysterious upper echelon of the new corporate elite. *Executive Suite*
(1954), based on Cameron Hawley's popular novel of 1952, sets the tone
of the classical corporate executive film in its generic tendency mainly
to further the mythology surrounding this business elite. As with the
ritualistic gunfight on Main Street that decides the fate of the town
in studio-era Westerns, the business executive film offers the climactic boardroom confrontation that presumably determines the fate of
the company. Hardly an independent gunman in the action-adventure
mode, the rising business leader in the classical corporate executive film
must act within the terms of the new professionalized bureaucracy. He
must project the right mix of selfless ambition and moral concern for his
family and the society at large. How accurate this apparent dedication
to family and larger social concerns might be as a portrait of real corporate leadership will be a primary subject of consideration throughout
this chapter.

Thematically, corporate executive films of the 1950s are notable for
how little they represent of the actual work done by big business, and
for how much they suggest about the absorption of the private family
into the corporate milieu. These texts tend, therefore, to be very close
to the genre of domestic melodrama, which already includes those films
involving the leadership of family business dynasties such as *Giant* and
Written on the Wind (both 1956).[7] In studio-era domestic melodramas,
a relatively constant sense of family values is tested against the social problems of a changing world. As Thomas Elsaesser observed of
this genre, "[T]he world is closed, and the characters are acted upon."[8]
Film melodrama's structural and aesthetic overdetermination of family
vis-à-vis societal problems also reveals the extraordinary expectations
placed on the family unit at this time to service the breadwinner's career
path and to negotiate the socioeconomic world generally.[9] David N.
Rodowick finds in domestic melodrama "the refusal to understand the
economy of the social formation in anything but familial, personal,
and sexual terms."[10] By personalizing political economic problems, domestic melodrama in its midcentury genre maturity constantly reduces
larger socioeconomic problems to a narrow family logic.

While this overall tendency also exists in the classical corporate executive film, there is an important difference. Where domestic melodrama emphasizes the proper arbitration of wider social conflicts
within the family, the conservative big business film emphasizes the

proper sacrifice of family needs to the needs of the company. The social milieu that surrounds the private family in melodrama is largely displaced in the big business film by an overarching corporate framework. Corporate omnipresence is taken for granted as the social reality base in these texts, and public success and leadership are measured by its terms. In the corporate executive film, therefore, institutional business authority does not so much reproduce family politics as it seems to absorb them into larger corporate contexts. Where the corporate discourse predominates at home as well as at work, isolation from the local community also ensues. Separation from a wider, homegrown social community inhibits the construction of personal, self-determining associations. Without the benefit of community alliances that could provide at least a grassroots buffer, the individual family unit of the executive class remains entirely beholden and vulnerable to prevailing corporate concerns. The constant insistence in the corporate executive film on an individualized, family-based frame of reference is therefore misleading. The executive character may be more emotionally centered in the family, but his/her sense of a public role and identity is tied up in the vagaries of internal corporate structures and interpersonal executive competition. This particular cycle of films thus attempts to resolve the difficulty of defining corporate behavior as socially responsible when executives and their families must constantly bow to corporate authority.

The four corporate executive narratives to be considered in detail in this chapter all insist or imply that ultimately what is good for the company will be good for the nation as well as for most families. In the equation of corporate with national strength the corporate boss may be associated with broad public issues. But one of the realistic circumstances overlooked in these four texts is the revolving door between company executive positions and government administration positions charged with business oversight. With the partial exception of the more progressive project *Patterns,* the films *Executive Suite, Woman's World,* and *Gray Flannel* all demonstrate how democratic principles of fair play ultimately prevail in the corporate setting. Overall, then, the classical corporate executive film mainly contributes to a mythological model of corporate culture in America. This model quickly lost credibility in the corporate business films of the 1960s and 1970s, as America's business goals became more controversial nationally and internationally. By the 1980s the corporate executive (or big investment broker) in film was already a subject of suspicion or ridicule, and by the 1990s this figure was often transformed into an intimidating overseer of transnational business-media conglomeration.

EXECUTIVE PROMOTION AND FAMILY ALLEGIANCE

Fitness means, not formal competence — there probably is no such thing for top executive positions — but conformity with the criteria of those who have already succeeded. To be compatible with the top men is to act like them, to look like them, to think like them: to be of and for them — or at least . . . to create that impression.

—C. WRIGHT MILLS[11]

The corporate executive films of the 1950s assume that the success dream of the individual corporate protagonist can be realized through allegiance to his superiors and their style of life. Unlike the private entrepreneur who builds and sails his own ship, the corporate exec seeks to be the captain of a ship already built and owned by others, and with established channels and reputations to uphold. Promotion to company president is the crowning achievement of the corporate careerist of the 1950s. Furthermore, the different companies represented in these films all have the same kinds of hierarchical structures, and the managerial elites that run them also share the same social and class assumptions, much like a private club.[12] The standardized plots in *Executive Suite, Woman's World, Patterns,* and *The Man in the Gray Flannel Suit* all involve the selection of one white male from among a group of vice presidents to head or be groomed to head a firm. This involves the positioning of his attitudes, ethics, and family in relation to that effort. Each protagonist tests his skills and principles against the will of a company president in a setting he may very slightly influence but cannot control.

The insider employee viewpoint that prevails in these films necessarily neglects the outside social impact of company competition and policy. The typical emphasis on the marital circumstances of competing executives, in fact, makes their narrowly constructed private life appear almost as significant as their job skills and performance. One reason for this is that substantive focus on social ethics, or the narrative's barometer of ethics, resides not with the company where the profit motive dominates, but with the employee's wife and/or family. The assumption is that the appropriate executive with the appropriate family support and values will inevitably be selected in the presidential power struggle, and that he will somehow simply import those values into company policy decisions. This narrative convention, however, does not consider the family's role in the larger community where the effects of company policy might be felt. Rather, the business executive's family is suspended within the corporate milieu. Consequently, family problems seem to correlate only with indigenous corporate concerns, while the greater socioeconomic environment goes largely unrecognized. This is particularly true in the two earlier and more conservative of the four films under discussion.

Executive Suite (1954), adapted by writer Ernest Lehman and directed by Robert Wise, opens with several angles on city skyscrapers, the kind of shots that were already becoming cliché. A voice-over asserts the regality of "sky-reaching towers of big business," followed by an insinuation: "You may think that those who work there are somehow above and beyond the tensions and temptations of the lower floors. This is to say that it isn't so!"[13] The viewpoint shifts to a subjective camera, eye-line perspective of a man leaving a building, who suddenly crumples to the street from a heart attack. He is identified as the Tredway Company's president, Avery Bullard, who is married to Julia Tredway (Barbara Stanwyck), daughter of the firm's visionary founder. Their marriage was partly responsible for Bullard's taking over the company after Julia's father died. Bullard's sudden death in the present leaves no obvious successor, and because of age or financial or moral corruption among the five sectional heads who might compete for the top job, the group of male candidates is soon reduced to two. One is a successful young production team head, MacDonald Walling (William Holden), who may have insufficient executive experience; and the other is the comptroller, Loren Shaw (Fredric March), who is an efficiency expert with the firm's money, but who is better with numbers than with people. The film's privileging of the production man Walling over the financial expert Shaw accurately reflects the history of American industry, which was still choosing production-oriented leaders in the early years of the 1950s.[14] As the managerial revolution took a firm hold at that time, there was a concern that the new business professionals who were promoted to the top at least appear to represent something more tangible than profit growth and stockholder dividends.

As if the contrast in job descriptions were not enough, director Wise continues in several ways to overload the job competition in Walling's favor. In Loren Shaw's search for sufficient votes in the decisive executive board meeting, he finally stoops to blackmail to thwart Don Walling's increasingly self-confident rise. Shaw assumes that businessmen need be driven only by the financial bottom line and individual pride,

1.1   *Executive Suite* (1954).
McDonald Walling (William Holden) wants the Tredway Company executives to elect
him president rather than Loren Shaw (Fredric March, back to camera), and he needs
the vote of Julia Tredway (Barbara Stanwyck, foreground) to do it.

but then he lacks the sense of teamwork that apparently comes for Don
from the input of wife and children. Shaw's bachelorhood contrasts
with the happily married Walling, who confidently looks for counsel
from senior family men like Fred (Walter Pidgeon), as well as to his
spouse Mary (June Allyson). Loren Shaw's lack of family seems almost
as blameworthy as his willingness to indulge in shady business deal-
ings. Moreover, two of the older vice presidents allied with Shaw (one
of whom is married) are shown in city apartments and in materialistic
relationships with young women. Walling's and Fred's good marriages
are further enhanced by their actual domestic environments. Walling
resides in a prominently featured, spacious, contemporary ranch-style
house. The older Fred resides in a gracious, two-story traditional home
with large formal rooms. Even at work Don is shown moving through
the open spaces of his big furniture-production lab with his colleagues,
while Shaw is shown compressed and nervous in his dimly lit office.

In this blatant manner, *Executive Suite* pushes its family-based ethics
as a deciding factor in the competition for company leadership. Just

prior to the long board meeting in the suite on the top floor of the Tredway Building, Walling privately approaches the company's largest shareholder, Julia Tredway, who is distraught and bitter over her deceased husband's sacrifice of himself and their marriage to the company. She has already given her signed proxy vote to Shaw. Don challenges her to think of her father's pride in the company rather than herself, and she throws him out. Later during the meeting, however, she makes an appearance and not only goes on to support Don for company head, but counsels his wife, Mary (who has initially discouraged her husband's possible promotion), that a president's wife has to learn to understand the company leader, even when he shuts her out. Mary will come to see that her husband's decision to assume the top position is worthwhile because of an increased pride in their status, and because their family is putatively serving in a higher cause. An American flag flies prominently at half-mast atop the Tredway industrial building where Walling works, suggesting a nationalistic purpose in the replacement of the lost patriarch. Women's limited role in corporate leadership is driven home when Mary is reduced to eavesdropping outside the executive suite meeting where her family's fate is being decided, just as Julia Tredway's once was. Insisting on having it both ways, however, the film ends right after Don is elected president, when he asks and learns from Mary that their son's Little League team won its game. Don can be a company president and still be close to his family after all.

Woman's World follows *Executive Suite*'s conservative and contradictory story premise but tries to broaden its audience appeal through higher production values (Cinemascope and Technicolor) and an increased attention to the place of women, romance, and family. The founder and chief of the Gifford Automobile Company (Clifton Webb) has chosen to find a replacement for his overworked and now dead general manager. He invites three regional vice presidents and their wives to headquarters in order to select one for the big promotion. Mr. Gifford's occasional tongue-in-cheek voice-over commentary is reinforced by his dapper and worldly demeanor, which sets the feminized and mildly comic tone for this ensemble narrative. The repetition of the film's cloying theme song, "It's a Woman's World," and the constant attention to formal wear and lush hotel settings, also remind the spectator that this is a "woman's film," a celebration of the wife's critical importance to her husband's job success through her enhancement of the proper executive image. Unabashedly direct references to her reproductive role as provider of future generations of business citizenry completes the picture of corporate expectations.

As a conservative business film, *Woman's World*'s primary intent is to reassure its mostly female audience of the potential for marital bliss within the corporate environment as a whole. This is confirmed by the decision to make New York rather than Detroit the unlikely home of the Gifford car company, which helps to lend its corporate meeting an ambiance of cultural sophistication. But the absence of real family viability in the big-city rat race of corporate industry is especially notable in the film.[15] Gifford is an effeminate single man who looks to his sister for advice about women. Similarly, the man whom he eventually selects as general manager also feels compelled to jettison his mate during the competitive review process. Once again, the message to wives is clearly that the promotion of their husbands to company president will not in any case be ideal for their family interests. This is an issue of internal family compatibility and has little to do either with corporate ethics or with wider corporate social effects. For the women characters are also isolated in their families. They may compete alongside their husbands for the big job advancement, but they build no bridges among themselves even when they are alone together. Each one remains individually bound both to her spouse and to his particular business perspective. Other than slight variations in dress and personality and place of origin, furthermore, these middle-class couples are virtually indistinguishable. It is curious then that this narrative form lays claim to the inner workings of the chief executive suite from the obscure perspective of a woman's family melodrama, when this approach can be seen to reveal the extent to which the family's income and social life are directly dependent on the male exec's employment.

One couple, Sid and Elizabeth (Fred MacMurray and Lauren Bacall), already suffer from Sid's ambitious overwork. Their marriage has gone sour and Sid has an ulcer, although none of this is mentioned to President Gifford. Only Liz's constant threat of departure from their marriage makes Sid realize that their relationship means more to him than the big promotion he has always strived for. Similarly, a second couple, played by June Allyson and Cornel Wilde, are simply unsuited to the game of executive posing: she makes one public gaffe after another, while he is concerned that "big business isn't built on personal relationships anymore." They are pleased to learn that they won't have to move to New York and can return to their home and children back in the Midwest without further fear of reprisals for their lapse in job ambition. In the case of both couples, the executive's nuclear family is sustained as an alternative to top-level promotion, if only as a one-way ticket back to Indiana. The corporate demands associated with the highest promotion will apparently require a devotion exceeding personal family concerns, although these demands are not also assumed by the film to contradict family values generally.

The third couple, Bill (Van Heflin) and his voluptuous counterpart Carol (Arlene Dahl), have no children. Carol is more interested in the glitzy high life of New York City than in domestic matters. Furthermore, Carol's raw expressions of ambition are accompanied by a show of sexual assertiveness toward President Gifford. Her forwardness is meant to help Bill secure the promotion, but it offends Gifford, who thinks at first that Bill has plotted it. Carol's behavior also runs counter to the corporation's desire to keep up family appearances. The corporation's idea of family values is not only to keep the woman out of the executive suite, but to keep her actively supportive of her husband from the home. Carol's transgression of those values—introducing feminine power framed as sexuality into industrial decision making—is enough to make her a complete liability to the company and to Bill, and serves further to justify women's exclusion altogether. Because Bill takes the initiative to dispense with her, Bill is rewarded with the promotion. Marriage is not an absolute requirement of Bill's job, although his allegiance to the company's family image certainly is. The Gifford Company's public image must be preserved at all costs, even where its top executive positions cannot be stretched to accommodate married men. This is an interesting contrast to the family and corporate leader message in *Executive Suite,* and it demonstrates the extent to which these films play to their particular audiences. The remaining irony involving the expressed corporate need for a leader who has no family encumbrance, meanwhile, is simply passed over in the text in favor of a display of the remaining couples' happy outcomes. Gifford, too, appears to take the moral high ground by closing ranks with his employed families over the dire threat of one woman's cleavage.

Large firms in America have promoted the image of the single-career executive family as a social ideal at least since the 1930s. Corporations found that families supplied a conservative employee base, where predominantly male executives could depend on their unpaid spouses to manage the domestic scene while they devoted their full attention to the company. In general, what the middle-class family represents to the

1.2   *Woman's World* (1954).
Gifford (Clifton Webb), the head of the Gifford Automobile Company, shows off a line
of futuristic car models to his vice presidents (from left, Van Heflin, Cornel Wilde, and
Fred MacMurray). They are being considered—along with their wives—for the job of
top company manager.

corporation has been a stabilizing force suitable to a high level of production, and more recently, a marketing target for a high level of consumption. Peter Biskind calls the family of the 1950s "the key economic
unit of the affluent society."[16] The consistent emphasis in the executive
film of the 1950s is on individual careerism and the wife's orientation
to her husband's job struggle, which reduces the mission of the private family to an ideological oneness with the expectations and reward
structure of the corporation.

As suggested, *Woman's World* seems to emphasize the company's commitment to family virtue, while all along the sexual function of its
automobile advertising ("Luxury on wheels") inclines in another direction. In the opening scene Gifford shows off his company's elite car
model directly to the film spectator as a beautiful (womanly) master-
piece of design, intended "to appeal to the snob in everyone," and with

a "hood that actually winks." His ironic presentation of a variety of auto "accessories," in addition to the fact that he is such a debonair, unmarried man, provide subtle indications of the substitutional logic of commodity reification that pervades the business environment of this film. The executive's libido is clearly meant to be directed toward the husbandry of the company and its gleaming (eroticized) commodities, while the wife, where she survives at all, is intended for a purely supportive role. The mainstream woman spectator is expected to laugh at the male fascination with automobile technology, while she learns serious lessons about how to help her spouse negotiate the public rituals of corporate life. The assumptions of corporate patriarchy are readily on display, including the wife's privileged role as beneficiary (along with her children) of the executive salaries and public prestige that the corporation can provide. *Woman's World* is an advertisement supporting the spousal role of corporate executives.

The repeated representations of big business from the standpoint of executive promotion further suggests that the family unit holds the reins of choice in the degree of its accommodation with the company. But this appearance stretches realistic and narrative credibility, even where the question is limited to one of time management. As the well-known writings of David Riesman in *The Lonely Crowd*[17] and William H. Whyte in *The Organization Man* make clear, the modern executive type not only works for the organization but belongs to it. The typical business executive "is unable to compartmentalize his life . . . leisure, home, friends—he instinctively measures it in terms of how well it meshes with his work."[18] Peter Biskind seems to share these sociological observations while adding his own ideological gloss on films of the 1950s. He notes how the "buccaneer model" of the capitalist, who was prominent in the decades prior to World War II, is contradicted by the "centrist pluralist" executive who characterizes big business in the 1950s.[19] Don Walling still shows traces of the old buccaneer in *Executive Suite* as a way to legitimize his bureaucratic advancement and masculinity. But just two years later in 1956, the restrained pluralist executive who chooses family over career in *The Man in the Gray Flannel Suit* is also made palatable. This film, like *Patterns* released in the same year, was considered quite liberal for its time simply because it paid lip service to issues of social welfare in the corporate context.

In fact, all four of the films discussed here intimate that, in the corporate bureaucracy of the 1950s, the young executive and his family are secure whether he accepts the big promotion or not. Hence, the appearance of conflicts between job and family are generally revealed to be a moot point for society as a whole. Either way, the companies represented continue to determine their standard for success and the types who might fit it. That the family might suffer from the bread-winner's job priorities is confirmed by Whyte's research, which concludes that "the men on whom The Organization depends most are generally the ones able to resolve successfully any dual allegiance."[20] This new team player reduces the traditional cultural ideal of independent hero to the measure of a competitive functionary, the bureaucratic careerist favored by the corporation. Far from the extremes of American cinema's dynastic capitalist of old, the modern managerial figure and his family observe strict behavioral patterns for corporate advancement.[21] These "patterns" have little to do with democratic procedure and freedom of expression, and everything to do with deference to a vertical corporate authority system whose reach extends into every corner of the executive's personal life and increasingly into the life of the nation.

The classical corporate executive film's promotion of this difficult new male image necessarily relies on a restrictive model for the executive's wife. After the war, when the middle-class nuclear family of male worker and domestic spouse was reinstituted as the norm, single working women usually lost their wartime employment status, while married women who continued to work were perceived to signify their husband's economic inadequacy.[22] But an increasingly urban and cosmopolitan society of leisure time and consumer options began to break down the Victorian sexual double standard, including the heretofore largely sacrosanct world of men's work. Even the ideal image of the executive wife began to change slightly during the 1950s. The softer versions of the executive protagonists' dutiful wives in *Executive Suite* and *Woman's World* give way to a more blatantly shrill and ambitious one in *Patterns,* and to a more sexualized one in *The Man in the Gray Flannel Suit.* Neither of these two latter narratives are comfortable with the wives' increased outspokenness, but they go to considerable lengths to demonstrate the male hero's ability to answer to his wife's demands in an assured masculine way. The gray flannel exec's *rejection* of promotion and the consequent reduction in his corporate authority, for example, impugns his masculine image so severely that only his wife's claims at the end regarding the high quality of his sexual and family performance can begin to shore it up. But even this is not enough, as I will explain in the next section of this chapter.

The executive wife in the films considered here is also expected to be an ambassador for her man and his company even as she is deprived of independence and real choice. She is meant simultaneously to be sophisticated and placid, astute but infinitely agreeable to her working husband's needs. At certain moments she may be shown within ear-shot of company decision making, or she may help her husband with specific suggestions, but her voice is restricted to articulation through her spouse. Her desire to speak for herself and her family must continually be couched in terms that her husband can make acceptable to corporate management. Ehrenreich and English describe popular culture's effort to cling to a romantic ideal of femininity at this time, when a supporting cast of "experts" appeared in the media to promote maternal self-sacrifice in the face of growing trends toward leisure and self-gratification.[23] Byars, too, looks back at related Hollywood genre films and social history to note that "as the melodrama developed in the 1950s, the family itself became less stable."[24] The high point of domestic melodrama, in other words, was a reaction to building pressures in the heterosexual family in the 1950s, which included the growing instability of a single income, and the fact that the patriarchal economic structure continued to demean the voice of women even as it expected more from them in the complex urban/suburban consumer domain.

The expectations surrounding the role of women in these texts also reinforces Heidi Hartmann's conclusion that "the underlying concept of the family as an active agent with unified interests is erroneous." She points to the severe inequality in gender roles that includes the low regard for nurturance in the home.[25] As well as being blamed for not being social secretaries for their executive mates, working businesswomen also realized lower salaries than men for comparable work. Women's secondary business roles and salaries carried over from their undervalued roles in the home (see Chapter 2). But the crisis of the modern middle-class family appears to have less to do with women's increasing employment outside the home than with the low esteem assigned to noncorporate family and community support networks generally.

Patterns is a particularly melodramatic but personally insightful film based on Rod Serling's 55-minute *Kraft Television Theatre* teleplay. Serling expanded the script into an 83-minute kinescope version directed in live-TV style by Fielder Cook, which creates the sense of a staged presence in the text. The plot involves an aging executive, Andy (Ed Begley), who has fallen out of favor with the company president and finds himself with nowhere to turn outside the corporation to which he and his wife have devoted themselves for so many years. President

1.3   *Patterns* (1956).
The aging and ineffective executive Andy (Ed Begley, left) is humiliated and goes after his boss Ramsie (Everett Sloan, middle). Andy is held in check sympathetically by the concerned new executive, Fred Staples (Van Heflin).

Ramsie (Everett Sloan) brings in a new administrator, Fred Staples (Van Heflin), to effectively replace Andy in his job as industrial relations man. Andy spells it out for his young new colleague Fred: "On our level you don't get fired. They give you a situation you can't live in. They keep chipping away at your pride and your security until you begin to doubt and then fear and finally hate. . . . The larger the salary, the more you become dependent on it. It means more than your pride." He might also have added, "more than your family," because his son also tells Fred that his father has been married to his job ever since he can remember. But Ramsie's response to all of this is to criticize his own father for the way he built the firm with "thank-you notes" and "a preoccupation with morality." Although he has inherited a successful business, Ramsie believes that he now must run it differently by keeping a personal distance from his employees, and by pushing them relentlessly to produce.

Ramsie's constant browbeating is the main reason that Andy's demise has been so painful, despite Fred's efforts to cover for Andy. Andy exemplifies the experience of a senior vice president who has not pursued top-level promotion but has been driven to apoplexy anyway. He and his family have had to endure his overwork, drinking, poor health, and pending forced retirement. Andy's condition compels Fred to tell his opportunistic wife, "I don't like stepping on another human being to get into a capital gains bracket." Andy's and Fred's fates obviously constitute the corporate cycle or "patterns" of the title, as each one in turn faces Ramsie's excessive demands on their lives. Fred decides with some trepidation to take the promotion not offered to Andy, but he seeks at the same time to remind Ramsie that his employees and their families are human beings. Fred goes so far as to allude to some of the pernicious effects of Ramsie's overzealousness. But Fred's social accusations ring a bit hollow because they remain unrepresented visually. In the closing scene Fred is ready to desert the company when his boss goads him to try to be his conscience, as if Ramsie were interested in entertaining policy debates on social issues. Presumably, Fred will do well simply to endure the same systemic colonization of his life that has destroyed Andy. The corporate executives of the 1950s can apparently be at best well-meaning players in a conformist economic club.

CORPORATE NATIONALISM

To the extent that business becomes truly national, the economic roles of the upper classes become similar and even interchangeable; to the extent that politics becomes truly national, the political opinion and activity of the upper classes become consolidated. All those forces that transform . . . localities and a scatter of companies into a corporate nation also make for coinciding interests and functions.

—C. WRIGHT MILLS, *The Power Elite*[26]

The ideological conservatism of 1954's *Executive Suite* and *Woman's World* is partly recognizable in the way it confirms the propriety of executive selection, reassuring the audience not only that a democratic process exists within the corporate system but that wife and family are adequately considered in this process. In 1956's liberalized *Patterns* and *The Man in the Gray Flannel Suit,* the appropriate executive candidate either accepts the proffered job kicking and screaming or rejects grooming for the top position because it is too debilitating for his family, nobly resigning himself to the next highest corporate rank. The two latter films assume neither a corporate democratic process nor a readily workable family consensus, but they do remain in awe of corporate economic power and leadership as a national force. The fixation on individual career advancement that characterizes all four plots is justified primarily by the tendency to represent the company president and those executives (and families) closest to him as martyrs of national leadership. They appear to respond to a call to action that suggests a modern heroic myth, where the preservation of the nation-state is made synonymous with corporate success and perpetuity (inevitably defined as growth). That established corporations in the pursuit of power and profitability might be vulnerable to the same temptations as the individual citizen (if not the same forms of accountability)[27] would appear to be an unpatriotic notion in the representational logic of these films. They simply leapfrog any association between corporate behavior and legal and political economic affairs, suggesting instead a vague, national level of destiny through technical and material "progress" for which the family should be happy to sacrifice.

A professional corporate culture was firmly in place and widely recognized by the mid-1950s. Many corporations took credit for victory in war, and went on during the Eisenhower years to support a social and political conservatism that enhanced government favors to large, established businesses. High government positions were often filled by former heads of major corporations. In the 1950s, the extensive involvement of big business in government became firmly established and had a selective tendency to restrict market competition in many fields.[28] Nevertheless, large firms and their political representatives continued to raise the banner of open-market competition as an ideal, even as they tried to dominate markets and control competition, including product inroads by new and smaller businesses.

It was the contributions of American industry during World War II and the Korean conflict that helped create public associations between corporate enterprise and a patriotic national mission. The close interdependency between business and government during the 1940s and on into the 1950s continued after the Korean conflict, as the Cold War prolonged the hysteria over Soviet invasion and perpetuated the demand for military-corporate preparedness. Defense budgets continued to rise, creating a huge government/industry/military revolving door that dictated the goals of public policy and monopolized the country's human and natural resources. Intellectual historian Richard Pells referred to this as a "transformation of economic structure," where "few foresaw the harmonious marriage of government, business, the military, and the unions that became an accustomed feature of American life after 1945."[29]

The continuing national ideological debates around "big business" and "big government" have been skewed by the fact that government is the largest customer in the U.S. economy. Add to this the fact that the largest government "entitlement" program of all—the business of national defense tied to the ever-growing fortunes of Pentagon contractors—has been largely exempted from discussion.[30] In that historical era of widely available resources and expanding demand, particularly among the growing but often cash-poor middle classes, it was easy to embrace theories that favored production (e.g., supply-side economics) as a solution to all social ills. As the second term of President Eisenhower (who was central to this trend) wound down in 1961, he took it upon himself to make his famous warning about the "military-industrial complex" and "the potential for the disastrous rise of misplaced power."[31] Political observers such as C. Wright Mills had already expressed their concern:

> All this had been going on for a long time and is rather well known, but in the Eisenhower administration the corporate executives publicly assumed the key posts of the executive branch. . . . Is there any need for subtle analysis of such matters when the Secretary of the Interior, Douglas McKay, blurted out to his friends in the Chamber of Commerce, on 29 April 1953, "We're here in the saddle as an Administration representing business and industry"? Or when Secretary of Defense Wilson asserted the identity of interests between the U.S.A. and the General Motors Corporation? Such incidents may be political blunders—or would be, were there an opposition party—but are they not as well revelations of deeply held convictions and intention?[32]

Besides encouraging the notion that all big business growth correlates with national strength and progress, and vice versa, the rapidly growing corporate culture of the 1950s also promoted, through the powers of advertising, the possibility of a rising living standard for the private American family. In *Executive Suite,* Don Walling's climactic, winning speech to his fellow VIPs reflects this same corporate version of political idealism: "Management man does not work to make money for himself and the company," Walling says. "Business is *people,* and when you help people to rise to their fullest, you make them fulfill themselves, you create more and better goods for more people, you make happiness!" Walling's notion that corporate enterprise exists primarily to "help people" has at least the rhetorical sound of a speech-making leader, and it garners the support of his uncorrupted peers. It is significant that Walling delivers his speech in the boardroom atop the Tredway Building, which has a Gothic cathedral design that lends a religious righteousness to the proceedings. While pulling a cheap table apart with his bare hands, Walling's inspired message—punctuated by the tolling of cathedral bells before a backdrop of stained glass—metonymically suggests that his visionary leadership will carry not only the company but the entire nation and its confused families to an American Promised Land of superior commodities. One need not belong to a corporate hierarchy to appreciate the cornucopia of goods that confirmed this approach. Mass production for profit could therefore equal the uplifting of one's fellow man. And Don Walling, the athletic white male, could become the transfigured prophet of a new, consumer-oriented corporate ethics.

Walling's managerial approach of the 1950s, while a departure from the older craft and entrepreneurial ethic, is still based in his role as a creative head of the company's research and development division. But his exalted assumption-of-leadership speech reveals a very traditional business rhetoric for rising careerists. Bureaucratic acumen and loyalty to the corporation and one's career—determined by comparison with others in the hierarchy of command—are the fluid standards of Walling's world. He embraces the profit and expansion goals of the company as his own personal sense of value and meaning, based on the assumption that corporate/consumer growth equates with personal and family well-being. William Dugger views the effects of corporate careerism on the family differently. Writing from the vantage point of hindsight, however, he notes how the family faces "increasing pressure to keep up with the rising standard of middle-class living accompanied by less secure employment and greater strains on middle-class children to become careerists themselves at earlier ages."[33]

In a time of plenty, however, big business could afford pious formulas of individual and corporate success, and the Hollywood film industry of the 1950s was hardly positioned to suggest otherwise. Hollywood's studio executives, when it came to movies about big business, had no motivation to risk alienating the major banks and corporations that now underwrote them. The political climate that bred the HUAC witch-hunt endured by Hollywood at the beginning of the decade contributed, along with McCarthyism and ongoing Cold War tensions, to the chill affecting candid representations of big capitalism. The major studios were already on the defensive because of the antitrust decisions that resulted in their loss of exhibition chains in the late 1940s, not to mention the growing competitive challenge of television. Movie attendance was way down and the cost of maintaining large studio facilities was continuing to go up.[34] The sum total of these circumstances helps to explain the narrow thematic focus of these corporate business portraits. Their insular preoccupation with intracompany rivalry and intrafamily maneuvering provides a skewed mirroring of actual corporate concerns, but an otherwise accurate facsimile of the blind careerism expected of corporate executives generally.

The fact that internal information on corporate operations was not readily accessible to the American public also gave these films a special educational place in popular culture. They had a contemporary relevance that most other genres—which looked to nostalgic or inaccessible worlds of the past, present, or future—did not. Maccoby points out that as early as 1940, "Walter Lippmann cautioned that careerism had taken over the schools and was undermining the spiritual tradition of Western civilization."[35] The impetus for what Lippmann called an "asocial careerism" did not, however, originate with the schools. Furthermore, according to Maccoby and several others mentioned in these pages, careerism was only one particularly obvious part of big business's impact on personal, family, community, and government life during this critical decade. The classical corporate executive film, therefore, in ways both manifest and latent, played a special role in creating a success mythology based on personal/family accommodation to an expanding corporate culture. Among other things, these films also continued, ironically, to insinuate that the private family was still the moral authority guiding Western capitalism.

SHORING UP THE NEW MALE BUREAUCRAT

Conservative films often preferred to separate man and family entirely. Corporate-liberal films . . . tried to bring the family to the battlefield.

—PETER BISKIND, *Seeing Is Believing* (312)

In many ways, *Executive Suite, Woman's World,* and even *Patterns* are all preparations for the 1956 blockbuster adapted and directed by Nunnally Johnson, *The Man in the Gray Flannel Suit.* This big-budget entry into Hollywood's popular trend toward "problem films" pays particular attention to middle-class unrest in the new suburbs. Johnson's film covers roughly 12 years of American history and is more psychologically and socially fleshed out than its peers. Its hero, Tom Rath (Gregory Peck), finds that his winning climb to the top of the executive pyramid is laden with a veritable parade of obstacles from all sides. There are signs that the stay-at-home wife and kids not only are feeling disillusioned—partly due to raised consumer expectations resulting from TV exposure—but are beginning to complain about it. Tom's wife Betsy (Jennifer Jones) and their three young children are unwilling bystanders to his constant absence from the home. Hence, the traditional big business film's presumptuous attitude toward the domestic sphere becomes more conscious here. Tom Rath's family difficulties are clearly foregrounded, but they are also largely separated from his problems at work. Therefore, Tom's final dramatic decision to forgo promotion in order to have more time for his family can hardly be construed as a general rejection of corporate executive lifestyles and attitudes. Moreover, while the message foregrounded in Johnson's film is the balancing act between domestic and corporate time commitments, it is mainly the values of domestic life that are investigated. Corporate ethics are not in question. Hence, the main implication of the narrative is Tom Rath's representation of a new, more flexible and pluralistic male executive image, which does not assume that the greatest success lies only at the top of the corporate ladder, although it does not actively question that apparently benevolent authority either.

At story's end, Tom's modification of career aspirations to suit family needs is made acceptable from a masculine standpoint in several ways. One of these is the example set by his boss, Ralph Hopkins (Fredric March), who pays a personal price for having neglected his own wife and children. Hopkins has devoted his mature life to becoming president of the UBC Television and Radio Network, leaving his family cash-rich but thoroughly estranged. His wife leads her own life in quiet isolation from him, while his 18-year-old daughter elopes with a middle-aged playboy. Mrs. Hopkins (Ann Harding) justifiably blames her husband for their daughter's bitterness. And at a critical moment of defensive pique, Ralph bursts out to Tom: "Big successful businesses just weren't built by men like you . . . 9 to 5 and home and family. . . . Without men like me there wouldn't be any big business." Despite Tom's rejection of further promotional grooming, Hopkins seems to assure the corporation's interest in supporting its executives' family concerns by promising the young man job security.[36] Hopkins's patriarchal role as corporate head is also mirrored by Tom's fatherly role in his family. Hopkins's interest in America's mental health problems — which prompts him to spearhead a national fund-raising campaign using his television network — is represented as his dominant working concern.[37] The corporate network as big parent will answer to the country's needs, despite Hopkins's awareness that he has been unavailable to his own family. There is at least a comic irony in the fact that Hopkins's choice of philanthropy might relate to his own poor state of mental/emotional health as network chief.

The tendency of patriarchal capitalism to appear to address social needs even as the family life of corporate employees is undermined by the expectations placed on them is only part of the equation. According to Dana Polan, ours is "a capitalism that encourages excessive expenditure, that desires a desire that is not sublimated or organized within the frame of the Oedipalized family."[38] In a sense, then, Freud's patriarchal family logic becomes overdeterminative in corporate capitalism, where business careerists are more driven than driving in their work, and where paternal and maternal domestic roles are also increasingly defined by the marketplace. Corporate capitalism encourages a materialistic status seeking through a psychology of consumption, a displacement of interpersonal autonomy and values with an orientation toward the solutions of materialism and all its related symbolic values. As Galbraith concludes, "Production only fills a void that it has itself created."[39] In this metapsychology of patriarchy, according to Heidi Hartmann, it is not the individual male breadwinner who is the cause of the problem; he is a pawn: "patriarchal control is now exercised by the corporations or the experts, rather than the small guy out there, one to a household."[40]

Tom's standing in *Gray Flannel*'s narrative is stabilized by the fact that he has already proven himself to be acceptable to the ruling elite represented by Hopkins. And one may speculate that the public recognition of Tom's employer, the TV network, will continue to lend Tom social standing despite his refusal to ascend to the uppermost corporate rank. But Tom's preservation of his own sanity in his final reembrace of family will no doubt degrade his status and probably his satisfaction in continued long-term employment with UBC. Corporate executive success is hence defined in Nunnally Johnson's film as once again mainly a sacrifice of time with the private family in the name of greater responsibilities to the growth of the company and nation. While an economic or social role for the corporation is at least mentioned, its social

1.4   *The Man in the Gray Flannel Suit* (1956).
Tom Rath (Gregory Peck), home from work, observes his children fixated on a
TV Western show, perhaps featured on the UBC network where he works. He is
concerned that growing job responsibilities and domestic television are leaving him
estranged from his young family.

effects through its products and advertising and political influence are
not. The corporate executive remains isolated in an enclosed world of
decision making, the effects of which are hardly known or seen beyond
his insulated executive class.

For executive managers striving to improve their careers and domestic life, the question of the direct impact of corporate culture on their
family remains. In *Gray Flannel,* this question may be answered by observing casual juxtapositions rather than explicit story emphasis. The
seemingly obvious ties, for example, between Tom's public relations
writing career in television and his children's fixation on the noisy new
box in the living room are at least superficially recognized in the text by
offhand comedy. For Tom, the living room TV signifies mainly irritating
noise (inane chase-and-shoot Westerns) and a rather useless distraction
for his children. Tom remains fixed on the pecking order at UBC as if it
were an unrelated entity, considerably removed from his very specific
problems at home. His spouse Betsy — once Tom has accomplished pro-

motion to the precise salary she has learned to determine is necessary for them, a determination based on her image of the ideal home and its cost—is more emotional about Tom's personal history in wartime Italy than about his current employment in television.

The first half of the film is partly devoted to two extended flashbacks of Tom's military experience as a paratrooper captain on the Italian front, which works both for and against him in preparation for his battles on the job and at home. Tom engages combat and romance while on the front. He stabs a German soldier, destroys his closest army buddy by mistake with a hand grenade, and impregnates an Italian girl while his wife awaits his return to the United States. Tom excuses this latter behavior by explaining to Betsy that going from a life of nine-to-five commuting to wartime killer of 17 men, and then back to commuting again, is not without its emotional side effects. Tom's combat "traumas" help excuse his initial lack of career ambition, although this is a lack that, as I have suggested, the narrative seems constantly determined to recuperate.[41] Historically, Tom embodies national pride in wartime victory and European reconstruction (support for his foreign-born son), as well as a positive spin on corporate television's public relations and active fulfillment of its social responsibility. Tom's quiet dignity also appeals to his boss Hopkins, who views Tom as a substitute for his own son lost in the war. Tom combines a patient assertiveness appropriate to his bureaucratic position with an understanding paternalism in his domestic roles as husband and father. And it is these qualities that define him as the mature, masculine bureaucratic ideal of the 1950s. Following Biskind, Elizabeth Traube notes, "Domesticated masculinity was presented as the liberal solution to an incipient crisis in the 'father-absent' middle-class family," although this was, she finds, "a highly unstable solution to the masculinity crisis."[42]

This narrative's inclination to disavow the family's growing dependency on patriarchal corporate media and its expanding social influence may also be seen as closely tied to the need to reinforce the masculine image under bureaucracy. Despite the new male figure's integration into the methods and thinking of professional managerialism, he must continue to appear to possess assertive and independent traits. The male stars chosen for all four of the corporate executive texts emphasized here—from William Holden and Fred MacMurray to Van Heflin and Gregory Peck—obviously possess a physicality meant to offset their confining institutional roles in business suits. Tom Rath's rapid integration into the corporate perspective, for example, begins with his very first assignment, when he is asked along with others to help compose a major mental health speech for his boss. But just when he seems prepared to cave in to accepting Hopkins's own draft of the speech, Betsy insists that Tom be forthright in challenging his boss's version. She wants her husband to challenge "that mass nonsense that sells cars" with a more sophisticated appeal to his presumed audience of physicians. Tom's subsequent, successful version gives voice to an image of Hopkins as a wise, superior authority. It will also permit his audience to seem to reach its own conclusion that Hopkins and UBC should lead the health campaign. With this coup, Tom silences his main competitor at work and solves the bureaucratic game, which he has dubbed "a tricky business with a lot of tricky angles." This homegrown victory reveals the liberal corporate executive plot's need to somehow invoke a more personalized voice of spouse and family, as if it might actually guide the direction of corporate operations. The contradictory placement of the private family vis-à-vis the corporation is not to be missed here, as contradictory messages are typical of Hollywood cinema. Hopkins neglects his family in order to run the company successfully, and Tom Rath makes use of his family (or wife) to benefit the company and win the offer of promotion.

In one sense, Nunnally Johnson's film boils down to the simple premise (enshrined in the happy ending for the Raths) that dad can heal the ills of the modern family with a little more free time, while corporate leadership takes care of itself. But Tom's middle-class, single-income family is also already recognizable for the problems that would soon make it an endangered species in America. This occurred both because of the middle-class family's high consumer expectations, which flew in the face of inflationary conditions that quickly deflated the single family income by the late 1960s, and because of the consequent tendency of overworked adults in a mobile society to neglect more personalized forms of family effort, which probably boosted the sudden explosion in the national divorce rate. But it is also noticeable here more than in earlier executive films how Tom struggles in his marriage in a way that mere job promotion or work reduction cannot resolve. Betsy resents her secondary voice in Tom's employment sphere, and this is compounded by her disillusionment with his wartime romance that left him the father of a son out of wedlock. But Betsy also wants a new house in a better neighborhood and she wants it now, in indirect exchange for which she is willing to forgive her husband's wartime indiscretion. Betsy's impatient materialism seems to be one step ahead of Tom's next possible raise at work.

The pressure Betsy exerts on her husband and his career also takes the form of a challenge to his pride and to his manhood (subtle sexual blackmail). The background to their relationship is explained in the novel: Tom met Betsy at her debutante's ball, and he's been afraid ever since that he couldn't provide for her at the level to which she's been accustomed. Betsy confirms in the film that one of his key appeals for her was his ambition, which she claims he lost during the war. It is Betsy's drive and class consciousness that defines what the new executive's spouse should demand that her breadwinner provide. Once expected mainly to bear responsibility for moral and interpersonal family/community concerns, the modern middle-class wife represented by Betsy now seems increasingly preoccupied with deciphering the hierarchy of commodities that define her husband and family's status. As she makes clear to Tom, she will stand by her man in relation to his economic willfulness. In a seminal study of motherhood in crisis, Nancy Chodorow observed how historical changes in the modern American economy, which included rising costs and high unemployment, sharpened the contradictions within the family.[43] But possible correlations in the film between big commercial interests and "private" family/community problems remain obscured by both sexual jealousy and the pretense of job and family choices. The film's conclusion buffers Betsy's outspoken class ambitions by highlighting her magnanimous decision to allow Tom to pay child support to his impoverished son in Italy.

The extent to which this particular narrative limits the question of family survival to minor adjustments in careerism and cash flow do not appear to mitigate the underlying forces of commercial objectification that are apparent just below the surface. In the story's second half, Tom's family inheritance is threatened when his deceased grandmother's caretaker tries to lay claim to it, forcing the war veteran to seek legal services. Tom appeals to an old-fashioned local probate judge (Lee J. Cobb), who conducts a personal investigation of Tom and his snide, working-class adversary. This extensive pursuit of an individual small claim is as surprising as the Raths' community involvement is unusual in the corporate executive cinema. Johnson's film seems determined to reassure its audience that the nuclear family—with the support of established local community institutions—can provide the stability necessary in rapidly changing times. Far from serving as a model for family independence or alternative lifestyles, however, the Raths' community affiliation is driven mainly by financial necessity. Moreover, their legal case with the judge reveals the kinds of adversarial relationships encouraged by consumer competition. In this corporate culture of opportunism, the get-rich-quick attitude filters down to the cranky caretaker, whose sense of injustice and cynicism inclines him toward litigation. No wonder the avuncular judge has a dyspeptic condition.

At story's end, when there is not enough money for Betsy's big dream home, the plot elides the spurious dichotomy between corporate advancement and family time and provides instead a dramatic deus ex machina—a positive legal settlement of Tom's inheritance. Tom and Betsy are gratified to learn that they can not only move into his grandmother's big home, but also complete the sale of her remaining property to make way for a housing development. This Hollywood closing constitutes an implicit admission that even a man of Tom's stature may not be adequate to the rising expectations of the American Dream, the new success mystique. In the end, Tom Rath, with all the privileges of the executive class, must fall back on his grandmother's wealth to preserve both his marriage and the prerogative of a reduced job commitment.

BEYOND THE CORPORATE-FAMILY EQUATION

If A is success in life, then A equals x plus y plus z. Work is x; y is play; and z is keeping your mouth shut.

—ALBERT EINSTEIN[44]

The Man in the Gray Flannel Suit is revealing in the subtle way it exposes Hollywood's industry turf wars with television by simply downplaying TV's growing cultural influence. Johnson's film has little more to say about television than does *Desk Set* (also 1957), and both could just as well involve any typical corporate setting. When Tom Rath complains to his boss that the television has taken over his children, network head Hopkins promptly replies: "Kick that TV in. Kick it in and stomp on it. Don't let anything keep you away from your family." But there is no mention of how these television executives might interrogate, much less regulate, the power of the commercial medium that employs them. Like the motion picture, television was treated in its early days as something of a novelty. But by 1957 it was already in 67 percent of American households and clearly the most powerful tool of mass influence in history, owned by corporate networks and driven by corporate sponsorship. It provided as never before a platform not only for product sales but for attitudes conducive to mass consumerism, including audience passivity and what Riesman called "other-directedness."

Johnson's film comments on the small, monochromatic TV picture and its mass audience programming from the superior perspective of a wide-screen, high-budget entertainment production.[45] The TV icon within the larger text is reduced to an annoying toy for the children, to simply one more throw-away commodity. By separating television from its essential placement in the commercial cycle of entertainment and advertising relationships, and by emphasizing a network head's direct use of it for his philanthropic campaign, the film largely misrepresents cultural realities. This was probably due in part to the film industry's actual or perceived competition with television, which tended to denigrate its social and cultural impact. I have noted how the TV set is circumscribed as a domestic distraction, a novelty time-killer for children, while Tom's network job demands are isolated as a critical duty to be performed outside the home, affecting society only in a broad, indirect way.[46] As a result of this discrete nuclearization of private and public functions, the executive family can appear to possess a slim margin of self-determination, such as whether or not to pursue executive promotion.

The executive's preoccupation with his corporate standing and income level in these films is a realistic reflection of corporate life, mirroring as it does the strict attention not only to the particulars of career desire but to a corporate, bureaucratic mind-set generally. The big business heads in these movies do sometimes die of stress-induced heart attacks and ulcers, but this is attributed to nothing more definite than "overwork," a generally accepted and often respected condition in a social Darwinian economics. The claustrophobic interface of job and family in these narratives gives the impression of a general consensus of shared needs, while the largely passive role of the family as a consumer unit is barely touched upon. Because no significant societal context beyond the corporate world is shown to exist in these portraits, the executive's family is necessarily swallowed up by prevailing business values. There is no incubator of local community interaction where identity formation initiated in the family might grow separate from the ongoing pressure of corporate values. Hence, *Patterns* and *The Man in the Gray Flannel Suit* both convey the corporate domain's tendency to punish and marginalize those who are not already ambitious or independently wealthy enough to make themselves eligible for the elite executive class.

They also hint at a larger, persistent, escalating promotion of consumer attitudes led by corporate/industrial sponsorship, and how that growing movement was beginning to threaten directly the localized world of family and community experience. Individual consumer appetites were encouraged as a way to realize a superior selfhood at the same time that corporate work was becoming more alienating in the way it separated economic specialization from inherent social function. Participatory citizenship in local communities was being adversely effected by corporate agendas. Richard Godden finds the increasing growth of such consumer agendas to be particularly troublesome:

Since American "citizens" find their collective welfare in a private consumption basket, their "citizenship" and "collectivity" are liable to wither to a defence of personal appetite. I exaggerate . . . to underline the continuing power of consensual ideas in a society whose system of production is geared to the privatization of need and the fragmentation of sociability.[47]

American politics have always been characterized by an antagonism between laissez-faire "private" enterprise and a public concern for the greater social welfare, which usually means a resort to regulatory government measures.[48] But this is not a theme of primary concern to the heroic tradition in the mainstream business executive film, which rather accurately reflects the insularity of business/family rituals in corporate career life.

As I have pointed out, the corporate executive cinema of the 1950s is also a cultural commodity that plays to the melodramatic film styles and sociosexual interests of the time rather than to economic particulars. Through its overwhelming focus on individual job competition, it encourages attention mainly to the employee's exact job/income bracket as the measure of prestige. This is reinforced not only by the indications of wealth and class in the decor of the offices and homes occupied by the main characters, but also in their dress and formal manner of speech. These sunny Hollywood tales largely take corporate perpetuity and the family's corporate complicity for granted. While the narratives demonstrate clearly enough how social status derives from corporate job position, they also continue nevertheless to insist that the executive's personal independence and moral fortitude somehow spring pristinely from him, and/or from his isolated and yet somehow self-restoring family unit.

In sum, through the corporate executive film, the Hollywood studio industry enlarged the myth of masculine accomplishment to include a form of career success marked by both professionalism and bureaucratic conformity. The corporate managerial ethos expressed in these films certifies efficiency, predictability, and control. These texts mute any pejorative effects of corporate commerce on the society at large by allowing only very generalized verbal references to them. Perhaps the kind of arbitrary conjunction of signs that partly defines contemporary postmodernism [49] begins for mainstream Hollywood in that moment when Hopkins tells Tom to smash his television! This is an effective joke coming from a TV network head, particularly because the American audience knows Tom will do no such thing (without a family revolt), and that even if he did, the expanding forces of a mediated sign culture would hardly be daunted by the absence of one terminal receiver. The film's overall blend of television's irritating effect with a serious and positive TV network image remains contradictory.

Since the 1950s, Hollywood's big business films have usually painted darker pictures of corporate hierarchies and of the ambitious nuclear family as its complementary institution of socialization. No longer represented as the idyllic moral stepchild of the corporate system, the embattled family unit began to look more like its victim. The romantic couple is in retreat from corporate life in two films from 1960, *The Apartment* and *From the Terrace,* in which Jack Lemmon and Paul Newman, respectively, enact the roles of executives who are unhappy with the corrupting influence of urban corporations and their antifamily atmosphere. (The *Godfather* films of the early 1970s touch a nerve with their nostalgic extended family, whose business nevertheless thrives through gangland intimidation and murder, and the complete exclusion of wives from the family enterprise.) By the 1980s and 1990s, popular corporate executive films feature a more intimidating internal business atmosphere, which is seen to impact not only the employee's private family, but the viability of a separate private world altogether. The family is either absent or under direct assault in major recent films such as *Wall Street* and *Robocop* (both 1987), *Class Action* (1991), *The Firm* (1993), *Disclosure* (1994), and *The Insider* (1999). These examples demonstrate a level of disillusionment with the competitive extremes of patriarchal capitalism that would have seemed heretical in the 1950s. The stress and violence commensurate with America's particular version of oligarchic corporate empowerment, coupled with the low priority assigned to the common social welfare, have resulted in a high-intensity, low-trust culture that reflects what Godden has called "the fragmentation of sociability," or perhaps more precisely, the devaluation of noncommercial sociability. The steady erosion of the traditional American family may be attributed in part to the very excesses of a capitalist consumer system that has (d)evolved in the name of providing for it.

Despite the family focus of the corporate executive film of the 1950s, therefore, as the more recent versions of this narrative type suggest, family values appear to have deteriorated in a corporate culture that has served as the economic and political gravitational force and center of American life and national identity. Looking back from the present, William Dugger concludes that the giant corporations of capitalism have been "eat[ing] away at the alternative lifestyles and institutions that once provided a degree of balance to the society. As a result, the United States is becoming hegemonic rather than pluralistic. . . . The meanings, values and beliefs of the capitalist corporation have replaced those of the church, the community, the family, and the school." [50] But there is no suggestion of such tendencies in the midcentury corporate executive film, which prefers only the most superficial narrative opposition between executive business practice and family life. A more realistic corporate agenda—altogether missing from the postwar films discussed here—is summarized by C. Wright Mills in 1956: "Today, the success of the corporation depends to a considerable extent upon minimizing its tax burden, maximizing its speculative projects through mergers, controlling government regulatory bodies, and influencing state and national legislators." [51] In view of these practical concerns, the career-quest paradigm in the classical corporate executive film is best characterized as a narrative of omission. It throws a narrow border around the world of corporate economic power by reducing its dominant influence in American society to a bureaucratic, insulated executive pecking order. If the top job was not for everyone, the image of the corporate executive leader that emerges from this important film cycle is that of a man whose biggest problem is either sacrificing private time for the sake of somehow uplifting the corporation/nation, or keeping his little family happy while maintaining the status quo at work. But we are discussing, after all, the mythical, mass-market entertainment products of Hollywood studios, those corporate institutions that were mainly invested at the time in reflecting the way America wanted to see itself.

I have yet to hear a man ask for advice on how to combine marriage and a career.

—GLORIA STEINEM

I do not believe there is such a thing as female writing. There is the hysteric's voice which is the woman's masculine language . . . talking about feminine experience.

—JULIET MITCHELL, *Psychoanalysis and Feminism*[1]

CHAPTER 2
THE EMERGENCE OF THE CAREER WOMAN

Unlike corporate career films, where men have traditionally dominated on-screen as in real life, there are, since 1944, approximately as many business films about female as about male entrepreneurs. In the last three decades women corporate executive characters have also become increasingly prominent on-screen. Clearly, success in business careers has obviously not always meant the same thing for women as for men, particularly since the general expectation for women to work (discounting the years of World War II) did not become widespread until the 1970s. By this time, national monetary inflation, marriage at a later age, and soaring divorce rates drove women in great numbers into higher education and the paid workforce. Young career women who also wanted to start a family had to find ways to accommodate the additional demands of motherhood in their success equation. While there has always been an expectation that men would develop and advance their business and career work, women have only in the last three decades found themselves pursuing careers with the increasingly accepted notion that their economic needs and career goals are as pressing as are men's, particularly owing to their increasing roles as heads of households. Since the 1930s, women in ever growing numbers have had to prove themselves worthy in a variety of business and career circumstances, and Hollywood films have traced their difficult but mostly successful attempts at ever higher levels of socioeconomic accomplishment. Hence, business success for women in films of the 1940s and 1950s has different connotations than their understanding of success in films of the 1980s and 1990s. It is therefore useful, initially, to consider middle-class working women in cinema in relation to their historical era as well as their marital and maternal status. Also, because the woman's specific marital and family status as an employee seems as important to her identity status as the exact nature of her career (at least from a historical perspective), I have expanded the business category in this chapter to include some women's career pursuits beyond business per se.

This status is important because Hollywood's overall portraits of single and married working women (particularly if they are also mothers) differ markedly. Certainly, American cinema's mirroring of career women generally reflects deeply embedded assumptions about work and gender roles that do not begin to change noticeably until the 1970s. As a starting point, therefore, I look first at classical films to determine how gainfully employed women are represented in relation to new social facts and tenacious cultural myths. The first section of this chapter focuses on the large number of studio-era films featuring the single working mother. It also extends into the 1960s and includes the single or married childless woman who tries to balance her career with her romantic life or with her husband and his career. The next section takes up the sexual/gender revolution as represented in films of the 1970s. It goes on to trace women's rise into corporate managerial ranks in the 1980s and 1990s, and the plight of increasingly desperate married or single working mothers in this recent era. The third section goes beyond the film survey approach; it considers the significance of the usually marginalized and desperate working mother character from a psychological, ideological, and historical perspective. The social survey emphasis of sections one and two helps set the stage for the more intensive psychoanalytic reading of three films from three different eras in the third section that involve gainfully employed moms and their unhappy offspring.

Since World War II, Hollywood films have represented middle-class working women as a troubled lot, tortured as much by their successes as by their failures. This is not to say that businesswomen characters are made to appear inadequate to their jobs, but rather that in films up through the 1970s, their jobs are treated as compensatory or secondary to romance, marriage, and most of all, motherhood. It is a truism that women have ultimately been measured against the cultural priority of motherhood, while men have ultimately been measured against the cultural priority of being family providers and public leaders. And this paternalistic conception of women's domestic priorities necessarily extends to how they have been perceived in the workforce. Only since the late 1970s have the challenges for successful working women and ambitious moms been taken more seriously and become more commonplace in Hollywood films, even as the working woman's portrayal remains largely contentious, and as the nuclear family ideal, if not the actual nuclear family, continues to reign supreme.

The stereotyping of women as home managers and mothers has persisted despite Susan Van Horn's discovery that the number of married women in the paid workforce doubled between 1940 and 1960.[2] During World War II, the government encouraged women to take jobs because of military needs, but by 1955, women were discovering "new work motivations based on the need for family goods and services."[3] This significant change from military requirements to domestic consumer needs as a motivation for mothers to work occurred, according to Van Horn, "in spite of the prevalence of negative opinion regarding married women's work for pay and the lack of supportive ideologies for new [work] activity."[4] Particularly in a consumer-driven economy, social conventions can be forced to yield to economic necessity, or — under circumstances of growing affluence — to the latest perception of what is considered necessary. Consumerism is in fact a significant form of ideology, particularly in the absence of a dominant and conflicting religious ideology in the West to hinder women's employ.

The negativity toward working married women that Van Horn refers to is certainly apparent in classical Hollywood's screen treatment of gender relations. Molly Haskell notes that "the trust that accompanied [heterosexual] attraction" in films of the 1920s and 1930s, became "a thing of the past" in the more pessimistic and "sexually suspicious" 1940s.[5] That decade, for example, prominently features married women both as femmes fatales in films noir (e.g., *Double Indemnity* and *The Postman Always Rings Twice;* see Chapter 3) and as ruthless controllers or saboteurs of the family (e.g., *The Little Foxes, Harriet Craig,* and *Bright Leaf*). It is only in the popular Hepburn and Tracy comedies such as *Woman of the Year* (1942) and *Adam's Rib* (1949) that gender role adjustments are more directly addressed by the two-career middle-class couple, although significantly, children are not included in these youthful marriages. And where the Hepburn-Tracy pairing is presented as a married couple with children in later comedies such as *State of the Union* (1948) and *Guess Who's Coming to Dinner?* (1967), the characters played by Hepburn are not gainfully employed. In American cinema, working women of any class who are actively married and have children hardly exist as film protagonists until the 1980s! This disregard by the movie industry flies in the face of the fact that workforce "participation rates for married women with spouse present" again doubled between 1960 and 1980 to 60 percent for women in the childbearing years.[6] By 1985, 62 percent of American mothers were spending a significant portion of their adult years in the workforce. Hollywood could no longer look upon this phenomenon as a temporary condition, especially in the face of women's increased demands for social, sexual, and income equality.

It does appear that women's longing for social, sexual, and economic freedom has been greatly motivated by the desire or need to be gainfully employed, to stand at least as equals to men in the prestigious arena of job and income significance. A consumer economy that wanted to sell women refrigerators, stoves, and vacuum cleaners in the postwar era could just as well sell them business suits, cars, and homes in the decades that followed. Hollywood films confirm that the revolutionary change in feminist consciousness that took a firm hold within America's middle class by the 1970s was inextricably tied to the growing numbers of middle-class women who had entered or were entering the workforce. Because of American consumer society's emphasis on economic wealth as the basis for social power and usually esteem, women's social authority and freedom increased alongside increases in their career and economic leverage. But the gradual demise of strict patriarchy in the economic and domestic environment has not liberated women or children from the growing pressures of a graduated consumerism, which continues to dominate psychological as well as sociological experience. This domination is apparent in the formulative psychology related to self-worth and success established in the child's early relationship to his or her mother. While this relationship is noted in certain films throughout this chapter, the closing section zeroes in on this problematic relative to the working mother as it is highlighted in the film noir tradition.

FROM SHAMED WORKING MOMS IN NOIR AND CLASSICAL MELODRAMA TO EMBARRASSED ONES IN COMEDY

There are so many things that we should have and haven't got.

—VEDA TO HER MOTHER MILDRED IN *Mildred Pierce* (1945)

Classical Hollywood films about working women assert that while paying jobs might equate with greater economic independence, they do not necessarily equate with greater happiness, particularly for working single mothers. The disjunction between business success and domestic failure is striking in films such as Michael Curtiz's melodramatic noir *Mildred Pierce* (1945) and Mitchell Leisen's maternal melodrama *To Each His Own* (1946). In both, the tortured mother seems to devote her entire career toward positioning herself for a full reconciliation with an estranged child. The young unwed mother, Josephine Norris (Olivia de Havilland) in *To Each His Own,* is pressured to hide the birth of her son and then to give him up at birth. She throws herself into work as a substitute for her loss, and eventually uses her business success in cosmetics as a device to win her son back. Josephine's personal longing rather than her commercial life is foregrounded. *Mildred Pierce* does trace the developmental progress of divorced mother Mildred's business and class ascension, but her sense of success is also all along intertwined with winning her child's admiration and love. Mildred's quest eventually ends badly as she is forced out of her own business and loses her daughter to prison. Josephine Norris, meanwhile, who has long suffered the absence of her son, is finally reconciled with him at the height of her own business and romantic success. Both stories show the mother's conviction that maternal love, however pure or imperfect, is alone insufficient and must have the additional sanction of a rising financial and class status. It also appears that the single mother of the studio-era film feels guilt for the absence of a male figure and breadwinner for the child, and she therefore seeks to make up for it financially as well as emotionally. It is an interesting commentary on American values that the fundamental mother-child bond in these narratives is constantly disrupted by the single mother's felt need to validate herself through class advancement, even where that compulsion can be seen in *Mildred Pierce* to contribute to the alienation of the child in the first place.

By the 1950s, central working mother characters are often found in "social problem" or "message" movies. The single mothers with one child in both the 1953 version of *So Big* and in *Peyton Place* (1957), for example, are gainfully employed and, up to a point, insistent on their independence. Jane Wyman plays the desexualized schoolteacher turned successful truck farmer in *So Big.* She is determined that her success not be wasted on her son, who is sorely tempted in his architectural career (due largely to his mate's class ambitions) to "sell out" to crass but high-paying commercial influences.[7] In *Peyton Place,* Lana Turner plays a sexually repressed dress shop owner who tries desperately to prohibit her daughter from the same error of unmarried motherhood that she suffered. The lesson she must learn is to overcome her own rigidity (and frigidity), and eventually to accept marriage herself, as well as a reduced preoccupation with business success. In each of the four aforementioned films, in fact, the economic independence won by the single mother may not be lasting or sufficient either to guarantee reconciliation with her offspring or to bring family closure for herself. For that, she must look to the concluding appearance of a spousal figure (or, as in *So Big,* a grown son who will listen to her) for complete emotional and usually economic stabilization.[8] The importance of the paternal role within the family and in commerce is preserved in these films, and the economic and sexual double standard thus prevails. Molly Haskell, an early observer of women characters' fate in classical Hollywood cinema, has noted "the double bind of masochistic rationalization triggering the woman's film," where "what adds to its conviction on one level subtracts from it on another." And so does the working mother of classical cinema who strives for economic progress also experience maternal guilt for her domestic absence, the now well known "double bind." She usually tries in several ways to compensate for this absence from her children and/or her heterosexual mate. Thus, as Haskell describes it, women "moved up the employment ladder and down from the pedestal, paying for the one with the fall from the other."[9]

This double bind does not end with the demise of classical Hollywood cinema, however, but continues right through the 1990s, particularly in regard to single working mothers. In addition to the single working mom characters in the four dramatic films cited above, many others can be added, including *Imitation of Life* (1959), *Marnie* (1964), *Up the Sandbox* (1972), *Alice Doesn't Live Here Anymore* (1974), *An Unmarried Woman* (1978), *Mommie Dearest* (1981), *Places in the Heart* (1984), *Marie* (1985), *Murphy's Romance* (1985), *The Good Mother* (1988), *The Grifters* (1990), *The Rapture* (1991), *CrissCross* (1992), *Gas Food Lodging* (1992), *Striptease* (1996), and *Erin Brockovich* (2000). The historical continuity of the double bind for single working mothers contradicts the optimism of commercial ad copy addressed to women, including the well-known dictum in the 1970s that "You've come a long way baby." That such encouraging words from a tobacco company are aimed mainly at young single women with leisure time is quickly apparent if one conjures the image of a breast-feeding working mom puffing away on a Virginia

Slims cigarette and wearing a business suit. The success mystique for the gainfully employed single mother in dramatic films continues to be a contradictory proposition.

The double bind in career and motherhood is really a triple bind that is particularly apparent in working mother comedies, where a loving man typically rescues the mother from becoming too devoted to career life at her child(ren)'s emotional expense. Films in this group include *Miracle on 34th Street* (1947), *The Thrill of It All* (1963), *Mister Mom* (1983), and *Mrs. Doubtfire* (1993), among others. At least in the two more recent films, the mother's career quest does not undermine her domestic nurturing to the point that audiences assume the necessity for her to remain in the home at all times, as do the earlier films. On the other hand, all four of these films continue to insist on the need for the right man to complete the family ideal. This is the romantic or third aspect of the double bind. Business success for women and particularly mothers continues to be weighed, then, in traditional family terms in comedy right up through the 1990s. I will have more to say about these recent films and gender, work, and family in the next section of this chapter.

With gender role typecasting already well established before 1945, the highly revealing roles of working mothers in Hollywood film can be seen to fall into three primary categories: the good mother, the well-meaning sacrificial mother, and the bad mother. The good working mother appears mostly in comedies, from *Miracle on 34th Street* (1947) to *Mrs. Doubtfire* (1993), where she is shown to have something to learn (mainly the value of a good man), but is flexible enough to learn it. The sacrificial mother, meanwhile, is typically found in domestic melodramas and often does not work outside the home, as demonstrated in *All That Heaven Allows* (1955), and by the black housekeeper in *Imitation of Life* (1959). In both texts of domestic melodrama directed by Douglas Sirk (which have echoes of King Vidor's *Stella Dallas* [1937]), the expectation of the mother's sacrifice for her children is readily apparent, whether she finally martyrs herself for them or not. In *All That Heaven Allows,* the Jane Wyman character's relationship with her children suffers because she defies social constraints by choosing to see a man apparently below her class rank (defined, of course, only in monetary terms). The problem stalls their relationship and is defused only after her kids grow up and leave home, and her beloved's yard work develops into a respectable tree nursery business. Obviously, marrying up or down in class can also be a shortcut to a woman's respectability or social collapse, although upward marriage must also be for the right reasons. Downward class marriage for mature women is hardly a topic of Hollywood cinema, even if for love or simply support in parenting. In choosing to give their children more than what they had, parents in American cinema also continue to define the "more" mainly in financial and class terms, the assumed keys to happiness.

Exactly how the sacrificial working mother's children suffer from her employment outside the home is painstakingly delineated in *Mildred Pierce* (1945) and *Imitation of Life* (1959). The obsessive working protagonists in both are driven, self-centered women who cannot entirely escape some degree of responsibility for the imprisonment or death of their "family" members in the end. Both films feature a daughter who suffers from her mother's absence at work, although the problem is not simply one of time commitment but of the distracted mother's social ambition. It is the particular way each white mother embraces society's class values that has serious consequences. The parallel working mother plots that exist within *Imitation of Life* further reveal the problems each daughter develops as a result of being left to her own devices in a classist and racist environment. The light-skinned daughter Sarah Jane (Susan Kohner) of the housekeeper Annie (Juanita Moore) rejects her darker-skinned and shabbily dressed mother and passes herself off as Caucasian. This breaks Annie's heart and leads to her death. It also serves as a lesson to the white mother and head of the household Lora (Lana Turner), who has been too self-absorbed in her rising success as an actress to notice Sarah Jane's growing alienation from the domestic and larger social scene. The maternal dynamic in Lora's home where live-in Annie serves as a housekeeper and cook has all along exhibited society's norms of racial inequality despite the love between Annie and Lora. For these working mother characters, employment stability or success once again gives birth to trouble with children. The actress's overattention to fame is problematized here, especially since Lora's career ambition seems to go well beyond her more than adequate support of the family group. The fact that she is hardly seen doing her work does not diminish the obvious impact of her career on the household. Lora is the head of the household and is clearly implicated in Sarah Jane's behavior and Annie's consequent death because of her self-absorption in work, despite her personal inability to overcome the racism that Sarah Jane experiences outside the home. Culturally observant immigrant director Sirk is particularly convincing where he suggests that the image-conscious, class-bound society that has created the distracted actress Lora is the same society that has been guilty of racial stereotyping. The sacrificial working-mother type, therefore, becomes particularly revealing as a conflicted position when other social problems such as racism are also thrown into the mix.[10]

In contrast to the sacrificial mother, the bad mother figure is such an intimidating character on the social and psychological level that gainful employment becomes virtually irrelevant. The emphasis in the bad mother plot is precisely on what has or seems to have taken place between the mother and the very young child in the private confines of the home. Realistic, dramatic versions of these psychologically oriented tales include the dictatorial mother figure in the melodramatic *Now Voyager* (1942), the Oedipal mother in *Suddenly Last Summer* (1959), the guilt-ridden rejecting mother in *Marnie* (1964), and the psychotically brutal mother in *I Never Promised You a Rose Garden* (1977). All four texts play on the mother's repressive influence on the child, and the need to bring it to light by way of psychotherapy. Bad mothers in classical cinema are also found in political tales (*The Manchurian Candidate* [1962]) and in horror (*Psycho* [1960], and *Carrie* [1976]), where the distortion of the nurturing mother-child bond has extreme consequences. But the bad mother does not make a strong appearance in film as a realistic, gainfully employed woman until 1981 in *Mommie Dearest,* which shakes the very foundations of the heretofore positive assumptions regarding the role of the sacrificial working mother. This story of child abuse based on the book written by Joan Crawford's adopted daughter Christina not only opens the gates to future films about how sacrificial mother types can become monsters, but it also delineates how studio Hollywood enforced a success image on Joan Crawford's private life that helped push her ambition to domestic displays of authoritarian violence against her children. This reality-based film demonstrates clearly just how severely the success mystique, particularly as defined by institutional pressures, can distort and corrupt the maternal family role.

Since the beginning of the American woman's mass migration into the paid workforce in the 1940s, the myths surrounding idyllic motherhood and the dangers of her overinvolvement beyond the nursery have persisted in strange ways. Michael Rogin has demonstrated, for example, how women's increased socioeconomic role during and after World War II added to both masculinist and patriotic paranoia. The growing "infiltration" of women into the paid workforce became merged with Cold War obsessions about the lack of male discipline and the fear of communist treason. This conflation of fears of possessive motherhood and of communist infiltration within the nation is made in such films as *My Son John* (1952) and *The Manchurian Candidate.*[11] Certainly the latter is the quintessential Hollywood film of all-controlling "momism," which attempts to blame the politically ambitious mother (Angela Lansbury) of Raymond Shaw (Laurence Harvey) for manipulating Raymond at the unconscious level. The mother-child bond normally founded in nurture becomes for the man-child here a subconscious trigger for political murder. *The Manchurian Candidate* is quite sophisticated in the way it finally suggests how America's primary enemies are homegrown megalomaniacs. Raymond appears to be the result of an excessive national mythology of maternal perfection alongside a reality that can encourage, particularly for the nonworking mother, exorbitant career power expectations that can only be projected through the child.

Momism becomes recognizable as another variation of the pressure that an excessive success mystique can create. By blaming historical McCarthyism (the fixation on the perceived omnipresence of communist infiltrators with foreign allegiance) ultimately on the regressive paranoia of mother domination, the film also reveals an infantile and Oedipal fear of maternal power in American culture at large. Because Raymond's mother works at the pre-Oedipal or subconscious "brainwashing" level of mind control to empower herself through her son, the child's own growth and development become secondary. This same phenomenon of momism is also blamed for the origin of criminal psychopaths in films as diverse as *White Heat* (1949) and *Psycho* (1960). Its enduring quality also lasts into the 1970s through Milos Forman's 1975 film adaptation of Ken Kesey's novel, *One Flew over the Cuckoo's Nest,* which features the ball-busting Big Nurse overseeing a psych ward. I will say more on the psychological aspects of this pattern of generational legacy in the last section of this chapter.

In contrast to problematized working single mothers and the aggressive momism phenomenon, gainfully employed single women without children consistently fare better in Hollywood cinema. In the 1950s, the single businesswoman can be found in films that are either progressively resistant to or conservatively consistent with the gender expectations of the status quo. *I Can Get It for You Wholesale* (1951) and *Lucy Gallant* (1955) both feature dedicated entrepreneurs who work in women's clothing, and who are determined to be successful in work even as they are on the lookout for a worthy man to complete their dreams. In the former film, Harriet Boyd (Susan Hayward) is so driven to success that she cons her sister out of inheritance money to help capitalize her dress business venture with two men. Because she is successful in her design work as well as ambitious and attractive, she lands the job opportunity of her dreams with one of the world's biggest designers, who is also a romantic interest. But she finally resists this wealthy paternalistic authority in her career and decides to return to her hardworking but desperate partners, the younger of whom she remains endeared to. Her stance in this exceptional little film by Michael Gordon (from a Jerome Weidman novel scripted by Abraham Polonsky) is finally for gender equality in romance and work. In *Lucy Gallant,* directed by Robert Parrish, Lucy (Jane Wyman again) builds her own successful business, only to give it up in the end for a paternalistic marriage. Lucy's decision is prompted by the problems facing her big women's clothing store, which are thrown up to her by the men on her own board of directors. (The boardroom scene here is very reminiscent of the one in *Mildred Pierce,* where Mildred loses control of her business because she too has not paid sufficient attention to financial and logistical details.) Lucy has the option to save her position as head of her board with money contributed by her longtime admirer (Charlton Heston), but she makes instead what is meant to appear as the more noble choice. She marries this wealthy oilman, whom she has long resisted, and terminates her business for a homemaker's role and the desire for children. The film makes clear that she has finally realized her proper place and will find happiness under her husband's patriarchal authority.

In further contrast to Jane Wyman's dramatic role in *Lucy Gallant,* a greater interest in the woman's ability to direct her own career success and romantic connections is also apparent in the Judy Holliday comedy vehicles *It Should Happen to You* (1954) and *Solid Gold Cadillac* (1956). Whether fighting initially for self-recognition in the former film, or fighting for a group of lowly and abused stockholders in the latter, Holliday's characters represent a naive but very game honesty that flusters stuffy businessmen and endears her to the struggling middle class. Class advancement is not her primary motivation so much as the need to be recognized and appreciated as a citizen with basic rights that have to be tested in order to be realized. While Judy's characters do find token romantic closure in both films, it is the democratic principles of the rights and inspirations of the common people, under circumstances that can otherwise also encourage injustice, that are the central themes. Hence, good career women may find dignity in ways not so very different from good career men, whatever the specifics of their romantic and family arrangements. Judy Holliday's roles in these texts are also reminiscent of James Stewart's grassroots business and career roles in films a decade earlier (e.g., *It's a Wonderful Life* and *Mr. Smith Goes to Washington*). Holliday's characters must, like Stewart's, begin from basically nowhere and work their way up. All of these are populist-influenced narratives that want to believe rather nostalgically that the best impulses of the honest heart and native wit of the man or woman can go a long way to right the wrongs of corruption in commerce and government. Nor does the blond and charming Holliday permit herself to become a sex object or romantic fantasy, since her career interests are more than just self-serving efforts leading eventually to marital bliss. Judy Holliday's dizzy spunk overshadows her lower register of sexuality. This quality also made her appealing to large female audiences hungry for alternatives to the working woman extremes played either by the morally impeccable but entirely traditional Wyman or by the blond bombshell Jayne Mansfield.

As comedy material, Holliday's businesswoman roles clearly contrast with Jayne Mansfield's leading parts in *The Girl Can't Help It* (1956) and *Will Success Spoil Rock Hunter?* (1957). Both of these are breast-fixated explorations of the already wealthy woman, who in the first case is assigned for career grooming to make her a star, and in the second case is already a wealthy movie celebrity, who provides a commercial endorsement merely to create a phony romance to win back her movie star boyfriend. Work experience for Mansfield's role in each film is a self-centered exercise en route to the discovery of her true maternal instincts as a potential wife and mother. Unlike the softer body lines of Judy Holliday, Mansfield has the benefit (or burden) of the cultural sexual ideal of the hourglass figure, which she exploits as part of her body and voice caricature of Marilyn Monroe, already defined as a sex object. Under the sexual double standard of the 1950s, the working woman in film as in everyday life could be acceptable only if she controlled her sexual impulses in private, whatever the image she projected for the sake of commerce. These films in fact mark a growing separation between what is acceptable sexually in commercial and career promotions as opposed to personal and local community standards of behavior. The very traditional girlfriend (Betsy Drake) of Rock Hunter (Tony Randall), for example, finds herself going to great lengths to match the breast configurations and tight dress styles of her apparent competition, Rita Marlowe (Mansfield). Rita's exaggerated sexual display and "kissable lips" lipstick promotions—which Rock Hunter has encouraged not only as the adman but as Rita's new "lover boy"—reflected a new boldness in advertising that was beginning to change public and private views of women's behavioral prerogatives. Sexually liberalized and yet body-objectified, both comedies also want to poke fun at the performative, distorting role of advertising and celebrity. They deny its social influence by recuperating moralistic family conclusions. Because the career objectives of the women in these sex comedies are contained within romance and marriage, they appear finally nonthreatening, just as do the women in their comic and adolescently teasing sexual display.

Closer to the Judy Holliday or girl-next-door image than to the Jayne Mansfield sex object are the roles of Doris Day as single working woman in *Teacher's Pet* (as a journalism instructor; 1958), *Pillow Talk* (as an interior decorator; 1959), and *It Happened to Jane* (as the entrepreneurial owner of a small Maine lobstery; 1959). These typically ebullient characters thrive on optimism and spunk, and they are not afraid to be assertive in their career pursuits. They also never forget in these comedies, however, that they are single women whose career success would be empty without the companionship of a good man. Pure and engaging in their friendliness and optimism, they stand for an endearing if somewhat tomboyish and well-scrubbed feminine charm. In other words, their physical sexuality is played down to reduce any additional threat to the male characters. Doris Day's roles in these romantic comedies of the 1950s show the advantage of womanly resourcefulness in business atmospheres that, owing to the heavy-handedness of male power figures, apparently need it. Like Judy Holliday's roles, Day's industrious young characters represent an optimism and a challenge to stuffy institutions or picky masculine figures that both genders can relate to.

Age groupings of career women portrayed in dramatic film are also indicative of prevailing myths. Older single business characters of the 1950s such as those played by Joan Crawford in *Johnny Guitar* (1954) and *The Best of Everything* (1959) are mainly frustrated, lonely women who seem to have chosen or become devoted to careers where their romantic lives have failed. On the other hand, young, single working women characters of the time seem to require a background explanation for their career aspirations. And their romantic experiences are frequently tumultuous and often unsuccessful. Director Raoul Walsh's *The Revolt of Mamie Stover* (1956) offers an unusually honest and candid class study, which demonstrates that a young woman (Jane Russell) can be just as venal and self-centered as a man, whether the game is business profiteering or romance. As a character, Mamie Stover does share a common history with Lucy Gallant in that they are both motivated by their father's failure. Lucy's dad committed suicide on the eve of her intended first marriage, while Mamie's father raised her in abject poverty. Films about strong business and career women continue to offer special rationales for the occupational ambitions of their heroines until the mid-1970s. Where such strong rationales are not forthcoming, working women protagonists at the time tend to be either tentative characters, as found in *The Apartment* (1960) and *Rachel, Rachel* (1968), or careerists under the tutelage of more experienced men, as are those in *Rear Window* (1954), *Madison Avenue* (1962), *The Americanization of Emily,* and *Sex and the Single Girl* (both 1964). In one way or another, all of these examples of middle-class working women seem to support Jeanine Basinger's observations on that era's film romances. In this film category, she notes, the idea is almost always reinforced "that a woman's best choice in life is love. This will be her basic career." [12]

But inflation and a general leveling of men's salaries meant a loss of purchasing power precisely at a time when single-income families were being encouraged to purchase more goods. The revolutionary encroachment of commercial television into America's homes in the 1950s and 1960s obviously helped push privatized consumerism to new levels. And while new appliances freed married women from a certain amount of domestic labor, cash also had to be found to pay for these goods, as well as the growing array of less essential items increasingly considered necessities. John Kenneth Galbraith describes the economic ups and downs of the inflationary economy of this era, which ran on what he described as "surplus commodities and demands," and the incurring of debt by the masses. [13] Advertising inflamed desire for products and their associated prestige, pumping up middle-class expectations to the point that families had to look to the wife's "supplemental" income. Initially, Hollywood treated promotional commerce as if it were a passing fad worthy only of the self-conscious sex comedy popular at this time. In the 1963 Doris Day vehicle, *The Thrill of It All,* a mother married to a successful obstetrician finds that her wholesome image on TV can sell domestic products for high-paying male advertisers. But her family is thrown into commodity chaos because of it, and she is happily restored to the status of mother and doctor's wife in the end. Women were expected to remain not only passive homemakers but active consumers in their assumption of new responsibilities related to an increasingly competitive, image-driven society. The tension mentioned earlier between women's traditional domestic roles and their increased exposure in public careers and in sexualized media images nearly reaches the breaking point in this 1963 film. The power of television, which so quickly elevates the Doris Day character to celebrity status and a big paycheck, is soon reduced to comedy by her pratfalls related to the sale of domestic commodities. It is only this that inclines her back toward the benefits of motherhood and homemaking, and the safety of passive consumerism rather than a career in advertising (see Chapter 4). She projects the kind of innocent sincerity that sells products, but she apparently lacks the organizational talent to control the tangible benefits of her success. This is an updated version of what befalls businesswomen Mildred Pierce and Lucy Gallant, who can start successful enterprises but cannot do the financial follow-through. The American moviegoing public was still not ready for young, competent, much less sexually assertive career women whose idea of success might apply both to their own family and to their career of choice.

Writing from the perspective of 1978, Nancy Chodorow concluded that the domestic "absent father–present mother" syndrome had all along been fundamental to consumer society's lopsided gender expectations and nuclear family structures.[14] Traditional gender roles had always been synonymous with mainstream family values, since those values were based on both a sexual and an occupational double standard. But domestic support and child rearing by wives and mothers was being newly defined in relation to their targeting by advertisers and producers, who invaded the home with a cornucopia of commodities and images meant to banish every form of deprivation, to the point of *creating* needs when product demand was not forthcoming. Mothers such as the one played by Doris Day become less defined simply in terms of personal nurturing, and more recognizable as purchasing agents. This becomes increasingly important with the multiplication of product brands, and with their varying costs and advertised associations with particular lifestyles and class status. To keep abreast of the newly affluent society, however, women increasingly needed not only discriminating purchasing skills and class awareness, but "extra" income to keep their families on track toward an ever rising consumer standard. That some women, including mothers, might find great satisfaction in careers without entirely compromising their mates and/or children became a subject of considerable contention in the 1970s and 1980s.

THE 1970S AND AFTER: TRANSITIONAL CONSCIOUSNESS GIVES WAY TO CLONES, COMEDIC SUPERMOMS, AND COMPETITIVE SABOTEURS

I've heard the ticking of my biological clock, Jack . . . and I've been thinking, let's merge, you and I.

—KATHERINE TO A CORPORATE COLLEAGUE IN
Working Girl (1988)

The 1970s mark a turning point in feminist consciousness and the first signs of a change in Hollywood cinema's plots involving career women and mothers. The decreasing demands of domestic labor and the increasing monetary needs of single, head of household, and family women meant more females in the workforce and less justification for "male only" white-collar jobs. The mass consumption of domestic labor-saving devices had the unexpected side effect of adding momentum to the feminist revolution and to the demand for gender equality in the workplace. But Hollywood's response to these social and attitudinal changes was belated. Throughout the 1940s, 1950s, and 1960s, unmarried working mothers on the screen usually appeared interested in male business support and the search for a mate. By the 1970s, however, films about middle-class working women begin to shift their focus to more specific, practical struggles with employment, sexism, and domestic management, where camaraderie with other women, or the lack of it, takes on added importance. The new consciousness among these characters for gender freedom and equality results in a host of films focused on women's issues in every phase of life.

The young married mothers with one preadolescent child in groundbreaking films such as Martin Scorcese's *Alice Doesn't Live Here Anymore* (1974) and Paul Mazurski's *An Unmarried Woman* (1978) suddenly find themselves without their husbands due to death or divorce. In the former, Alice (Ellen Burstyn), the widow of a truck driver, has few job skills and is unable to get her dream of a singing career off the ground. Despite frequent job rejections, approaches from unwanted men, and her final employment as a diner waitress, the dignified Burstyn as Alice seems middle-class, even when her concluding romance with a gentleman farmer (Kris Kristofferson) does not alter her need to continue her employment. (The long-running TV sitcom *Alice,* which followed this film, appears to confirm the cultural interest in independent working women at the time.) In *An Unmarried Woman,* the suddenly abandoned Manhattan wife and mother has a career at a fashionable art gallery as well as child support and upkeep from her estranged husband, which allows her the leisure to seek solace among her women friends and from a professional therapist. Erica Benton (Jill Clayburgh) wants to restore her shaken self-confidence and discover her identity outside of the marriage that no longer exists. After several false starts with men, she eventually manages to improve her romantic life with a seemingly ideal lover and successful artist, Saul Kaplan (Alan Bates). But she chooses to remain single in the end, perhaps in part because she does not have to worry about money and can continue to pursue the urban lifestyle to which she is accustomed. Although not primarily a woman's business career film—since Erica is hardly shown at work, as if this were unworthy of attention in her construction of a new identity as single woman—*An Unmarried Woman* does encourage the possibility of options other than marriage or mere survival for the growing number of single careerist mothers heading households. (Census figures from 1992 indicate that the number of traditional family households dropped by almost 25 percent between 1970 and 1992, while households headed by single women almost doubled.)[15] Erica does secure a higher-paying job and the self-confidence to choose to live alone with her daughter.

Kramer vs. Kramer was released the year after *An Unmarried Woman* in 1979 and looks at the deserted working spouse as a father (Dustin Hoffman). His main problem, besides locating a new job and a new woman, is running the household for his young son. Having first deserted her family to "find herself," Kramer's wife (Meryl Streep) returns suddenly to take custody of her child through a lengthy courtroom hearing after she manages (offscreen) to establish gainful employment. Her career stability becomes important mainly as a child custody issue, while the nature of her work pales in comparison. The film's condemnation of child abandonment by the mother, and of dated child custody attitudes toward men in a time of rapid family sex role changes, are the dominant themes of this controversial and widely seen film. The divorced parent themes of these texts all speak to the soaring national divorce rates at this time, which were obviously affecting the jobs and the parenting of men and women. No wonder Hollywood seemed anxious to focus on private parental tribulations rather than the career side of divorced life.

Similarly, the gender struggle of single women in work and leisure is also underscored in the popular "dramedy" *Annie Hall,* and in the much darker *Looking for Mr. Goodbar* (both 1977), which feature Diane Keaton as either costar or star. In the former, Woody Allen's love story provides a whimsical view of men and women who unsuccessfully try simultaneously to build both a relationship and a career. While it suggests that women should have the prerogative to pursue their careers above devotion to romance, it also mildly reminds them that good romance will not always follow career success. The focus, however, is on the ironically named Alvy Singer (Allen), who loses his lover Annie (Keaton) in the end to her ambition for a singing career. The film's romantic poignancy finally gives hesitant encouragement to men such as Alvy, who support their women's career desires and freedom, even at the risk of losing them. In contrast, Richard Brooks's *Looking for Mr. Goodbar* is a strident thriller based on Judith Rossner's novel about an actual murder case involving Teresa (Keaton), a teacher of the deaf whose career provides the only apparent stability in her search for independence. Teresa suffers from a hereditary bone disease that seems to contribute to her restless frequenting of singles' bars. The film functions mainly as a warning to all single women who expect that sexual freedom will necessarily accompany the independence of a career life.

Meanwhile, the traditional either-or dynamic of motherhood versus career is further interrogated in Herbert Ross's *Turning Point* (1977) and in George Cukor's last film, *Rich and Famous* (1981). Both delineate ambiguities in the cultural attitudes that surround motherhood and work. Both also feature married mothers who long for or achieve success in the arts, but who remain conflicted about their work and family status. Men are kept largely in the background while dual women protagonists in each film struggle with each other and with the compromises they have had to make in choosing to pursue one arena or the other, or both. New opportunities and choices for these middle-class women create their own kinds of problems.[16] Their creative expression through the arts and as mothers guiding children is underscored, although the competitive atmosphere that exists between these women friends is also tied to their own personal conflicts about career versus family commitments. Concerning their pride as mothers or artists, they appear trapped in the same competitive rat race for success—albeit more in terms of image than merely money—as are male careerists in business.

The ethics of corporate, government, and media bureaucracies gained increased attention following the Vietnam War and Watergate scandal. And not surprisingly, working women characters in Hollywood films were frequently used as sounding boards for some of these ethical dilemmas. Assertive newswomen—played unsympathetically by Faye Dunaway in *Network* (1976), and sympathetically by Jane Fonda in *The China Syndrome* (1979)—find the television workplace a battle zone between the commercial interests of sponsors and ratings, and the factual concerns of professional journalism. This trend is only superficially continued into 1980s films such as *Broadcast News* and *Switching Channels,* in which TV newswomen are more accepted, but where commercial controversies surrounding the media are already being reabsorbed into preoccupations with romance and careerism. What is new to realistic dramas after *Network* is the tendency to recognize that the assertiveness of career women in both work and romance is not necessarily a bad thing resulting from unfortunate childhoods or neuroticism, or that their career success is necessarily a second choice to romance and marriage.

Films of the late 1970s concerning single working mothers also take on decidedly more grim and often metaphoric images and forms. Some of the most popular movies of the time feature working "mother" characters who are antagonistic and even monstrous. Consider the knife-wielding religious fundamentalist mom in *Carrie* (1976) and the coat hanger–happy Joan Crawford (Faye Dunaway) in *Mommie Dearest* (released in 1981). The proximity of horror to issues of childbirth was already literally presented in Roman Polanski's screen adaptation of *Rosemary's Baby* (1968). The diminutive tortured mother (Mia Farrow) is surrounded by satanic cultists and betrayed by her husband, who naively plays into their scheme because it benefits his career as an actor. The success of this prototypical film appears to have spawned several films in the 1970s with strong, supernatural overtones. *The Exorcist* (1974) is an exorbitantly successful shocker in which a lone career actress seems inadvertently to be punished by her heretofore healthy 12-year-old daughter's sudden possession by the devil. The radical intrusion of evil possession into this single working mother's life only exaggerates her vulnerability; she becomes reliant on male order in the form of Catholic priests. The more realistic and claustrophobic chiller *The Stepford Wives* (1975) was less successful commercially but is quite literal in its frontal attack on marital patriarchy. A social survey worker (Katherine Ross) visits Stepford, Connecticut, and attempts to liberate the doll-like wives there. The normal Stepford women are being victimized by an insidious male conspiracy that replaces their bodies with look-alike automatons meant for smiling sexual and domestic service. Avoiding the technological issues of cloning, the film indicts conservative masculine desires both to confine women to the home and to insure their utter passivity and agreeableness. Adapted like *Rosemary's Baby* from an Ira Levin best-seller, *The Stepford Wives* attempts to sound the death knell of oppressive attitudes toward women, especially if they also choose to work outside the home. One year later *The Omen* (1976) is released, and then its immediate sequel, *Damien* (1978). Both present an unsuspecting married woman who unknowingly finds herself with a demon child. And in all three cases of devil incarnation, social rank is no protection against the unknown dangers surrounding the motherly role. The horror genre has always been interested in the perversities and gore of new and strange images of birth (and death), but the sheer number and popularity of the negative maternal images in the 1970s reflect a new level of cultural paranoia that seems attributable to women's massive entry into the workforce, a revived new feminism, and widespread social disillusionment on the heels of the Vietnam War and Watergate.[17] Or is there yet more to be read into these troubling images of body possession and the birthing of evil that relates to economic drive and upper-middle-class complacency?

The late 1970s mark the appearance of innovative generic blends of horror with science fiction that begin to look beyond helpless motherly types and domestic slaves. Major films such as *Demon Seed* (1977) and particularly *Alien* (1979) blend themes of horrific reproduction into the contexts of advanced technology and corporate-government aspirations. This constitutes a significant departure, politically, from the Cold War nationalism and momism that drove most of the science fiction plots of the 1950s. Old nationalistic and economic righteousness now begins to yield to concerns about huge and nefarious homegrown institutions dominated by their own market agendas. The conflation of natural birthing with the intrusive powers of corporate-government technology is literalized in *Demon Seed*. Here a dutiful wife (Julie Christie), who is married to a high official in a secret government-corporate project in cloning, is forced to endure a robotic implantation and birthing. The biological reductionism that reads motherhood as a purely reproductive function easily lends itself to ideas of deadly distortions in nature. *Alien,* for example, represents lethal otherness as an egg-laying monster. The film's heroic woman astronaut Ripley (Sigourney Weaver) battles the female black monstrosity—which is equipped with a phallic version of vagina dentata—in order to save herself as well as rescue a "pussy" cat, which confirms her human maternal function (the cat becomes a little girl in the first sequel, *Aliens*). The fight between the two maternal figures in *Alien* is brought on by the astronaut's employer, a profit-fixated intergalactic conglomerate back on Earth, which seeks to learn the secrets of the almost indestructible creature's power. Success for these futuristic heroines is mainly an issue of surviving the mandates of corporate technology for the rights to autonomous human reproduction. The close association between a perverse alien reproductive power and a controlling corporate entity is also a central theme in the postmodernist *Blade Runner* (1982), in which genetically engineered human replicants are created as a slave race intended for dangerous industrial labor in off-world colonies.[18] Natural maternity and Mother Nature herself are on the verge of extinction in this clone-oriented corporate dystopia of 2017. Closely related is a new variation on *The Stepford Wives* called *Cherry 2000* (1988), in which robotic women made for love and domestic work can be purchased on the open market. They require only food/fuel and technical maintenance, much like one's car. In the 1980s, the image of female monsters or clones for housework and sex that are sought or created by patriarchal technology begin to make traditional representations of maternity and women's family roles appear to be icons of nostalgia. This also applies to *Back to the Future* (1985) and its sequel in 1989.

In the 1980s, the circumstantial complexities of contemporary lifestyles were reaching such troublesome proportions that working women seem forced to excessive measures. No fewer than five films were produced about employed women in crisis at this time, all of which were based on true stories. The biography of Loretta Lynn is played sympathetically by Sissy Spacek in *Coal Miner's Daughter* (1980), which traces Lynn's long climb to success and all the marital and personal problems that burden her after the singer's success dream is attained. Spacek performs again in a biographical story called *Marie* (1985). Marie is a divorced mother of three, who successfully fights her employer's corruption in a state parole system, and thus ends the political career of a Tennessee governor. Perhaps it is her status as an innocent working mother that helps to make her success possible, since this was not the outcome of another true-life whistle-blower whose story was adapted to the screen as *Silkwood* (1983). Meryl Streep plays the brave worker in a nuclear parts plant whose romantic life suffers as she becomes more politicized and involved with union activities. She dies mysteriously in a car accident while on her way to testify against her corporation's cover-up of potentially disastrous practices at their plant. Two other sympathetic biographies concern both the writer Marjorie Keenan Rawlings, who is played by Mary Steenburgen in *Cross Creek,* and the race car driver Shirley Muldowney, who is played by Bonnie Bedelia in *Heart like a Wheel* (1983). Each of these characters dump their

2.1   *Working Girl* (1988).
Tess McGill (Melanie Griffith) is the street-smart clerical assistant to company
executive Katharine Parker (Sigourney Weaver), who steals her ideas. Jack Trainer
(Harrison Ford) becomes allied with Tess, who acts the role of an executive to gain his
support in making her business plans heard by the corporate CEO.

husbands and confront sexism along their independent way to proving
themselves through their career success. These films seem less inspiring
than they might have been because of their protagonists' career obscu-
rity and each film's hindsight perspective, and perhaps because women's
career success stories were by then becoming so commonplace in cultural exchange.

Working women comedies of the 1980s are both more direct and
more contentious about the dilemmas of female corporate employees
than were their predecessors. The ensemble comedy *9 to 5* (1980) shares
with the romantic comedy *Working Girl* (1987) considerable enthusiasm for resolving the working woman's many problems in corporate
employment. The former poses a group of clerical single and married
women against their abusive and sexist male boss, whom they kidnap in
a good-old-girls' conspiracy that puts a stop to corporate sexism if not
patriarchal rule. *Working Girl,* on the other hand, reaches a larger audience by pitting woman against woman for career advancement and the
mutually desired man. The savvy, working-class secretary Tess (Melanie
Griffith) wins out in career and romance against her pretentious yuppie

boss Katherine (Sigourney Weaver) because she is only slightly more honest but considerably less jaded. In both comedies, however, honesty becomes a relative term in the heat of business and gender competition, which are viewed equally as a kind of game. Prevarication and misrepresentation are the modus operandi for these characters who are saturated in an environment of aggressive sales and marketing, which nevertheless leads to a highly ironic, overriding assumption of corporate goodwill in the end. These comedies about women in big business in the 1980s reflect women's desire not only to protest their lowly traditional fate as passive corporate service personnel, but to prove their qualifications for top executive positions. These two comedies have the energy that comes with the underdog's newly clarified hopes for executive success.

The same patriarchal assumptions regarding the benefits of corporate authority are also reflected in these films' treatment of the father's place in the nuclear family structure. Ellen Seiter finds that family-oriented films of the 1980s recognize domestic crisis but continue to reassure us of the man's dominant place. Thus, *Ordinary People* (1980) and *Three Men and a Baby* (1987) seem to prove male characters the more capable parents. Meanwhile, maternal melodramas such as *On Golden Pond* and *Shoot the Moon* "show the pain and destruction which traditional male behavior causes in the family," even as they conclude "that the only hope for saving the family rests with women adhering to their nurturing, patient, forgiving roles as wives, mothers and daughters."[19] In contrast to the texts referenced by Seiter, however, is the central maternal figure in *The Big Chill* (1983). Glenn Close plays the role not only of a married mother but of a successful doctor, whose security in her economically balanced marriage provides the primary strength for her larger peer group. Ironically, most of the members of this group have forsaken their student radicalism to accept career and professional positions within an admittedly hollow but profitable marketplace. An increasing cynicism toward institutional settings and the possibility of individual success within them becomes apparent for men and women in American cinema as the 1980s wear on.

In the late 1980s and early 1990s, working mother dramas such as *The Good Mother* (1988) and *CrissCross* (1992) feature single women who, when they place their desire for a man alongside maternal responsibilities, still meet with very lamentable results. In the former, the divorced mother (Diane Keaton) is a lab assistant who admits that her work is "just to put food on the table." She soon learns that sexual fulfillment is not acceptable for unmarried mothers in certain courts of civil law, especially if her daughter is at home and her lover is a "mere artist" without the social stability of a salaried job. She loses custody of her child to her former husband. In *CrissCross,* Goldie Hawn plays the economically marginal single mom who has lost her husband to trauma stemming from combat in the Vietnam War. She is also subsequently used by an undercover cop to bust a drug ring. Her son is almost killed in the process, and she gains little but disappointment when the agent (now her lover) reveals himself as such and simply drives off at film's end. Equally disheartening is the experience of the married TV career mom (Sissy Spacek again) in Joan Micklin Silver's *A Private Matter* (a 1992 TV movie),[20] who discovers a likely thalidomide poisoning of her unborn fetus and seeks an abortion. This effort gets publicized and stimulates a media onslaught and witch-hunt tactics from the antiabortion extremists who make her life miserable. She finds that a successful middle-class marriage and career as the star of a local children's show are not sufficient protection against public expectations enforced on motherhood. This look back at a real event of the 1970s demonstrates the persistence of patriarchal norms in a time of change. The first thing that happens, given the conservative public reaction to her desire to terminate her pregnancy, is the TV station's decision to discontinue her now suddenly controversial children's show. The historical basis for so many of these career women films therefore testifies to their social and cultural relevancy, and to the degree to which career women's success is also strictly judged in terms of their personal and private lives as well.

Baby Boom (1987), like the aforementioned *Working Girl,* provides a fantasy that combines a New Age feminism with corporate job success. Both texts place a contemporary woman's economic struggle at the center of the narrative. But in doing so they also move gender relations back into an old-fashioned romantic mode. The driving motivation for the "working girl" from Staten Island, Tess, is to be accepted into the big-league Manhattan business establishment, which she accomplishes with the help of a male exec (Harrison Ford) with whom she becomes romantically involved. The female corporate executive in *Baby Boom* (Diane Keaton) has already proven herself an effective administrator, only to be forced to start all over again when she inherits a baby. This shifts her priorities from the company and her live-in mate to her role as a mother, which drives the old boyfriend away and precipitates the end of her company employ. She eventually grows a small business in a small town with some romantic support from a local male veterinarian

2.2   *Baby Boom* (1987).
J. C. Wiatt (Diane Keaton) has trouble balancing her executive career with the
responsibilities of raising Baby Elizabeth (Kristina and Michelle Kennedy) on her own.
It is the corporate job that has to go. She builds a company from scratch and finds a
good man, fulfilling a romanticized dream for the working woman with a child.

(Sam Shepard). As in *Working Girl,* the protagonist's new lover is of the
appropriate economic rank, charm, and liberated gender attitude, and
his status as a potential husband helps to confirm her overall success in
her personal as well as work life. *Baby Boom* further demonstrates how
adopted motherhood can be made to function alongside the demands of
gainful employment. Mary Desjardin believes that this film rewards the
career mom with superwoman status by rendering "comic the contradictions facing women who are told they can have it all." [21] The text hu-
morously enshrines the supermom who can both reject and then finally
take advantage of corporate economics. By growing her own independent business in baby food after first leaving corporate security, the
protagonist proves that resourceful middle-class mothers don't need
corporate salaries to survive. How she leverages and expands her new
enterprise into a big success worthy of corporate attention remains very
sketchy. This narrative gap has resonance in her product logo, which
features her adopted infant's smiling picture on every food jar. This
strategy reiterates the significance of the happy product image over the

dicey details of everyday financial struggle. Devotion to the long hours necessary to make a new business thrive have more often undermined family time and family commitments. Hence, in its selling of super-mom idealism, this comedy pushes a very sugary form of pablum on the viewing public. In the end, her former employer wants to buy out her successful new baby food line. When she presents herself as a hard bargainer, the company hires her back at an elevated executive position in charge of that food area. In both of these two comedies, then, the single businesswoman gains success in work, romance, and domesticity. To accomplish this outcome, however, each narrative shows to what extent she must inevitably bend her behavior to accommodate dominant economic patterns. The emphasis remains on her ability to prove herself executive material in corporate settings while still upholding her feminine charms and devotion to romance and family.

Comedies of the 1980s are also very much about career men's new sensitivity to the nurturing side of family responsibilities. The feminization of the career man is a central topic in career comedies including *Tootsie* (1982), *Mr. Mom* (1983), *Parenthood* (1989), and *Mrs. Doubtfire* (1993). Since the first and last of these involve male cross-dressers, I will consider them first. Sydney Pollack's vastly popular 1982 "dramedy" starring Dustin Hoffman as the out-of-work actor, who gets a TV soap opera role while dressed in drag as the respectable Dorothy ("Tootsie"), suggests both the career desperation and the role flexibility demanded of the performative new man. In his Dorothy persona both on and off the set, the man learns the woman's point of view and expands his feminine sensitivity. Dorothy's success as a TV character ironically represents both traditional womanly sensibilities and feminist gender values, which also becomes an education for the TV public when Dorothy/ Michael Dorsey finally feels compelled out of personal honesty to expose himself on the air as a cross-dresser. His feminization is clearly a humanization of the male perspective. The hardest thing Michael has to do is confess his true gender to the woman he loves (Jessica Lange), having already grown close to her in the guise of her professional colleague and intimate woman friend. Personal honesty and an open heart finally outweighs the lie that career success can sometimes become. In the more recent *Mrs. Doubtfire,* a resourceful divorced father (a voice specialist for cartoon film sound dubbing) resorts to the impersonation of a female housekeeper in order to be close to his children, and ultimately to convince his estranged careerist wife of his creative usefulness and value as their father. In times of business and family crisis for men, too, career devotion may have to be postponed to serve family needs. Both of these texts point to the new gender role fluidity required by the challenges of postmodern work and family life, where men or women can be fired from their jobs or dumped by their spouses, and yet still find ways to bounce back through the prioritizing of romance/family alongside career dedication.

Mr. Mom is a rather conventional family comedy while Ron Howard's *Parenthood* (1989) probes newer ground as a family ensemble piece. In the former film, the husband (Michael Keaton) stays at home with the kids after he loses his job, while his wife (Teri Garr) takes up a successful career in advertising. All the clichés are here, including the overwrought father householder with the confused children, his jealousy toward his wife's boss, and her jealousy toward a lonely neighbor woman who has taken a great interest in his daytime presence at home. The plot merely works to recuperate the couple's true love and family devotion, to reinstate the husband's career potential, and to give the wife career success and get her out from under an amorous and useless boss. In the realist comedy, *Parenthood,* however, career agendas for women and men are not so happily combined with family needs. The plot offers three distinct parental situations. Both parents are available in the first two family circumstances, but the third isolates the fate of the single working mother as the most desperate of all. This harried mom (Diane Wiest) suffers through her three young children's seemingly irreconcilable problems, but she is not able to fall back on remarriage, choosing instead to be active in a new family created by her daughter. This qualified happy ending places personal and family satisfaction above and in contrast to mainstream notions of economic success. And it also serves as a reminder of just how far the working mother and her children, because of the rising expectations of middle-class life, have been forced away from traditional family and community supports and onto their own limited private resources in order to survive economically and to find happiness. One of the two married couples is headed by an ad executive (Steve Martin), who loses his job largely because of family distractions, but regains it in the end. Nevertheless, his work is clearly an unpleasant sacrifice for the sake of his family's chosen lifestyle. This kind of job enslavement is not new to fathers or mothers, but its representation here is a reminder of how exceptional such a portrait of middle-class working experience is in Hollywood film generally. Career pleasure, despite career success, cannot be assumed, particularly where personal and family life are full of the kinds of setbacks for which public recognition and money really cannot sufficiently compensate.

On a similar but far more serious note, writer/director David Mamet's postmodern drama involving a single woman psychiatrist/writer, *House of Games* (1987), reveals how thoroughly deceptive the current world of professional work and romance can become. Holding all of her profits from a best-selling book appropriately entitled *Driven,* the practicing psychiatrist Margaret (Lindsay Crouse, Mamet's wife) finally murders the con man Mike (Joe Mantegna), who became her lover, fed her fascination with the confidence game, and then grifted her out of her income. Mamet here suggests not only the deterioration of professional ethics and romantic trust, but a more far-reaching breakdown. Through a stylistic repetition of words and dialogue voiced by the stiff characters, he points to a pollution of basic perceptual and language processes under the weight of incipient fleecing. Their interpersonal communication is reduced to the deceptive logic of the interminable scam. Con artists create situations in which they can extract the cash in the possession of their victims. This suggests the direction of the spiraling excesses of consumer desires. For eventually the grifter's appetites reach an abstract dimension, like a house of games, which joins performative spectacle to pure exploitation. The cynicism required to sustain this personally manipulative mind-set is apparent at the film's conclusion. After Mike is struck by two bullets from the bitter Margaret's gun, the con artist mentor/lover remains unbowed in his disdain for his assassin's bourgeois economic and romantic outlook. In fact, the grifter's house of games is premised upon the lack of need for real violent coercion when having one's way with a "mark." Mamet's film suggests the overzealous seriousness with which professional careerists can take themselves, pumping up their egos with their ability to get what they want from their clients without giving much back in return. The career quest too can turn into a house of games, imitating the one-upmanship of corporate executive competition. Having achieved successful status, women professional characters, like men, are neither free from nor above competitive envy, particularly if they are single. Single women careerists in dramatic films of the 1980s and 1990s are about putting career first and men and family later, since steady work seems the best way to assure stability and comfort, if not complete fulfillment. The wise, elderly female mentor of the psychiatrist character in *House of Games* has no idea how far her protégé has strayed from professionalism in her "exploration" of grifter logic, or what Margaret really means in her final, darkly ironic reassertion of her mentor's lesson in psychiatry: "Learn to forgive yourself." Emotional healer Margaret exceeds the house of games in her embittered fall into murderous lawlessness.

Less violent but sharing similar themes are Michael Apted's *Class Action* and Norman Jewison's *Other People's Money* (both 1991), which feature single women lawyers without children. The young barrister (Mary Elizabeth Mastrantonio) in the former film must resist the appeals for a corporate cover-up from her immediate supervisor and lover, who sets her against her father (Gene Hackman) in a major case involving car accident deaths from poorly mounted and thus dangerous gas tank and fuel lines. (The case has the earmarks of the Ford Motor Company's Pinto disasters, which lasted throughout the 1970s.)[22] And in Jewison's film, the young attorney (Penelope Ann Miller) defends herself personally and the old wire company of her father (Gregory Peck) publicly from an antagonistic corporate raider, Larry the Liquidator (Danny DeVito). Both texts demonstrate confused personal allegiances and ethical quandaries that result from the introduction of each lawyer's father and family into the plot. Each attorney is tested in relation to her dad, who in each case represents community sentiment versus either a corporate cover-up or a hostile buyout. These attractive young executive attorneys are expected to honor their fathers and the old sense of fair play over more lucrative but jaded career opportunities typical of the 1990s, which in each case involve giving in to powerful but ethically undesirable men. It is in the context of reconciling with or outright supporting their fathers, as well as their communities, that they ultimately win their cases and demonstrate professional ethics.

A recent film that is very close to the young single lawyer texts just mentioned is *Erin Brockovich* (2000), involving an energetic, foul-mouthed beauty (Julia Roberts), divorced three times and with three young children to feed. She ends up as an ambitious file clerk in a small law office. This career vehicle for Roberts is based on the true story of a woman who personally organized a major case against a power company that resulted in one of the biggest lawsuits in U.S. history. Erin's boss and father figure in the film (Albert Finney) seems even more nonplussed by her behavior than does the Gene Hackman character with his daughter in *Class Action,* and he (Finney) is legally on the same side. The film is clear about the nature of the horrible chemical pollution practiced by the giant utility, and about how the company sought to cover it up with brazen lies, and by buying people off who had suffered the deaths of loved ones, or physical malformations, vicious cancers, or a host of other side effects. Brockovich is able to build the case and outduel the company's legal staff (which just keeps offering the victims more money), and to get a judge at one crucial stage in the court battles who lives near the site of the water pollution and does not appreciate the company's misrepresentation of the problem. Brockovich works day and night for the victims and neglects her kids, taking a personal interest in what has happened to the hundreds of people who have lived or are living in the community near the plant. But however inconvenient her sacrifice is for her children and her personal life, the campaign becomes grandly lucrative in the long run and seemingly therefore worthwhile. This makes for a nice Hollywood ending based on the facts, although whistle-blowers seldom fare so well in life or in the movies that are based on their lives. Her children survive adequately with the help of Brockovich's babysitter and part-time lover, enabling her to pursue her goals without becoming overwhelmed with guilt.

Comedies of the 1990s—in contrast to what 1980s comedies of gender vengeance like *9 to 5* suggest about bold women in patriarchal corporations—give way to more all-inclusive social satires involving the competitive excesses of American mothers out in suburbia. *Serial Mom* (1994) and *The Texas Cheerleader Murdering Mom* (1995)[23] blend a mother's cheerful concern for advancing her children's social status in and around school with a homicidal competitiveness, which seems to borrow its virulence from the rapacious tendencies of capitalism. Disregarding their innocuous working husbands, these well-to-do moms don't need to be in the workforce to feel the heat of rabid one-upmanship coursing through their veins. The very absence of significant motivations for these homemakers' radical violence is a sure sign that the abrasiveness of the commercial marketplace has invaded and polluted the positive nurturant function in the no-longer-hallowed personal space of domesticity. It becomes harder still to keep mother on a virtuous pedestal—to see her as somehow separate from and above more compulsive extremes that she may deem essential to promote her family's status.

While it is true that most of the films mentioned throughout this overview follow a conservative tendency to blame and punish careerist mothers in particular for social instability and for the decline of the patriarchal family, I hope to continue to demonstrate how other causes for a prevailing domestic anxiety and alienation are also decipherable. The many preceding examples make it clear that while work and family circumstances have changed significantly for women over the last half century, the social expectations for mothers and their families have not.

A woman's work, even if she is single and childless, continues to be defined in long-range terms of domesticity and the ultimate model of the good mother. This irreconcilable career-versus-family tension creates the kind of circumstance that tends by the 1990s to push the more traditional sacrificial mother type over into the realm of the bad mother. And it is this circumstance that will be investigated in the closing section of this chapter. I will seek to trace in greater depth and detail the psychic history of the single working mother and her offspring in three films from the still unfolding and revealing Hollywood countertradition of films noir.[24]

CONSUMERISM'S LEGACY OF NARCISSISM AND DISPLACEMENT

When a child of any age can't get love, well, it takes what it can get, any way it can get it.

—MARK RUTLAND TO HIS LARCENOUS WIFE IN *Marnie*

Certain films involving working mothers go beyond a claustrophobic domestic melodrama to emphasize the economic and psychoanalytic dimensions of the mother-child bond. As a rule, these texts fall into the films noir tradition, which constitutes a shadowy reflection of mainstream business narratives in Hollywood film. To convey important historical changes in the mother-child bond within the noir text, I will begin with the postwar *Mildred Pierce,* followed in 1964 by the high-key-lit but noir-toned *Marnie,* and then in 1990 by the brassy hustle of *The Grifters.* In each case, the child of an employed but mostly unmarried woman grows up with serious issues with the mother and a marked inclination toward criminal excess. In addition to implying that single mothers who work outside the home are twice guilty for not being married and for neglecting their children, these three films taken together suggest a historical drift toward a significant deterioration in the mother figure's ability to guide her offspring. Consumerist messages increasingly encroach upon the private sanctity of early mother-child intimacy, and thus upon the child's emotional attachments and career choices.

As a mixed-genre text that imposes a noir thriller onto a family melodrama, *Mildred Pierce* was intended by Warner Brothers producer Jerry Wald to follow on the success of an earlier film adaptation of a James Cain novel, *Double Indemnity.* The earlier film superimposed a flashback, bookend structure onto a chronological crime narrative.

Wald and director Michael Curtiz also wanted to bring into the foreground of *Mildred Pierce* the maternal/generational theme that had remained latent in the earlier film. The generational theme is central to this Joan Crawford vehicle based in motherhood, business, and class desire. Furthermore, their addition of a murder spectacle to the film, which was not in Cain's novel of the long suffering mother, was intended to expand the movie's viewership to a larger male audience.[25] The fact that the murder intrigue in the narrative also increases the burden of guilt heaped on the working mother is only partly mitigated by the story's flashback framing, by Mildred's voice-over, and by an important shift at the story's climax. The structuring of the entire narrative around the daughter's act of murder nevertheless succeeds in sharpening the film's portrait of a spoiled child and the workings of class desire within the family. Mildred is not free from blame in this scenario, even as she appears to be as much a victim as an instigator of her difficult circumstances.

Mildred Pierce is more than a domestic melodrama with a homicide, because it constantly foregrounds the mother's entrepreneurial agenda in relation to her daughter Veda. Initially, the plot records Mildred's egocentric mothering of Veda, who, as Albert LaValley suggests, is meant to carry Mildred's own "unconscious in both its idealized and darker aspects."[26] Mildred's determined efforts to establish a profitable restaurant business do bear fruit, but her increased social power and sense of self-worth does not change the psychological dynamic in her relationship to her daughter. In fact, Mildred's business success only seems to accentuate the darkening ambitions of her favored offspring. Where Mildred has expected her improved social status and material gifts to Veda to serve as a guarantee of her devotion, Veda has apparently learned from earliest childhood to mistrust them. She therefore flaunts as self-serving her mother's socially approved acts of generosity. Veda wholeheartedly embraces her mother's preferential treatment as proof of her rightful sophistication. But she does not adopt her mother's work ethic as a necessary means to class mobility. She rejects work because she has learned that Mildred will work for her. Veda can gain her rewards by manipulating her mother's insecurities and need for approval.

Veda is only nine years old when the central story begins, but her mother's special attentions to her (rather than to her tomboyish younger sister, who soon dies) already gives evidence of their interdependency. Mildred will do almost anything to meet Veda's impetuous demands as the price of her own inflated expectations for her daughter. Mildred

2.3   *Mildred Pierce* (1945).
Mildred (Joan Crawford) stands by with concern as her daughter Veda (Ann Blythe) and Monte Beragon (Zachary Scott) proceed to spend her hard-earned money and begin an affair. Even the vain Monte figures things out before his death.

vicariously encourages Veda's snobbery as a projection of her own class desires. By foregrounding Mildred's troubled bond with Veda in relation to the mother's business agenda for success, the text also shows the way market values can infiltrate maternal dynamics and become an unconscious as well as a conscious aspect of the parent's legacy. Mildred establishes early on that she feels guilty as a formerly married woman for having to work her own way up, and she consoles Veda with material gifts meant to substitute for her presence in the home.

Mildred's effort to give her daughter aristocratic status, however, is continually overshadowed by Veda's ungrateful reception of her mother's "sacrifices." To win Veda back, Mildred finally consents to a loveless marriage deal with Monte Beragon, who gives her his esteemed family name and estate in exchange for a third interest in her restaurant enterprise. Monte's rapid financial sabotage of her business, however, soon drives Mildred to tuck a .38 revolver into the pocket of her large fur coat and go after him, only to learn that he and Veda have also betrayed her sexually. Veda needs for her mother to discover her sexual liaison in order to fully enjoy her mockery of Mildred's personal sacrifices for class status, even as Veda has been materially advantaged by and adopted them herself. But when Monte suddenly reverses himself and shows some maturity by taking Mildred's side against Veda, it is Veda who picks up the gun and shoots Monte, thus isolating herself as the ignominious scapegoat, the impetuous child who refuses to grow up. In the terms set forth in the narrative, Mildred seems for a while accountable for Veda's attitudes. This is due both to her willfulness in divorcing Veda's father and to her personal preoccupation with her growing business affairs. But Mildred's final effort to spare her daughter from the law by taking responsibility for Monte's death—as well as her final resumption of a relationship with her estranged husband Bert—largely recuperates her to good maternal intentions.

And yet Mildred's concluding attempt to rescue her daughter from prison is for a crime she herself almost committed. The true significance of the murder may be read into one important prop in that scene— Mildred's fur coat. In addition to being an obvious sign of her economic success, the coat as represented here also has Freudian overtones. The immediate aftermath of Monte's murder in the closing section of the film shows Mildred attempting to report Veda's act of murder to the police by phone, as Veda literally hangs on her mother's coat sleeve begging. Veda threatens Mildred by reminding her that she is a suspect, since it was Mildred who brought the gun and first threatened Monte. Veda's subsequent shooting of Monte thus remains inextricably bound up in a regressive competition with her mother. Mildred's continued primal (pre-Oedipal) connectedness to her daughter is enhanced by the coat's hairy associations with the woman's pubic zone, as well as by its womblike embrace of the body. Veda is more threatened by a possible break in her conspiratorial, codependent pattern with her mother than by her act of violence. And that pattern has developed through the way Mildred has all along attached her interpersonal ties with her daughter to the existing class system. This implies that the spoiled Veda is guilty mainly of embracing her mother's psychosocial values, which she has read in the particular terms of "love" her mother has established. Unconsciously, then, Mildred has impeded Veda's potential for emotional independence and cognitive growth, as well as her entry into the symbolic realm of object relations considered essential to maturation in Freudian-Lacanian psychology.

At the very least, therefore, Mildred bears some responsibility for creating in Veda a new variation on the femme fatale, who uses her sexuality to spite her mother in her competitive pursuit of selfish economic gain. Neither Monte nor his marriage to Mildred can survive the interlocked forces of this same-sex, parent-child struggle. The plot movement toys with the demonization of the maternal feminine, but Mildred can be faulted mainly for acting out as mother the specific form of substitutional logic that she has inherited from the prevailing values of her society. Mildred is defeated not by her hopes for her daughter's growth and prosperity, but because she has embraced the values of a hierarchical class system that have alienated her from what might originally have been worthy in both her husband and her daughter. Veda, however, becomes the easier mark for blame, despite her devoted embrace of her mother's class values and the absence of any alternative measure for evaluating her own self-worth. Like the homicidal acts in other films noir, Veda's aggression cannot be contained within either the mainstream business or family discourse, although it has sprung from an obsessive class desire that haunts both. This film's successful genre combination of melodrama and thriller becomes an unintended treatise on how the selfish class desire of one generation can become further exaggerated in the excesses of the next.

Exactly how a mother should raise her child has been an active debate in popular culture since the 1940s, when social expectations were increasingly being led by experts' opinions.[27] Feminist critics have also been particularly alert to the co-optation of the role of motherhood by patriarchal forces and institutions. Following in part on Julia Kristeva's work on the "abjectification" (degradation) of maternity, Barbara Creed describes how a mother's earliest attachment to her child is already doomed to negative connotations under the ideals of patriarchy:

> She is associated with the world of nature — and consequently denigrated — because of her reproductive and mothering functions. She teaches the infant to abhor what she herself comes to represent within the signifying practice of the symbolic. An ideology which denigrates women is also endorsed by woman: patriarchal ideology works in and through woman.[28]

Because the mother must encourage the child's identification with alternative love objects that will foreclose the totality of her own nurturing authority, the entry into symbolic understanding tends to denigrate the mother's entire position as within the orbit of the infantile. Nancy Chodorow takes this a step further in her recognition of the specific forms these cultural interventions may take. She notes the commercial aspect of intrusions into the earliest life stages, where "the reproduction of these social relations of parenting is not reducible to individual intention but depends on all the arrangements which go into the organization of gender and the organization of the economy."[29] And it is exactly through these socializing forces of economy and gender that Mildred's parenting of the increasingly venal Veda may be read. Their story suggests a process of contamination in parent-child intimacy that consequently stunts child development into obsessiveness.

What *Mildred Pierce* also helps to clarify, however, is the way the dominant economic discourse in American patriarchy denigrates men. The male characters who struggle to get ahead here are equally poor models of family and social leadership. Monte is a parasite, and Wally—who for a price helps Mildred get her business started—is exploitative in sex and commerce. Wally has driven Bert out of their real estate partnership because of his own greed and lust for ownership. A single man, Wally loves fast profits and fast women, and is thus a threat to family ideals, as opposed to Bert, who shows some potential to become a supportive family man. In Wald and Curtiz's effort to make *Mildred Pierce* a woman's film and a masculine thriller, the text both punishes and absolves the maternal feminine for its tendency to excess. It is the combination of feminized consumer impulses (Mildred's and Monte's) and masculine indifference to production or family leadership (Burt's lack of income and ambition at the outset and Wally's chauvinistic opportunism) that contribute directly to the Electra complex that is Veda.

The contradictions in patriarchal myths surrounding motherhood are also at the heart of the social class discourse in Hitchcock's transition-era thriller *Marnie*. The artificial studio lighting and backscreening, and the formalized acting and blocking in this 1964 production, contribute to a sense of claustrophobia surrounding the main character and her business milieu. Marnie is shown to have become a career thief because of her repression of an accidental murder she committed as a child, and because her mother, Bernice Edgar (Louise Latham), has continued to deny that past in order to hide her former life as a prostitute, victimized by poverty and sexually exploited. It is Bernice's class alienation that undermines her daughter's confidence in social relations and lays the groundwork for Marnie's fixation on the singular power of money. This wealth is further to be attained through disguise in a serial pattern of burglaries of large businesses. The film begins with a full shot on Marnie's large purse, tightly clutched under her arm and stuffed with stolen cash. Like the cunnic symbol in dream literature, the purse

2.4   *Marnie* (1964).
Marnie (Tippi Hedren) is driven by cash rather than romance with the wealthy
business owner Mark Rutland (Sean Connery), who pushes her into abusive but
perhaps also therapeutic directions.

suggests that Marnie equates/confuses the possession of money with
her sexual identity. This single image of the fetishizing of capital is also
carried through in later scenes of Marnie's own visual (via a camera
zoom in/zoom out) fixation on the business vaults that contain the objects of her desire. Marnie's covert assault on a hierarchical business
patriarchy is more than a retaliation against class and gender exploitation. Her aggressive fetishization of money/power is also a reactionary
response to her painful family history that entraps her in a cycle of
displaced desire for her mother's love. The mother-related motivation
for Marnie's childhood act of homicide is comparable to Veda Pierce's,
since both girls kill inconvenient men to reunite with their mothers.
These acts constitute both class defiance and psychological parallels to
the father-son dynamic of Oedipal competition. They call attention to
the female child's special problem of separating from the mother and
maternal authority in a commodity-driven culture.

Only the threat of prison drives the frigid Marnie to marry the vain and wealthy Mark Rutland (Sean Connery), whose surname invokes animal sexuality. Unlike the emasculated or greedy males in *Mildred Pierce,* Mark dominates Marnie in marriage and even rapes her out of sexual frustration and a proprietary class perspective. Mark's technique of confrontational psychotherapy with Marnie also holds Bernice fully accountable for her daughter's frigidity and criminality, while his own interest in the mother remains strictly self-serving. In any case, Marnie's victimization by her mother's disdain is clearly enunciated in the film, which leads Rebecca Bailin to note that the screenplay is by a woman, Jay Presson Allen, and that a progressive female enunciation is present in the text as a whole.[30] In the end, Mark and Marnie drive slowly away from the physically and emotionally crippled mother and toward a self-consciously painted backdrop that features a huge ocean liner. The ship hovers over Bernice's Baltimore row house like a monster of desensualized enterprise. And near Bernice's door, joyless neighborhood children chant of sickness (and of Marnie's particular cash obsession): "Call for the doctor, call for the nurse, call for the lady with the alligator purse."

Julia Lesage has pointed out that "rescue by a male is one of the major hegemonic female fantasies."[31] But Mark's attempt at the psychological rescue of Marnie (preceded by his rape of her and Marnie's attempt at suicide) is at best foreboding. Marnie appears to remain only partially reconciled with the blood-dripped images associated with her tortured mother. Her mother's own initial, youthful exchange of sex for a boy's sweater, which led to conception, Marnie's birth, and eventually Bernice's prostitution, is clearly linked to Marnie's blackmailed marriage to Mark. Michele Piso has observed that the entire series of relationships in the film are inflected with the pale of commerce, which stifles the "feeling bond . . . Cold to the touch, the purely economic transaction maintains vertical relations of power and privilege" that "deny the reciprocal incorporation of human desires and differences."[32] The gender and class and psychological antagonisms that characterize the experiences of Mark and Marnie and Bernice are not so easily resolved by the social institutions of marriage and psychotherapy.

Marnie's mother, like Veda's, has already been affected by exploitative class experiences and consumer desires, which further invade the emotional sanctity of their early bonding with their daughters. As a result, the eventual healthy confrontation with a sexual and symbolic "other" essential to the full development of both sexes[33] in the Oedipal stage is already confused with the authority of commercial exchange. Maternal succor and the foundation of gender identity already show the intrusion of depersonalizing relations with economic power and substitutional commodity objects. Andreas Huyssen and other postmodernists have suggested that "the decay of ego formation in the family" is due to an "invasion of the psyche by the laws of capitalist production";[34] and further that "twentieth century capitalism has 'reunified' economy and culture by subsuming the cultural under the economic, by reorganizing the body of cultural meanings and symbolic significations to fit the logic of the commodity."[35]

Most recently, the direction of future generations under the expansive regime of a commercially dominant sign culture may be traced through *The Grifters* (1990), which provides an even more explicit metaphoric articulation of the working mother and family in crisis. This late or postnoir film is reminiscent of *Marnie* in its focus on a solitary child who is seriously mother-impaired. But the singular "accident" that coagulates Marnie's distorted ties to her mother is not duplicated in Stephen Frears's production, where a seemingly universal pattern of economically inscribed relationships is indicated. The young Marnie's contemporary male equivalent in *The Grifters* is Roy Dillon (John Cusack), who reflects an entire history of disadvantage, indifference, and disconnection. Both Marnie and Roy may be repressed figures, lacking an identity beyond their compulsive criminal functions. But unlike Marnie, Roy has no mother's hidden memory of a particular event with which to begin the psychological resolution of his past. The cause of his grifting, therefore, other than his youthful mother's inadequacy and absence as a parent, is made to seem broadly indigenous to a generalized contemporary scene.

The basis for Roy's conflict with his mother and their choice of careers is directly referenced in the text. Lilly (Anjelica Huston) was 14 at Roy's birth, and he left her when he was 17 because they continued to be more like competing siblings than mother and offspring. They appear to require a third party to parent them both. Deprived of nurturing child care, they have fitted themselves to a pattern of deceptive profiteering that reflects their distrust of traditional authority and enterprise. Roy and Lilly take their cue as con artists from the drive to prove themselves tougher than any emotional deprivation, and more resilient than any limitation in superficial bourgeois identity. They bypass emotion by stripping themselves of social sensibilities in order to exploit those of others. This behavior appears to reiterate their own experience of maternal betrayal. I would suggest that *The Grifters* projects such a profound mistrust of mothering under the extreme stress of social commerce that it points to an altogether new mother-paradigm in American cinema.

As a contemporary noir text, *The Grifters* also offers some striking stylistic contrasts to *Mildred Pierce*. Where Michael Curtiz's postwar adaptation of James Cain's novel constructs a dark watery world of disorientation at the western edge of the continent, Stephen Frears's adaptation of Jim Thompson's *The Grifters* represents the same Los Angeles location as a washed-out, surface metropolis of aggressive deception. A complexity of character and family and class motivation in the earlier film gives way to a contemporary flatness of character and reduction of motive in the latter. Mildred as the obsessed, overprotective mother who lavishes gifts has her contemporary polar opposite in the self-centered and underprotective mother Lilly who narcissistically hoards. The murder mystery that misleadingly sets up the viewer in the earlier film becomes the revealed mystery of the hustle itself in the latter. The deceptive world of appearance and reality in 1945 becomes the aggressive world of appearance that is the reality in 1990. (Jim Thompson's novel was published in 1963 and reflects the 1950s era, but it is updated in the adaptation to an unspecified contemporary time frame.)

The Grifters is consistent with the worldview of its main characters in its unwillingness to moralize or to provide a resolution for its bottom-line orientation. Even the bad mother Lilly suffers egregiously without being allowed to become the martyr to maternal desire that Mildred Pierce becomes. Lilly saves her son's life in a medical emergency, but she is revealed to have the most self-centered motivations of all. Lilly is so engrossed in deceptive practices that her advice to her son is more threatening than supportive: "Get off the con, Roy, you don't have the guts for it." And in fact Roy's minimalist, anonymous existence in a cheap hotel is less severe than that of his mother, who is consistently shown in her car or overnighting in motel rooms with her handgun under her pillow. Lilly is the furthest possible remove from a maternal model, and she is therefore hardly in a position to direct the career choice of her emotionally undernourished son.

She is much closer in style to her younger counterpart Myra (Annette Bening), with whom she is forced to compete for her life savings and her life. Myra is not yet subjugated by a big racketeer as is Lilly. Rather than being simply tough as Lilly is, Myra is a performance-oriented seducer who seems to enjoy the comic aspect of paying her back rent with her

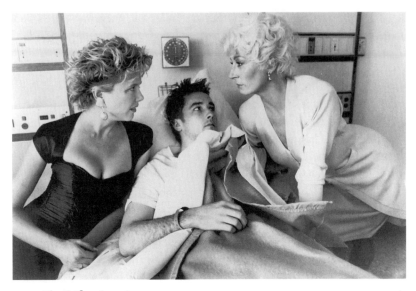

2.5   *The Grifters* (1990).
Grifter Roy Dillon (John Cusack) finds himself overwhelmed by a grasping criminal of a mother, Lilly (Anjelica Huston). She suddenly wants to run his life after years of absence. Lilly also wants him to dump his girlfriend, Myra (Annette Bening), who has "long con" ideas for Roy's future.

body instead of cash. She also believes she can recruit Roy and score a fortune from the "long con" she learned from an earlier lover, and thus retire to financial freedom and presumably happiness. The in-group, staged setup of the long con plays on the greed of the pre-identified cash-rich mark, whose money will then be divided among the players. Myra is clearly a child of the commercial entertainment age who feeds off and reiterates desire in her narcissistically inflated and meretricious spectacle of herself. She is also a slightly younger mirror image of Roy's mother.

Roy's mother Lilly in *The Grifters* may be tougher than the mothers in the two earlier films, but she is also more desperate and cold-blooded, short-circuiting her ability to support or guide at all. Lilly snuffs out first Myra and then her own son out of fear of reprisal from her racketeering boss, who has already tortured her psychologically and physically. She requires cash to leave town and escape his fury. Lilly's murderous acts not only indicate the difficulty in simply assigning personal blame to a bad mother or child, but suggest the denial of further confidence in the patriarchal maternal ideal altogether. Lilly's tortured existence signifies a new level of disconnected self-preoccupation that simply overwhelms the possibility of nurturing motherhood. In the closing scene, Lilly strikes her son with a briefcase full of his own money because he won't give it to her. This blow smashes the glass he is holding into his neck and cuts his jugular, sending him to the floor and to his death. Lilly thus gives new meaning to the word "cutthroat." She sobs only momentarily over Roy's prostrate body before she quickly scrapes up his blood-spattered cash, exchanges her vehicle for his, and drives away into the hazy, barren streets of L.A. In her viciousness built on the substitution of money power for love, Lilly becomes the ultimate bad mother. As such, she is also recognizable as a creation of the substitutional tendencies of capitalist society, just as are the femmes fatales Myra or Veda, who become sacrificial figures. Both the sacrificial and bad mother types are born of a misplaced intimacy and object-love. *The Grifters* refuses to confirm the nostalgic myths of a nurturing and sacrificial motherhood, and pushes that mythology to the brink of extinction. It also shares this characteristic with the urban gangster film. In Francis Ford Coppola's otherwise brutal Mafia world of *The Godfather* films, the sentimentalized mother and the crime family represent a contradiction that would seem to undermine any great social significance attributable to insular family values. Where a criminal marketplace driven by violent force prevails, the glorification of motherhood becomes a captive phenomenon that has social relevance only as an excuse for family business clannishness. The glorification of the mother within the patriarchal Mafia family is only possible because of her complete separation from the "business" affairs of the men.

As I have suggested, in line with the observations of certain social and psychoanalytic observers of recent years, the problem for the average contemporary child is that the mother's authority in the child's socialization has been greatly modified, even in the earliest years. Stephen Frosh, in *The Politics of Psychoanalysis,* explains that for psychiatrist and cultural analyst Chistopher Lasch,

[i]t is the surrounding social world (mass production and consumption, with its attendant fetishizing of images and manipulation of democratic structures in the interests of bureaucratic administration, etc.) that gives rise to the solicitude/distance dynamic of mothering that in turn leads to the development of the narcissistic personality. . . . [T]he child is thence left with enormous fantasies of maternal possibilities, but no hope for their fulfillment, giving rise to the self-bolstering, self-avoiding pattern.[36]

What Lasch and Frosh are describing amounts to a new factor in the maternal and Oedipal setting faced by the child, where parental authority is invaded by a new third term. *The Grifters* suggests an exaggerated version of this invasion of commercial signifiers, which cannot nurture in any direct way, but which dominate the contemporary regime of values. In the panic of abandonment experienced by Roy and by his mother before him, they are driven like Marnie to accumulate security in the form of a covert cash reserve or "stash." This substitute object or stash no longer serves the temporary symbolic function of aiding the child's separation from maternal dependency that is necessary for entry into the symbolic adult world. What the stash does represent is an extended dependency that is comparable to the larger cultural overinvestment in substitutional commodity forms. The new socioeconomic attributes that become formative of identity involve a relational mode of thinking, which moves away from Freud's original formulation of fixed instincts and repression. This new relational system tends toward narcissistic patterns that bypass the pain of mother separation and the law of the father, which has meaning in the Oedipal framework, and insinuates instead personal identification with highly mediated and seductive commercial forms of address.[37]

Roy and Lilly are prototypes of this privatized environment of radical displacement, where capital and commodities are transformed into virtual surrogate parents with all the attendant cathexis associated with unresolved parental dependency. Stephen Frosh elaborates:

With the demise of the powerful patriarchal family comes the post-Oedipal image of the pre-Oedipal world, the consumer narcissist faced with the feeding, invading, obliterating other which has no specific personality, but which creates desires in the same instant as it fulfills them, leaving the genuine needs of the individual untouched. . . . [T]he administrative society operates more forcefully through its ability to protect people against their real (pre-Oedipal) desires by manipulating what seem to be their needs.[38]

Just as maternal patterns that foment narcissism are social constructions, so, Frosch suggests, is their remedy. For him, "escape from narcissism is a social rather than a psychological project."[39]

The new conflicted mother image no longer hides the phallus in the fur coat as the distraught Mildred once hid her gun. The contradictory terminology of the "phallic mother" takes on meaning in the simulational multiplicity of contemporary phallocentrism, where nurture and sexual difference are quickly derailed into the rootless objectivity of commercial relations. The questions of whether mother is married or single, or goes into business or not, must be viewed in the real value terms of a mass culture that the declining family no longer influences in a significant way. The mother's arm that swings the cash-filled valise at and into her son's throat in *The Grifters* not only rejects patriarchal motherhood's figurehead status as a moral arbiter, but represents the evacuation of hope for significant maternal nurturance as an antidote to a nation bent on consumer solutions and values as they also influence career choices and behavior on an everyday basis.

The paradigm of this new career mother in cinema reflects an extreme contradiction, with the supermom as wealthy provider enshrined on one side of Hollywood's imagist "coin" (*Baby Boom*), and the bad mother as hoarding narcissist emblazoned on the other (*The Grifters*). To stretch the metaphor, the spinning of this coin suggests the circularity of the postmodern sign. Far from being oppositional, these image polarities within the business career film must be considered together as two sides of the same desperate syndrome. Together they constitute the dynamic of the cultural marketplace of surrogacy that displaces real desires into substitutional needs. Unlike *Mildred Pierce* in 1945, *The Grifters* no longer gives voice to and then represses ideological contradictions between commerce and domesticity. Instead, it demonstrates the reduction of maternity and family autonomy to a reflective complicity with the image/products of social power. The criminal psychology so prevalent in *The Grifters* begins to look more and more like a mainstream psychology of commerce that cannibalizes the foundations of maternity, family, and community. Lilly is the only central character in *The Grifters* who survives. But she is so destructive in her motherhood and enslaved by her criminal work that her survival suggests total cultural defeat. In such an environment, even the best of mothers is left to contemplate the loss of autonomous personal influence in the determination of future generations.

Under such circumstances, the increased opportunities in the business and employment marketplace for women, while supportive of women's independence and rights, do not in themselves answer to the growing problems of pervasive commercialization in the socialization process that affects children, parents, and employees of both sexes. In all three of these examples, the working mother becomes determinative of her child's fate mainly in negative ways that reflect her own inability to intervene for her child's sake or her own against a potent success mandate that encourages envy and greed. This success mandate can be seen to corrupt not only the mother's business pursuits but the nurture of her children as well. The child is left both to long for the parent's unconditional love and to rebel against or compete with the parent as a result of the class values that are enforced. Noir-oriented treatments of commerce and parenting, particularly involving the single working mother, survey the darker family psychology behind the career success mystique.

Judge your success by what you had to give up to get it.

—AN OLD PROVERB

CHAPTER 3
THE ENTREPRENEURIAL IMPULSE

Any consideration of the business and career film would be incomplete without specific attention to the entrepreneur, who plays such a central role in American economic history and ideology. Entrepreneurial business success is what most people have in mind when they conjure an image of the American Dream. This particular avenue of success suggests both individual independence and self-initiative, and a sense of the glory of personal and family fulfillment through those means. The dynamics of small business enterprise are also very different from career business tracks involving corporate employment and perhaps multiple employers over time. Success in small business requires considerable personal investment risk and complete, diligent commitment, which offers little or no separation between business and private life. And while there may be autonomy of decision making within sole proprietorships, there is no control over market pressures defined mainly by larger enterprises and their superior resources and political connections. Furthermore, while small business in America best represents the essential ideal of self-initiative and opportunity in a putative free market, statistics are also consistently clear on the failure rate of new businesses in the first three years (over 80 percent). This flies in the face of the idealism regarding new business opportunity and success generally. In fact, nowhere is the contrast between commonly accepted business ideals and marketplace realities greater than for the beginning

entrepreneur. This contrast becomes readily apparent in most entrepreneurial business films.

There are several examples of films about mom-and-pop businesses
during the Hollywood classical period, when small enterprises were a
way of life for so many. But the numbers of these films have declined
with the historical rise of chain stores and franchise operations in the
culture as a whole. While small businesses continue to exist throughout
the American economy, they have had less impact on the political and
economic domains than have corporate interests. Most new businesses
take years to grow to a size where they can be considered economically
and politically influential, and this is usually brought about after they
go public and become eligible for either mergers or buyouts. Because
of the proven effect and cost of advertising as a prime leverage to market expansion under capitalism, small businesses are almost forced to
grow and/or merge to survive for the long haul. The survival of George
Bailey's family building and loan business in the 1930s and 1940s in *It's
a Wonderful Life* (1946) is mainly an expression of hope for the continua-
tion of local, community-concerned enterprises. But George's nightmare vision into what things would be like had he not been around to
compete is also a warning about the fragile status of small, community-
conscious businesses in the face of larger, blockbuster networks that can
underprice them or simply buy them out. Capitalism is really geared
toward corporate and conglomerate monopoly status rather than the
survival of entrepreneurs. In recent years start-up, small business activity has increasingly adapted to advanced communications systems
and networks that are geared to national and global markets. Public
interest has also moved of late to more technologically inclined entrepreneurs, and thus cinema has gradually begun featuring protagonists
who exist in this setting.

Part one of this chapter is devoted primarily to a survey of Hollywood cinema's representations of men and women entrepreneurs and
their success goals. True of men and women who start or run small
businesses is their particular sensitivity to local conditions and everyday
life. Their enterprises represent very localized staging grounds where
the all-important interactions between their personal development as
businesspeople and cultural-economic changes take place. Individual
or family business responsibility obviously involves constant decision
making that can be as decisive for personal ethical development as for
the survival of the business. An idea of how little certain gender configurations have changed in the small business workplace historically

becomes apparent in a comparison of *Shop around the Corner* (1940) with its technically updated but near remake in Nora Ephron's *You've Got Mail* (1998). What has changed other than technology is a further increase in gender role confusion and ego image vulnerability alongside a more diversified ego base. In comedy also, the one-dimensional curmudgeon boss has almost disappeared, even from corporate thrones.

The second section of this chapter views family business stories in film from the important perspective of immigrant, ethnic, and racial experience. America's history of the last three centuries has been characterized by the promise to house the world's politically and socio-economically oppressed peoples under a banner of democratic liberty, economic opportunity, and equal treatment under the law. And while this is tragically ironic in relation to the history of Native American and African American experience, the story of immigrants and their small businesses is essential to the "land of opportunity" mythology. Ethnicity and race is also a key element of personal, family, and community identity, and often does not mesh easily with majority assumptions of identification. The minority entrepreneur represented in film must contend with the special problem of adjustment to dominant white business and cultural forms, which include the political pecking order of established special business interests in the nation-state. This process tests the myth of American political economic inclusiveness and multicultural diversity from one era to the next.[1] All four minority entrepreneur films in this section are considered in relation to their representation of the process of "integration" with the nation's dominant political economic regime.

The two final sections of this chapter are devoted to a special category of films about ambitious individual women who choose highly specialized, illegitimate means of getting started or getting ahead in businesses—the entrepreneurial femme fatale. This figure has a special place in modern Hollywood film and American culture because of some very significant convergences between the lust for money and sex, and the sense of prestige and power that are attached to both. Historically, woman's success goals have been hampered by a lack of access to the legitimate business domain, which partly explains her incarnation beginning in films of the 1940s as a wizened dame with frustrated but recognizable entrepreneurial impulses. The continued presence of the business-oriented seductress in films of the 1970s, 1980s, and 1990s points to changing meanings in her political economic and gender significance. Not only is this contemporary figure represented as a danger to male lovers and coconspirators, but in some cases as a metaphorically native kind of resistance to or epitome of conglomerate businesses generally. Other than the manipulative use of sex in the contemporary femmes' drive for success, it is sometimes difficult to distinguish her goals of economic success from those of legitimate businesswomen. Therefore, the two closing sections of this chapter consider this particular type of femme fatale, from her illegitimate entrepreneurial roots in postwar noir to her corrupted entrepreneurial opportunism in films of the 1990s.

SURVEYING THE AGONY AND ECSTASY OF OWNERSHIP

Performance used to count. For 15 years we met our obligations with unions, with the mills, and with the bank. We don't get down on our knees to anybody.

—HARRY STONER (JACK LEMMON) TO HIS ACCOUNTANT PHIL, WHO HAS JUST ADVISED HIM TO DECLARE BANKRUPTCY IN *Save the Tiger*

All of the dramatic and comic films considered in this section contribute to the sense that the entrepreneurial business success mystique exists and has a potentially liberating role despite long economic odds to the contrary. The agony and ecstasy of entrepreneurship even among highly qualified members of the white majority further evoke the very tenuous nature of America's quintessential success dream, as well as the increasingly tenuous family institution that it is meant to support. In the classical *It's a Wonderful Life* and *All My Sons,* and in the later *Save the Tiger* and *Tucker,* the business portrait that emerges is one of extreme individual and family hope and community idealism more or less aligned against a well-organized and well-heeled corporate front of superior size and political influence. While the protagonists in each film are heroic in their social ambition, they also experience desperation and a sense of failure related to their perceived personal shortcomings. They have to believe in themselves just to start and/or sustain their small enterprises, which are economically marginal by definition. Rather than being confirmations of the small business success dream, the important films considered here mainly itemize the dream's easy drift into a nightmare.

One of the reasons Frank Capra's fable *It's a Wonderful Life* has endured in popularity is because it paints such a simple and straightforward portrait of the two extremes of business attitudes still in contention today.

The one version represented by George Bailey (James Stewart) favors the small businessman who stays put and places the greater welfare of his immediate community above all other concerns, including his own profit. Those businesspeople who define their career success in relation to their sociocultural contribution to the general betterment of society represent what I will call the "social concern model." The other model in the film, of course, is represented by the stereotypical fat-cat capitalist Henry Potter (Lionel Barrymore), whose eye never wavers from profit, acquisitive growth, and monopoly control. These are the goals of what could be dubbed the "self-involved model" of business practice. In the eyes of Potter, George Bailey and his father are not really businessmen at all but simply "chumps" who let the "riff-raff" dictate their own lack of profit and growth. In this Potter has some justification, since capitalism favors rapid growth and expansion, and tends to buy out or kill off small businesses that merely stand in place. The narrative stereotype in the entrepreneur film inevitably presents little capitalism as good, and big capitalism as bad. The public loves the struggling entrepreneur, the underdog, and disdains the corporate kingpin. This simple story formulation also overlooks the fact that some entrepreneurs intend to sell off their businesses to larger ones at a certain stage of growth, leaving themselves open for further options. Potter extends a similar offer to George, asking him to accept a $20,000-a-year three-year employment contract with him that would mean the end of George's building and loan business. Potter knows that George never wanted to run the Bailey Building and Loan or to stay in Bedford Falls in the first place, and that the little business continues to be a burden to the young man. More than obliterating the Baileys' company, Potter hopes to take advantage of George's financial weakness by converting him to the narrow profit goals of big capitalism. Potter wants to prove his point that you can't be a nice guy in business and hope to survive.

Capra's postwar film obviously sentimentalizes the representation of the two models of business success in several ways. There is blatant typecasting involving age, demeanor, family status, and personality. George is young, friendly, and generous, while the curmudgeon Potter is old, cold, single, and hoarding. Where George specifically looks to rescue marginal people at some cost to himself, Potter disregards them to focus on serving the rich for greater financial and political advantage. Moreover, Potter is willing to be fundamentally dishonest when it gives him competitive advantage, while George is honest and giving to a fault, which virtually destroys his business but for the mercy of the community. *It's a Wonderful Life* represents the small entrepreneur as superior in ethics as well as personality, while his nemesis is selfish and unforgiving at the personal and the business level. The extent of Bailey's innocence and moral purity as a family and business man set against Potter's cold-hearted and literally decrepit status is a blatant Dickensian contrast, were it not for the fact that Potter's business methods are closer to contemporary reality than are Bailey's, which lends the film its irony and lasting appeal. This kind of nostalgic representation in the film is also permitted by the leeway that audiences extend to fables, which are meant to carry symbolic and not necessarily realistic validity. This film finally has enduring appeal because American citizens continue to want to believe in the viability of good community intentions on the part of capitalist institutions. They want to believe that grassroots family business and active community participation and support at that level can redeem the problems of big capitalism that may destroy families and communities (as represented, for example, in socially conscious documentaries such as *Harlan County, USA* [1977] and *Roger and Me* [1989]). It is appropriate that Capra's film ends on Christmas, and that the George Bailey Santa Claus figure receives gifts in return from the townspeople he has so long supported. Of greater concern, however, is George Bailey's nightmare supplied by his guardian angel Clarence, which shows the hostile and lurid Pottersville that Bedford Falls would have become had George never been born. George's nightmare suggests the realistic side of Capra, an immigrant and public figure,[2] who knew well enough that Christmas only comes once a year, and for some hardly ever. An effective community rescue anything at all like the one in *It's a Wonderful Life* would be miraculous today. And so too, perhaps, would be the likelihood that a young man like George who is asked by his father to take on a weak business (Bud Fox, for example) would actually do so.

Arthur Miller's play *All My Sons* was adapted to the screen by Irving Reis in 1948. It follows a steel manufacturer, Joe Keller (Edward G. Robinson), who is so determined not to lose a big government contract during World War II that he lets a shipment of bad airplane pistons be distributed. The faulty parts cause the deaths of pilots, and as Joe later learns, the suicide of his eldest son. Joe had lied about the shipment when a case was brought against him, blaming his assistant and letting him go to jail. But when Joe's younger son Chris (Burt Lancaster) returns from the war and becomes engaged to the condemned man's daughter, Chris gradually learns the truth about what happened. Chris confronts his father in a moving scene, which soon drives Joe to take his own life. Miller's play shows how ethical lapses in business can have great personal and social consequences. It also demonstrates just how thoroughly one can blind oneself to ethical responsibility in the pursuit of income and market share. The film version of *All My Sons* delivers the same themes, but Irving Reis's stage-bound presentational aesthetic is weighted with words, which leaves the content feeling moralistic and wooden, and finally self-enclosed. On its own merit, however, the story is quite revealing. The degree to which Joe has isolated himself within the bubble of his business reality correlates with the extent of his ethical denial, as if his internal company status as the beloved boss could supersede the rules of the greater social world in which he must live.

Once his denial is stripped away, Joe Keller's only explanation for his cover-up is the desire to better provide for his surviving son, Chris, which is the same business motivation driving Mildred Pierce in her provision for her surviving daughter Veda. Once again, underwriting one's child's future is meant to excuse any behavior geared to family business success. This implies that one of the great strengths of family business, the internal confidentiality and common mutuality of purpose, can also become a curse, binding a family like Joe's in a web of lies and deceit, and ultimately tearing it asunder. Joe Keller's willingness to bend the rules for his children converts an initially supportive parental motivation into a serious social liability. Joe's justification for taking special license to get ahead financially is, moreover, a lesson to his children that any behavior in the name of "family" profit is acceptable. Chris, meanwhile, turns against the family patriarch due both to his brother's suicide and to the imprisonment of his fiancée's father, all because of Joe's desperate act to save his business.

Joe not only has placed the standard of financial success and class ascension too highly in relation to his children, but has overinvested himself personally in his business. His sons are expected to carry on this patrimony as a birthright, a sacrifice to him in the only terms he can understand. Under the circumstances, this expectation pollutes the family business success ethic, turning respect for the father into a personalized business obligation. It is not Joe's ambition for betterment but the way in which it is pursued that becomes critical. Joe's overdeterminative economic mandate thus creates an environment for him of temptation and crime, and for his sons of guilt and the need for retri-

3.1 *Save the Tiger* (1972).
The garment business of Harry Stoner (Jack Lemmon) is headed for bankruptcy despite a successful new clothing line. Harry tries to convince his financial manager, Phil (Jack Gilford), to help him create the opportunity for an insurance payoff, which could save the company and its employees.

bution. Based on this example, the seductive pull of capitalism appears so strong in its encouragement of egotistic authority as to require active legal oversight in order to protect family as well as public interests.

In marked contrast to the supportive role of the entrepreneur's traditional family in these postwar films, there is the innocuous state of the small businessman's consumer-oriented family and community in John Avildsen's *Save the Tiger* (1973). This post–Vietnam War Hollywood transitional film reveals a level of family miscommunication and business and social disorientation far beyond the moral clarity espoused by classical family business films. The mental disorientation of the garment maker Harry Stoner (Jack Lemmon) is matched by a rambling plot throughout which Harry experiences varying degrees of clarity. Those who know him personally, including his mostly baffled and ineffective wife, are at least sympathetic to the World War II combat origin of his often disconnected psychological state. Although Harry is unable to get through a simple public address to his buyers at his annual garment show, he is having a good design year. It is also apparent, however, that this will not be enough to rescue his company. For the protagonist Harry, as in so many other small business films, the issue is survival rather than success, and to what extremes he will go to persevere. Harry and his bookkeeper, Phil (Jack Gilford), know the company cannot hold off on its debt payments long enough to fill the new clothing orders, but the alternatives are tough: borrow money at exorbitant rates from the mob; declare bankruptcy and give up; or commit arson on their small storage plant and collect cash from their insurance company. Harry chooses the latter over Phil's insistence that they declare bankruptcy.

The film succeeds in re-creating the feel of Harry's mental state through dark and grainy documentary-like visuals and interior flashbacks of combat that leave Harry talking to himself, stuttering, or speechless. He also feels degraded by what he is expected to do for some of his male buyers, as well as by his choice for survival, which will destroy part of another business as well as his own. From the moment he rises in the morning his wife is on him to call his shrink, Dr. Frankfurter, for hypnosis. Harry has already sent his kids for schooling in Switzerland because he thinks America has itself become too crazy. He is nostalgic for things of the past and identifies with a sidewalk save-the-tiger campaign. He has gone from getting goose bumps every time he looked at the American flag to being disgusted with the lack of rules and order common to his era. But this doesn't keep him from a one-night stand with an attractive young hippie, whose knowledge of the world hardly extends beyond marijuana and rock stars. Harry doesn't like the pandering he has to do for his clients to get the needed garment sales. His father owned a pharmacy that no longer exists, and now Harry too is on the verge of losing his own business. After many years of building it up to the point that it has a modest reputation and 14 staff members requiring 71 models, Harry will risk everything just to get through one more season. Harry has been beaten down and has grown cynical trying to live the American Dream. Although he has purchased the palatial house and fine car, the almost certain loss of his company is meant to recall for the movie audience a clarity of purpose about business in America that no longer exists. The global market was rapidly changing the American garment industry along with numerous others by the 1970s, making it much harder for small businesses to get or keep a foothold in the face of multinational conglomerate competition. It isn't, therefore, only the tiger with which Harry can be identified, but the endangered species of the small manufacturing business in America generally.

Francis Ford Coppola's *Tucker: The Man and His Dreams* (1988) is based on the true story of Preston Tucker (1903–1966). Coppola takes this famous American entrepreneur's story to the level of corporate competition and big government oversight, where it officially ended. The story opens with a publicity film supposedly made by the Tucker Corporation, which covers Preston's early history as a car nut with important race car designer connections. In the little promo film, Tucker promises to put the Big Three automakers out of business in five years. Tucker gets his breakthrough in investment potential with a magazine article about his innovative "car of tomorrow." Because Roosevelt wanted to make some of the war vehicle plants available to auto companies other than the Big Three, Tucker was able to acquire the "largest factory space in the world" (the Dodge plant in Chicago before the war and now the Ford City shopping center) with $15 million to finalize the lease (which in reality had no clause that 50 cars had to be built by the end of the year, a dramatic device used in the film).³ Having shown Preston Tucker (Jeff Bridges) as an idealistic visionary who is good at inspiring others, Coppola reveals Tucker's weakness in practical financial follow-through, which he leaves to others. While a natural at creative enthusiasm, Coppola also shows Tucker openly offending the Big Three on car safety: "The entire auto industry is guilty of negligence. The Big Three should be indicted for manslaughter." Coppola has this comment repeated back to Tucker by one Michigan senator Ferguson (Lloyd Bridges, Jeff's actual father) who means it as a rejection when Tucker seeks political help for his new enterprise.

The Senator is revealed in the text to be the political power representing Detroit, who appears eventually to incite the Securities and Exchange Commission (SEC) to go after the Tucker Corporation for fraud in the conduct of its investor and shareholder operations. Spies and minor espionage were actually used against the Tucker Corporation as the film indicates, but not necessarily at any central behest of Senator Ferguson. On the other hand, the Senator did head the War Properties Disposal Committee, which had jurisdiction over Tucker's plant. The Senator was also a friend of competitive carmaker Henry Kaiser and of the SEC's Harry McDonald.⁴ Coppola obviously wanted a singular figure to serve as Tucker's nemesis, who could highlight the association between established industry and highly placed politicians who wield government authority. This also serves Coppola's portrait of a moral crusade by a visionary entrepreneur against big government and industry. Tucker was actually tried by the SEC along with six colleagues, all of whom were found innocent of the various charges involving mail fraud and the improper solicitation of stocks. But this legal process also left him bankrupt, without a plant, and with his files confiscated despite the finding of innocence. There would be no community Christmas party like the one for George Bailey. Tucker's safety innovations, however, including seat belts, pop-out front windshields, padded dashes, and disc brakes (not on the 1948 Tucker cars) would eventually benefit the public, though it took years for them to be included on American-made cars. The Big Three argued at the time that they did not want to introduce seat belts because they felt that such a move would be an admission that their cars were unsafe.

Coppola's *Tucker* borrows from the inventor's real history all the little-guy-versus-big-guy thematics, including the political dimension of a trial. The main weakness lies in the portrait of Tucker himself, who is so oblivious to adversity that the narrative never finds a way to penetrate the surface of his character. The real Tucker, as Coppola's work makes manifest, is defeated by what their defense attorney called "serious financial problems and outside interference," by which he meant politically motivated government interference rather than specific acts of espionage.[5] The central message of Coppola's film concerns the politicization of market competition in favor of established corporations. And coming toward the end of Reagan's union-busting and deregulation-oriented two-term presidency, this work stands out as one of the only major business films among the many released in this era to question the role of government political interference in the formation of a corporation potentially competitive with established ones. Entrepreneurial success apparently becomes economically and thus politically threatening only at this level of market competition. Tucker's closing defense at the trial (the real Preston Tucker never spoke at the trial) is worth quoting as Coppola's final comment on the importance of America's visionary entrepreneurs: "If big business closes the door on the little guy with a new idea, we're not only closing the door on progress but we're sabotaging everything that we fought for, everything that the country stands for." Some critics mentioned the director's personal identification with Tucker as a risk-taking visionary, although Coppola lacks the Barnum & Bailey approach to his film projects that Tucker has toward the development of his car. It is the razzle-dazzle Coppola associates with the real Preston Tucker that gets written into the script and the film score, which, however true to that public man, leaves the film hollow at its personal center, absent other more intimate data about him. Tucker's frequent joyful intonation of the self-referential "Hold That Tiger" song is very reminiscent of the rah-rah obliviousness of the Willy Loman character in *Death of a Salesman*. The cheery song shows Tucker's enthusiasm. But it also grows tiresome on such a smiling cardboard figure, whose true-to-life vision, which produced a small but viable line of advanced automobiles, loses impact in the film because of the thin characterization.

Taken as a group, the four entrepreneurial films discussed above run the gamut from Capra's humane idealism rewarded in the postwar era, to Coppola's humane idealism trounced in the Reagan years. For the combat veteran and garment business tiger Harry to try to rescue his struggling garment enterprise by arson is seen to be as desperately misguided as tiger Tucker's misreading of his politically connected competition is blindly idealistic. Entrepreneurial opportunity is grand, as American idealism would have it, but it is in the particulars of its realization, as these films suggest, that the personal and social benefits must be judged. Entrepreneurial success remains illusive in these narratives, even when its personal and social rewards are clearly set forth. And while the abuse of entrepreneurialism hardly justifies its termination, neither does the constant defeat of what's best in small business realistically encourage its durability. New ideas as well as opportunity, as the character Tucker and all of these examples suggest, can only be sustained where conglomerate political economic power is prevented from becoming entirely hegemonic.

The desperate conditions that "free market" hegemonic corporatism enforces on small business appear to be the subtext of two entrepreneurial comedies of the 1980s, which feature the organization of middle-class prostitution rings run on otherwise relatively standard business formulas. Whether the male founders of these businesses are a hustler and meek male (Michael Keaton and Henry Winkler as morgue employees in *Night Shift* [1982]) or a youthful, itinerant college business student (Tom Cruise in *Risky Business* [1983]), these plots place entrepreneurialism literally in the arena of sexual solicitation.[6] These enthusiastic representations of meretricious business largely imply that it is okay to market anything so long as the ends can be made to justify the means. This theme is the common thread shared by both dramatic and comedic texts of the period. President Ronald Reagan set the tone for this when he encouraged a freewheeling, deregulated, and politicized business environment.[7] The parallel is driven home in the suggestion that virtually any organized private enterprise is worthy so long as workers are kept in line and business appearances are maintained over all manner of sordid truths. These good-hearted-hooker business fantasies lampoon the American idealism of private initiative even as they comically provide romantic closure for the momentarily disenfranchised. They support the justification-of-ends argument by stretching the category of means.

The protagonists in *Night Shift* and *Risky Business* also learn their raw business savvy from other men and women hustlers with whom they come in contact. The association of the hero's personal economic need with the group needs of prostitutes is represented as an illegitimate but laughably positive example of the entrepreneurial impulse. The ethical questions for these protagonists get reduced to a comic concern for the projection of the proper "company image" for winning results. The unlikely business protagonists of these comedies finally get the money as well as the "girl" (the kindly harlot) simply because they follow the current social interpretation of "free market" capitalism. These are tongue-in-cheek (or wink-and-nod in the Reagan sense) confirmations of the poor ethical state of contemporary business, which offers little hope of significant economic reform from the weak financial resources of most new entrepreneurs. By flaunting sexual exploitation as the content of business as well as its promotional form (typical of advertising), these texts play on the invasion of commerce into intimacy. The two become interchangeable when moneymaking business with one's gang-banging female associates is also grounds for personal romance.

One of Hollywood's romantic answers to the economic excesses of the Reagan decade is the widely popular Cinderella romance *Pretty Woman* (1990). It features yet another good-hearted hooker, Vivian (Julia Roberts), who gradually starts a relationship with the handsome Edward (Richard Gere). Edward is a highly successful corporate raider who is toned down considerably from the Gordon Gekko version in *Wall Street,* and is closer to the debonair raider type first seen in *Cash McCall* (1959). Edward is a rich workaholic who makes bundles buying out companies and dismantling them for quick profits. Immediate cash gains rather than product production is his sine qua non. Edward's intense schedule also allows time and energy only for prostitutes, who are hired at his sexual convenience. The proletarian streetwalker Vivian gradually draws Edward into the charms of a relationship, while he teaches her the world of finer things. He also manages to make his money-shark colleagues look misguided as he leaves their ranks a wealthy man to pursue Vivian. His move, rather than going against the cultural grain of 1990, however, reflects the fact that junk bond–leveraged corporate raiders were falling at least temporarily into social disfavor at the time, owing to the prosecution of junk bond "kings" such as Michael Milken. At film's end, Edward has decided to build ships instead of tearing down companies. *Pretty Woman* completes the romantic comedy/drama cycle of the 1980s with a "working girl" fantasy so extreme in its nostalgia for good intentions that it makes *Baby Boom* (1987) and *Working Girl* (1988) look like hard-nosed business success stories. All three of these feel-good examples place class advancement in sexual and romantic terms in a way that softens the themes of corporate and political greed and power otherwise so readily apparent in this decade's dramatic films. In these three sex-as-business texts, 1970s feminism meets a 1980s corporate romance it can't refuse, and walks off with the promotion and the successful career guy.

Hollywood, in its effort to reflect the mood of a highly competitive society and its endless appetite for leisure escape, continued to provide large doses of entrepreneurial business fantasy and comedy in the 1980s and 1990s, as in Ivan Reitman's *Ghostbusters* (1984), Penny Marshall's *Big* (1988), and Nora Ephron's *You've Got Mail* (1998). The cartoonlike *Ghostbusters* poses a start-up business run by marginal characters, who become successful not only at weeding out mere ghosts, but at saving a city and civilization from evil forces. The Pillsbury Doughboy figure done as a nightmarish destroyer stalking down city streets is a particularly nice touch, suggesting a commercial empire in the process of being trampled by its own absurd promotional projections, which have overtaken signification even at the level of the imaginary. Also turning to the tone and literal domain of the imaginary is *Big,* which concerns a 12-year-old boy who suddenly finds himself in a man's body (Tom Hanks). For a while, the boy/man finds a brief home designing creative toys for a company that has otherwise lost its ability to connect with the playful fantasies of its youthful clientele. While *Big* takes place in a corporate rather than small business setting, the theme is lost innocence, which can apply to the frantic profit fixation of both settings. *Big* remains nostalgic about the loss of fantasy and imagination in the contemporary business world of anxious adults.

In a more adult context, writer/director Nora Ephron's recent *You've Got Mail* (1998) soft-pedals one of capitalism's most troublesome small business realities. Kathleen Kelly (Meg Ryan) has inherited a small children's bookstore from her recently deceased mother. Kathleen soon finds herself struggling to preserve her little $350,000-a-year specialty enterprise against the encroachment of a large bookstore chain owned and run by Joe Fox (Tom Hanks), who has taken over management of the business from his retired and oft-married father. Joe's personal connection with his book business adversary Kathleen began earlier and blindly through e-mail. For most of the film Kathleen does not realize that Joe Fox is also the increasingly personal e-mail confidant. *You've Got Mail* very egregiously foregrounds romance as the solution not only to Kathleen's personal loneliness, but also to the loss of her business. The inevitability of such a loss seems hardly contested by the film, despite a community show of support for Kathleen's book shop. Joe Fox's big box store of discounted books and cappuccino bar, complete with a special children's reading section, is presented as an impersonal but seemingly inevitable trend of mass marketing, and of the current high cost of business, which *is* a real problem. Joe also adds insult to injury by continuing to play Kathleen along on e-mail even after he wipes out her shop. The film's concluding scene has the rather destitute Kathleen falling into Joe's arms when he finally reveals his electronic identity. Gushing music is meant to help the viewer forget that Joe has completely manipulated her into emotional as well as economic submission. The best moment in the film occurs earlier when the depressed, bedridden Kathleen shows the gumption to protest his destruction of her independent neighborhood enterprise. He says, "It wasn't personal." To which she replies:

What is that supposed to mean? I'm so sick of that. All that means is that it wasn't personal to you. It was personal to me. It was personal to a lot of people. Because whatever anything is, it ought to begin by being personal.

Kathleen does not protest for long, however. Her career uncertainty in the end makes it easier for her to embrace the multimillionaire, who is somehow both quietly sensitive as a person and economically severe as a businessman. Not exactly a Cinderella type, Meg Ryan as Kathleen is reminiscent of Doris Day's spunk as well as the way her roles in the 1960s usually gave in to the status quo in the end. One can imagine Kathleen eventually beginning to think like a blockbuster scion's wife, worried about how her husband's retail chain will do battle with other big-store competition, either endlessly merging with them or being the object of hostile buyouts. Nora Ephron's earlier success with Hanks and Ryan in *Sleepless in Seattle* (1993) mainly used distance as the hindrance to a budding romance, while *You've Got Mail* uses the monopolizing-of-small-business problem as the socially relevant obstacle to true love. But the film's romantic closure seems badly compromised by the lingering memory of all Katherine went through as the proprietor of a business she grew up in alongside her mother's devoted and successful work. Such hard economic and emotional realities as she might have faced (but which are hardly convincing here) are not so easily resolved. Speculating on the story's future, there will likely be no appearances by Kathleen at the Fox chain store to do readings for children as she once did at her own establishment. For the small-fish entrepreneur, the personal as well as personal integrity seems to suffer another telltale defeat in a pond where the big fish, now more personally sensitive and charming, continue to play the role of opportunistic sharks.

In addition to fictional entrepreneur films swept up in the technological revolution, there is also a current feature documentary worthy of mention in this context, *Startup.Com* (2001). It is produced by D. A. Pennebaker and directed by Chris Hegedus (the team that produced the political documentary *The War Room* in 1993), who also shares director credit with Jehane Noujaim. The film encapsulates the giddy speed of business moves by two young men in the digital age. It traces the quick rise in the late 1990s of a dotcom with abundant venture capital, amounting to some $50 million and an employment force of 200. This is followed by the sudden fall of the company owing to software vulnerability, internal strife, and the crash of new Internet businesses and their inflated market positions in the winter of 2000. The rapid overvaluation of technology stocks and the Wall Street "correction" that occurred soon thereafter is another example of capitalism's essence as an image-driven culture. The economic rise and sudden "downsizing" that effected so many new businesses and their employees has surely done more than any film to shake the popular faith in market fashions, if not high-tech itself. *Startup.com* is nevertheless a sobering nonfiction reminder of the deceptive exhilaration and all too real letdown of fluctuating markets, where appearances and groupthink can drive personal as well as monetary investment. The two long-term friends who started the company, for example, grow completely at odds under pressure and the one fires the other from the business.[8] The documentary is also a reminder of the fragility of image-based business investment strategies in a highly volatile and competitive new media marketplace.

IMMIGRANT AND RACIAL ISSUES IN FAMILY BUSINESSES

You can be dark and have money, or you can be fair and have no money, but you can't be dark and have no money.

—A GOSSIPMONGER (MIRA NAIR) ACTING IN HER OWN FILM, *Mississippi Masala*

The United States was founded by mostly white European immigrants, who destroyed or drove the Native American population to the hinterland and for a while imported slaves from Africa to support a landed aristocracy. The American Indian and slave populations as well as each new wave of immigrants have made their contribution to what constitutes American culture today, although contributing to culture and having a say in its political economic direction are not the same thing. What has remained consistent about immigrant and ethnic experience in the American nation has been the key role of family small business as a starting point for survival and advancement. The process of adaptation to a "new land" through private enterprise requires capital investment and community outreach, a special commitment to a location, and a business identity. The business and career films in this category thus make their own particular contribution to the search for identity and success from a marginalized perspective. The minority entrepreneur must decide to what degree to "assimilate" into mainstream business culture, as well as choose between exploitative or community-friendly models of business practice. These remain critical questions not only for racial and ethnic identity but for national identity as a whole.

Gina Marchetti questions the seemingly pluralistic approach to immigrant culture and business usually taken by Hollywood cinema: "Hollywood loves to see itself as the big 'melting pot,' assimilating all in its fantasy image of America. However, access to that America has a price: the rejection of any marker of 'foreignness.'"[9] Robert Stam also questions Hollywood film's "co-optive liberal pluralism," which he finds is "tainted at birth by its historical roots in the systemic inequities of conquest, slavery, and exploitation." He looks instead to an ideal he names "polycentric multiculturalism," which "unlike a liberal-pluralist discourse of ethical universals—freedom, tolerance, charity—sees all cultural history in relation to social power. It is not about 'sensitivity' but about empowering the disempowered."[10] In the analysis of specific films that follows, I hope to show how Hollywood and the voices of more independent American cinema continue to treat issues of pluralism relative to business and career attitudes and goals.

The five films addressed in this section demonstrate how the entrepreneurial quest, while it is hardly unique to this country, nevertheless has special characteristics in American contexts. These films feature business conflict both within and between ethnic families and communities, as well as with the prevailing economic system. Some have challenged the notion that classical Hollywood cinema either stereotypes or simply ignores minorities,[11] although the small number of major films focused on this important subcategory of minority business since 1944 would seem to contradict this claim. This is also unexpected, considering that so much of the initial immigrant experience in America historically has been based in small family business activity, which congeals so well with American economic ideals. The nation's verbal commitment to the Horatio Alger success ethic (lifting oneself up through personal initiative from deprivation) was current up through the first decades of the twentieth century and very much reflected the national rural-to-urban as well as global immigrant migrations. But the emphasis on this ethic clearly had worn off by 1950, when the country's increased affluence began to shift attention to the needs of the growing, mostly white middle class. For American Indians, once enslaved African Americans, and immigrants, the central importance of small business did not change in the postwar era, but the nature of its challenges and demographic circumstances certainly did. As the films considered here indicate, small enterprise has in some ways usefully anchored minority individuals, families, and communities. Minority entrepreneurial business experience in film, however, also reveals special difficulties of adjustment to powerful economic and social forces already in place. For immigrants and African Americans alike, the process of individual and small business assimilation with the political economic dominant has been a loaded issue, particularly where racial difference also applies. I have hence arranged the films in this section in the following order to allow due consideration to the specifically racial concerns at issue in the last two: *House of Strangers* (1949), *Avalon* (1990), *Big Night* (1996), *Do the Right Thing* (1989), and *Mississippi Masala* (1992).

Gino Monetti (Edward G. Robinson) is the family patriarch in Joseph Mankiewicz's *House of Strangers*. Mankiewicz's somewhat stagy postwar film refers in dialogue to a time around 1912 when Gino brought his family to the Lower East Side of Manhattan from Palermo, Sicily, and started a cash-lending business. By 1932 the little enterprise has grown into the large and successful Monetti Trust and Loan Association. Gino employs all four of his sons at the bank, pays them low salaries, and treats them with no respect. The one partial exception is his oldest son, Max (Richard Conte), who has a law office in the bank and hence some independence from his father's business and salary restrictions. All the sons must have dinner with their parents every Wednesday or suffer the loss of their bank positions. So relentless is Gino's iron rule over the family that he has created a house of strangers where fear and jealousy rule. Gino, who inherited a small barber job in Palermo before seeking greater opportunity across the Atlantic, lives by his autocratic version of the American Dream: "Old world, your father a barber, you a barber. New world, your father a barber, you a presidenté." Instead of a president, Gino has become a family and community tyrant through his rapid rise to success within his immigrant community. Here he has largely made economic law for years, charging usurious interest rates on small loans for which he keeps no written records. The new Banking Act of 1931 changes all that and Gino goes to trial for "misapplication of funds." Max tries to get his brothers to distribute their father's legal culpability among themselves, but they want Gino's degrading treatment of them and dictatorship at the bank ended and thus refuse. When it is apparent that Max will lose his father's case in court, he tries to bribe a juror. But his brother Joe is on to him and has Max arrested for jury tampering. Max gets seven years in prison and his father loses all rights and control at the bank, which Joe now takes over and manages with his two remaining brothers.

The main story occurs in 1939 after Max is released from prison and comes looking for Joe and his other brothers for some sort of recompense. Max refuses Joe's small monetary offer and visits with his bitter father, who wants Max to exact revenge on Joe and reclaim control of the bank for him. "The bank is my life and my blood," Gino says. "You've got to make them pay." Gino's brand of patriarchal imperialism has been learned not only from his native Sicily but in part from that aspect of his American experience that has encouraged a particularly egocentric, self-interested form of business behavior. Gino's family legacy is such that since Max went to jail, his widow and remaining sons have all chosen not to live at the big family house. As Gino's wife explains to him shortly before he dies there, and after he has just reiterated all the things and money that they have acquired since coming to America: "We poor, Gino, . . . Before we had a barber shop, we rich, we loved each other. Now there's no more love, there's only hate."

When Gino dies, his widow harangues Max and her other sons at the funeral for continuing Gino's hateful ways, although it is not Max's mother but his American lover, Irene Bennett (Susan Hayward) who finally has the greatest impact on him. Max was already seeing the outspoken Irene before prison and while he was engaged to a very traditional Italian girl. He found that the passive, homebound ways of traditional Sicilian/Italian women, including his mother and her ineffectiveness with Gino, no longer appealed to him, though he has had a long struggle adjusting his old macho attitudes to Irene's independent ways. Irene has tried valiantly all along to prevent Max from being influenced by Gino's self-centered greed. She also works to help Max forget his desire for revenge on Joe. Irene finally convinces Max to leave with her for California and a new life. Just as Max prepares to depart the old family home where he is staying temporarily, his three brothers catch up with him and Joe demands that Tony pummel Max and then that he throw him off the balcony. At this last command Tony suddenly realizes that Joe is more like his hated father than is Max. Tony turns on Joe instead and is ready to kill him when Max recovers sufficiently from his beating to intervene. Max will leave his brothers in Manhattan to sort out all the family strife that still surrounds them and their father's loan business. Max will have to go farther west to escape the domineering business methods that Gino found could thrive on the East Coast of the United States. Now it is up to his son Max to realize the ethical propriety of a more democratically honorable legal and business career in California.

Max desires a less brutal and more elastic identity than his father's, beginning with his more gender-balanced and respectful relationship with Irene. His connection with her is obviously not only about romance but about a mentally open and ethical "assimilation" with a specifically progressive, community-oriented, fair-play kind of America that she represents. Meanwhile, Joe's undeserved and continued control of the bank by film's end points to his negative assimilation with the dog-eat-dog business values of America as experienced through his father's fascistic interpretation of them. Gino's sons Joe and Max exemplify the two extremes of immigrant business assimilation with American cultural forces: the one conjunctive with private profiteering; the other oriented toward community goodwill, diversity, and a more democratic economy. In *House of Strangers,* the question is clearly with which of these rival political economic cultures in America will the immigrant choose to assimilate.

Similar themes are also apparent in Barry Levinson's *Avalon* (1990) and in *Big Night* (1996), both of which dwell on the question of what it means for immigrants and their families to become Americanized in the 1950s. The extended family and immigrant community group in *Avalon*—which holds regular meetings and takes a collection to help members of the different families gain a toehold in America—slowly falls apart under the pressure of more opportunities, business success, and home mobility. The realities of the new consumer economy also demand constant business reinvestment for stability and growth, including heavy outlays for promotion, which can make but also break family businesses and immigrant allegiances. When the successful department store business that two cousins build together suddenly burns to the ground, it leaves them destitute because the capital that was to go to fire insurance went to TV advertising instead. The ideal of renewal through a vibrant economy is preserved in the conclusion, which points to the protagonist's entry into an advertising career as a TV time buyer. The immigrant group identity that was so strongly maintained in the beginning has gradually broken down under the pressure of economic necessity, which has mandated individualism and job mobility. But the entrepreneurial business ethic does continue partly to be an extension of the traditional family ethic in this film, continuing a fragment of the Old World.

In *Big Night,* the emphasis is less on the extended family than on the competition among immigrants who are in the same business but who arrive in America at different times. The older immigrant, Pascal (Ian Holm), has developed a successful Italian restaurant based on the notion that glad-handing and giving customers what they want is more important than quality. This contrasts with the recent immigrant brothers, one of whom is a consummate Italian chef and food purist. Their restaurant is failing because they try to serve risotto to an American public that knows only spaghetti and meatballs. In desperation they seek Pascal's help, who promises that he will arrange a "big night" of publicity at their restaurant with guest Louis Prima, which will solve their problem. The brothers' giant expenditure for their gratis feast wipes out their resources, but the event comes to nothing because Pascal lied to them. This destroys their business but does not win Pascal the services of the gourmet chef, who is too proud and "unassimilated" to work for such a market-driven saboteur. A common nationality is clearly less important than business ethics, particularly for those who still feel a personal pride in their work and attachment to their product. In *Big*

3.2   *Do the Right Thing* (1989).
Pizzeria owner Sal (Danny Aiello) stands with his sons, Pino (John Turturro, left) and
Vito (Richard Edson), against racial pressures in a predominantly black Brooklyn
neighborhood. This era's strong racial discontent is also an assumed part of this
community's sweltering summer heat.

Night, the ethical purity of craft in business contradicts assimilation.
The price for joining such a fully mercenary and commercialized mass
market system is simply too high.

Spike Lee's *Do the Right Thing* offers a contemporary setting for an already assimilated Italian, Sal (Danny Aiello), a white business insider in
a Brooklyn neighborhood populated mainly by African Americans. Sal's
Bedford-Stuyvesant pizzeria serves as the center for his working family
of two sons, the oldest of whom hates the local black community and
wants to move the business to a more complacent white community. In
his many years of effort to be a good neighborhood merchant, Sal must
now contend with a wider social phenomenon of economically disenfranchised black youths. He has hired Mookie (Spike Lee) to deliver his
pizza, and perhaps some goodwill along with it, but Mookie quickly
finds himself caught in the middle of tension between certain members
of his local racial majority and the pizzeria. These individuals are hostile to what they see as Sal's self-centered white pride and disinterest in
his black clientele. Sal is proud of his Italian American heritage and its
difficult historical assimilation into mainstream American culture. He

believes that his long-term community commitment gives him a certain status ("these people have grown up on my pizza"), and that his ability to overcome adversity in the past will serve him in the present. But he does not see the persistent racial and class divisions that have isolated black youths in the inner city, and that have displaced much of the rough gentility and sense of common purpose that might have helped small businesses in mixed neighborhoods survive in the past.

The voice of protest is literalized by the "Fight the Power" song prominently featured in Spike Lee's rhythmically orchestrated neighborhood film. Radio Raheem at times plays the song at full volume on his boom box, and it is also the main theme in the film's score. The lyrics are a call to action based on a frustration that Sal does not fully understand and cannot answer to. Nor does he realize that it isn't just a matter of defending his shop, but of finding a way to share power and recognize cultural difference. The wild-haired, comedic-looking militant Jimmie demands that Sal include African American cultural artifacts on the pizzeria walls to go along with all the pictures of Italian Americans. Perhaps Sal would have responded to this differently if Jimmie hadn't simply ordered it out of hand. Sal feels that he can do as he wishes in his own store, telling Jimmie, "In your own place do what you want." And of course this calls attention to the fact that Jimmie has no apparent family, community support, or resources with which to pursue a business possibility. Nor is his militancy shown to be fully representative of the black community in the film, which seems more closely attuned with the character Mookie, who feels both sides of the racial and class tensions in the neighborhood. Mookie also has a constantly complaining Puerto Rican girlfriend (Rosie Perez) who is taking care of their child, whom he mostly disregards. It's hard for Mookie to realize his family role or to see any promise in his low-paying job delivering pizza.

When the confrontation precipitated by Jimmie and Radio Raheem reaches the level of violent crisis and the police inadvertently kill Raheem after pulling him off Sal, Mookie's emotions get the better of him and he initiates the full-scale, climactic assault on Sal's shop. It isn't Sal specifically that Mookie means to attack, but rather the dominant centrality of a white business institution in his neighborhood where no black-owned businesses are apparent. The fact that a Korean-owned vegetable market has also just appeared around the block only furthers Mookie's sense of being colonized and unable to direct his fate. The closing scene has Mookie and Sal standing before the burned-out hull of the pizza shop throwing cash at each other, unable to bridge the economic divide that separates the levels of their opportunity. At the end, Mookie recovers the cash from the debris on the street, more desperate than Sal to get through the coming days with no job. Sal still has his sons and doubtless the commitment to open a new store with the insurance money, but probably somewhere else where he doesn't feel that he is on the front lines of America's continuing racial struggle. *Do the Right Thing* is a modestly stylized city block scene complete with an aging male chorus. And while it doesn't hedge in the way that it sees the minority problem, particularly in relation to small business opportunity, nor does it offer much insight for possible solutions. The frustration and impatience in Mookie's climactic attack is the more startling because it's so self-conscious. The overzealous response of white authority to black violence is a tiresome old story, and perhaps meant as a further reflection on black economic opportunity denied. Certainly there can be no positive business and cultural diversity where such strong racial and economic divisions continue to exist. Mookie will probably continue to think from job to job rather than in career terms.

Mississippi Masala (1992), an American film directed by Indian Mira Nair, presents some of the same ethnic and racial themes as *Do the Right Thing,* but with added romance and economic subtlety, and with a more optimistic conclusion. Replace the Italian American–owned pizzeria in the mostly African American neighborhood in Brooklyn with an Indian owned liquor store and motel in a largely African American section of Greenwood, Mississippi, and again the economic tensions between African Americans and immigrant merchants quickly become apparent. Nair's film presents a hodgepodge of Indians who stick together in mutual support of their various efforts at private enterprise. This community has also imported its own Hindu ritual and family traditions, which further binds its members to a sense of belonging and cultural identity in a foreign land. But inside the group, socioeconomic rankings based on skin color and financial wealth nevertheless prevail, just as in the black community. The international perspective in Nair's film is an important reminder that these are also global and not simply national problems. The crippling legacy of slavery in America, however, continues to impede the socioeconomic progress of blacks in contrast to immigrant groups that have no such burdensome history in the United States.

The film opens in Uganda, where the Indian Jay (Roshan Seth) was born and has grown up to become a successful family man and lawyer with property. A black African with whom he was reared has been a brother to him, and when Idi Amin seizes power in 1972, this "brother" encourages him to leave the country with his wife and young daughter rather than face political persecution and perhaps death because of their ethnic origin. The Uganda segment is done quickly with both provocative and frightening visuals and little dialogue, emphasizing the emotional distress of suddenly being uprooted from one's homeland. The film jumps forward to Greenwood, Mississippi, in the year 1990. Jay and his wife Kinu now own and manage a small liquor store. Their one child, Mina (Sarita Choudhury), is just reaching the age of 24, but she has only managed a job in the motel where they all live together. Her father wants her to go to college as quickly as he can finally find a way to afford it.

Mina, while also born in Uganda, has been raised in England and America and has never been to India, meaning that she has been close to her parents but not to the full Hindu cultural tradition. She is dark and attractive, and she appears to have a romantic choice between a wealthy fellow Indian, Harry Patil, or an ambitious young African American, Demetrius Williams (Denzel Washington), who has his own carpet-cleaning business with a friend. After dating for a while, she agrees to go off with Demetrius for a night in Biloxi. They are by chance discovered by two of her Indian neighbors who live in Greenwood, and suddenly everything changes. Her parents, who never approved of her liaison with someone outside their ethnic group, feel shamed in their own community. Her father wants them all to return to Uganda (Amin is now gone), and although his wife and daughter do not approve, they will respect his wishes in the traditional way.

Demetrius is also being pressured by his own community to give up the "foreign" woman some consider to be "white" and therefore trouble. He is furthermore ostracized by members of the Indian community, who make up his main clientele. And the white-owned bank threatens to foreclose on his commercial loan if he cannot make his next payment. Prevented from seeing Mina by her father, Demetrius promptly accuses him of being uppity and acting white against the black community, "comin' down here from god knows where and treatin' us like we're your doormats." In frustration and perhaps to save his hard-won enterprise, Demetrius brings suit for whiplash against the young Indian man, Anil, who is the Americanized son of the motel owner where Jay and his family live. Mina was driving Anil's car when she crashed into Demetrius's truck much earlier. In desperation, Mina tracks down Demetrius. He explains that his business partner, Tyrone, has given up on Mississippi and moved to L.A. The couple reconciles around Mina's idea to start up their own cleaning business together in hopes of leaving the racial confines of Greenwood as soon as possible.

At the conclusion, the film returns once again to Uganda, where Jay has gone without his wife to seek recompense for his former loss of property from the government. The legal/financial outcome of his claim against Uganda is not disclosed. But Jay does learn that his Ugandan brother was taken away and disappeared in the ensuing years, presumably killed by Amin's military, and perhaps for his association with Jay, an outspoken critic of Amin. The final shot has Jay holding a Ugandan baby amidst music and dancing, waiting to start his long trip back to his wife in Greenwood and their small liquor store. This is a hard truth for him after serving so long and well as a lawyer in the country he always considered home. Compared to those who at least live in the country they can call their birthright, Jay feels he is a homeless man whose profession in law has also been destroyed by political racism.

Mira Nair, who also directed the acclaimed *Salaam Bombay!* (1982), plays a gossip in her American film debut. She comments at a wedding on skin color among Indians, noting how difficult it is for anyone who is both poor and has dark skin to get ahead, which is true of Mina. Mina does not want to give her life to her parents' liquor store any more than Demetrius intends to follow in his father's footsteps. His dad is an elderly man stuck busing tables in a white restaurant, who is constantly called to task as "Willie B." by his white female boss. Siding with Mina and Demetrius, *Mississippi Masala* looks to the future when and where better multicultural and multiracial attitudes might prevail. It is the multicultural blending suggested by the low-key scenes of dance and music — from the new African sound to the Delta blues — that want to point to a common need and possible solution.

Jay writes to his wife from Uganda, confirming the cliché that home is where the heart is, which in this case is with her. Forced back upon his essential personal identity, he values his family above all things. Narratively, his decision appears to be like the standard Hollywood movie answer of romance/family as an option to a lost career and a meager family business. But more than that it is a recognition of his own essential identity in the new global multiculturalism, where he can find his place among his ethnic compatriots no matter in what country they reside. There are also hints that he may eventually regain some of his old capacity as a legal counselor in his own small community, although

3.3　*Mississippi Masala* (1991).
Demetrius (Denzel Washington) holds his Indian lover Mina (Sarita Choudhury)
in one of their few happy moments together amidst ethnic and racial turmoil.

fraudulent claims to collect insurance payouts will not be his métier. He will not trade his honor even as a poor entrepreneur living in a motel room. He has learned from the loss of his Ugandan brother and from Mina's departure that he is capable of big mistakes, and that career success is hardly the first priority at the deepest levels of human commitment. The Ugandan baby he holds in the end is not such a stranger after all.

He can take heart that Mina, too, has chosen love and hard work over against the socially esteemed choices of ethnic purity and wealth, where commitment to a Harry Patil might not be sincere. On the other hand, Mina's poverty and strict family tradition has held her to her parents to the point that she has suffocated, compelling her to find herself through romance when educational or career possibilities were not available. It is her parents' good intentions and mostly good judgment, particularly her mother's, that gives her the self-confidence to discover her own way. The long-term choices made by Jay and by Mina and Demetrius are shown to be good and ethical ones. But there are those in *Mississippi Masala,* whether of African American or Indian heritage, who represent the values of social appearances. Demetrius's former lover Alicia and the motel owner's son, Anil, aspire to the signs of prestige and success approved by mainstream culture in all its derivative forms. Neither of these individuals are presented as bad or cruel, but they are self-centered and willing to help others only when they also directly benefit. Their values lean toward the importance of the signs themselves, whether in the form of Alicia's flashy wardrobe and new boyfriend, or Anil's pride in his big car.

Mississippi Masala is an American but not a typical Hollywood film, and it apparently confused several critics. Many felt that the story was too broad and did not sufficiently focus on the romance of the young, mixed-race couple, who would in Hollywood terms typically be the film's heroes. Nair's film, however, is not primarily a romance but a multicultural, global reflection appropriately bookended by Jay's experience with Africa. It concerns not only obvious racial and ethnic conflicts, but also the clashes both within each of these groups and as they relate to dominant socioeconomic values. Independent characters who strive to find their own path and who necessarily make some mistakes are privileged here over those who only rely on group values to guide them. The impulsive drive of the younger generation is shown against the sometimes encrusted values of the older one, and assumptions regarding gender roles are made by all of the groups represented.

Overall, then, Nair's text shows the value of the individual who can learn to look beyond racial, ethnic, class, generational, and gender differences to the common humanity beneath. But this does not mean a melting pot blend that simply overlooks ethnic differences and homogenizes everyone into a common allegiance to the dominant values of mass consumerism. "Masala" means a spicy blend that preserves difference and is simultaneously enhanced by it. This film comes the closest to representing how Robert Stam's ideal of polycentric multiculturalism—which emphasizes essential political economic and particularly ethnic variety—might begin to be preserved and encouraged.

ENTREPRENEURIAL FEMMES FATALES IN THE FILM NOIR TRADITION

The very fact that we can speak of a woman "using" her sex or "using" her body for particular gains is highly significant—it is not that a man cannot use his body in this way, but that he doesn't have to.

—MARY ANN DOANE, *Femmes Fatales* (26)

I don't think what someone does for a living necessarily defines who he is.

—INDEPENDENT HIT MAN (JOHN CUSACK) TO HIS
GIRLFRIEND IN THE BLACK COMEDY *Grosse Pointe Blank* (1997)

The sexual seductress of Hollywood cinema has a long and varied international lineage, and alterations in her representation continue to the present day.[12] Molly Haskell concluded that while the original Italian and French silent film versions of this "vamp" figure were allied with "the dark forces of nature," the version that gradually developed in America was from the beginning allied with "the green forces of capitalism."[13] In Hollywood's studio-era films noir of the 1940s and 1950s, and in the noir tradition that followed, her role as femme fatale has tied her closely to undercurrents of sexual, social, and ideological unrest. While she has continued over the years to have a destabilizing effect on film narratives, her incarnations are also at times nonviolent and/or supportive of the protagonist, such as those in *The Big Sleep* (1946), *Point Blank* (1967), and *Something Wild* (1986). But my focus in this section is mainly restricted to the lethal seductress associated with business, whom I will trace through Hollywood's noir history from *Double Indemnity* (1944) to *The Last Seduction* (1994). This figure abjures traditional romance and passive domesticity, choosing instead to apply her sexuality to homicidal plots in the service of commercial power. From the classic noir period beginning in the 1940s through the neonoir film era of the 1960s and 1970s, her signification of an economic and sexual repression and desire gradually grows more conscious and culturally mainstream. The fourth section concerns the postnoir films of the 1980s and 1990s,[14] where women's acceptance at the highest levels of the business and professional workforce transforms the contemporary seductress into a literal figure of abstracted image power. Overall, then, the deadly dame's narrative positioning has continued to unfold as a barometer first of women's economic repression and desire, then of her victimization as unconscious repository of capitalist greed, and finally of her embodiment of the process of consumer reification and fetishism.

It has been widely observed that the femme fatale in films of the 1940s is a timely indicator of wartime misgivings about sex roles, marriage, and sexuality. Thomas Schatz points out that "changing views of sexuality and marriage were generated by the millions of men overseas and by the millions of women pressed into the workforce. The postwar 'return to normalcy' never really materialized—the G.I.s' triumphant homecoming only seemed to complicate matters and to bring out issues of urban anonymity and sexual confusion."[15] It seems no coincidence that the rise to prominence of Hollywood's lethal siren occurred simultaneously with wartime and postwar readjustments in society. The massive entry of women into the workforce encouraged during the war was suddenly discouraged at war's end, but not altogether reversed. There was also the Korean War (1950–53) and the extended Cold War, which further reminded Americans of life's fundamental insecurities, including economic vulnerability and the "occasional need" for women to work outside the home. On the other hand, there was continued resistance to women's gainful employment by those men who wanted to be the sole support for their family, and at a time of economic expansion in the 1950s when this was still quite feasible for the middle class.[16]

Mainstream dramatic films as diverse as *The Best Years of Our Lives* (1945, the Virginia Mayo role), and *All about Eve* (1950) offer negative images of resourceful working women, but it is the deadly femme noir who most directly assaults sociopsychic conventions and thereby invokes the most telltale narrative dislocations. Historically, the returning veteran who had "sacrificed" for his country in a strict military system assumed that he would again wield economic authority and thus retake command of the family home front. This militarization of male circumstances and attitudes further increased the defensive stance against women in the paid workforce, particularly if they demonstrated economic independence. Ambitious women evoke a certain paranoia that is readily apparent in the metaphoric plots of classic films noir, where they are made to appear beautiful but also treacherous, criminally depraved, and castrating in their desires. Often serving as catalysts for criminal behavior in men, they encouraged the blame heaped on women's sexuality and furthered the calls for her sexual repression and economic restriction to the household. But these dark sirens of classic noir, it must be remembered, use their sexuality as a means to an end that society was not otherwise supporting in the traditional family structure.

Two familiar examples of films noir, which originated as novels by James M. Cain in the Depression-tainted 1930s, demonstrate how the deadly seductress threatens the moral and legal codes of marriage as well as the economic codes of society at large. In *Double Indemnity* (1944) and *The Postman Always Rings Twice* (1946) an unhappily married woman becomes sexually involved with another man in order to engage his help in murdering her husband for escape from a dull marriage, but particularly for profit and business opportunity. To murder him only for romantic freedom would not have been necessary, and any motivation other than money and business leverage would have been difficult for America's mass audiences to comprehend. What makes her so threatening to traditional marriage and phallocentric authority is her longing for financial independence by way of sexual initiative. In the examples here, her allure results first in an adulterous affair, while the real goal of her seduction is realized through the murder-for-profit conspiracy with her lover. (One might also ask whether straight treatment of an adulterous affair at the time was not made more feasible for clearance by movie censors if murder for money followed by punishment was thrown into the mix.) In *Double Indemnity,* the wife takes advantage of her illicit lover's insurance business knowledge as well as his muscle, while in *Postman* it is in part her lover's handyman abilities and youthful athleticism that attracts her to the possibility of a future working enterprise together.

Either way, her male partner in crime is hardly a model citizen who is simply overwhelmed by her seductive powers. The main difference between them is that while she is exhibited as the fetching and restless wife, he is a willing and opportunistic outsider already mistrustful of social authority. She merely activates his sexual energies in the cause of a lucrative alliance. After their murder of her spouse and during the period of the legal investigation, they become unsettled and suspicious of one another, scrambling to guard their personal positions and to preserve the insurance payoff. Each one suddenly becomes a mirror for the selfish greed of the other, and their heterosexual attraction becomes a burdensome obligation based in mutual survival and profit. The fact that the woman is represented as the primary sexual deceiver despite her new partner's wavering sexual allegiance after the murder (particularly in *Postman*) is worthy of note. In the classical era, women clearly had fewer behavioral and income options than men, which partly explains the need for scheming tactics by the seductress in the first place. It is further apparent that these films are mainly about her effect on him, the narrative subject. His insecurity and disorientation as a noir protagonist commands each film's predominant visual perspective, which is often supported by his voice-over commentary (*Double Indemnity*). His point of view defines the particular tone of *his* desire and disillusionment. But the degree of paranoia he feels after their crime is also tied up in the intimate proximity of the woman—not a stranger but one in whom he recognizes a part of his own lustful and criminal opportunism and culpability. She brings out his greed and recklessness through sexual attraction, whereas he is to her a tool in the service of her own ambitions. The ignominy heaped on the woman does not obliterate the problem of the man's vulnerability to her sexuality, which stimulates his self-confidence and willingness to take huge risks for the pecuniary advantages they both crave. Interpretations of her desire that are limited to sexual seduction, therefore, overlook her predominant desire for monetary power. It is also in the exact means to this economic goal, and not in their sexual union, that the seeds of discord are sown and cultivated in these film narratives. The classical-era femme fatale thus provides a window on the desperate underside of the American couple's success dream, where the woman's longing for class mobility is initially tangled up in an unfortunate dependency on her husband's finances and authority, leading to a desire for independence that only another man and cash (an alternate coupling) can make possible.

Viewed as a figure of marital disaffection and revolt, the disruptive noir temptress can also be seen to look toward the future and more liberated views of women's self-assertion in marriage and work. Writing in the 1970s, Janey Place viewed the classical seductress as an important female archetype, and the otherwise gender-regressive film noir form "as the only period in American film in which women are deadly but sexy, exciting and strong."[17] But Laura Mulvey's original work on the dominating masculine perspective in Hollywood studio cinema was less optimistic about the woman's representation as a figure either of power or freedom.[18] It could be argued that the prevailing male gaze upon the seductress provides the most obvious confirmation of the woman's visual objectification. On the other hand, that male gaze is also problematized and punished in the noir narrative. Both members of the wayward heterosexual couple suffer, though the punishment meted out to the seductress is inordinate by comparison. The frequency and similarity of her incarnations in noir films of the 1940s points to a wider cultural anxiety with the ambitious woman's willingness to use sex as a way out of her financial and business dependency on men. The desire to see such demonstrative and thus "threatening" women put back in their domestic "place" largely reflects economic patriarchy and male role uncertainty at the time.

Significantly, in classic films noir, the avaricious siren does get her due in the end, but it is not conventional social institutions such as big business and the law that bring her down. The profit and image concerns of the insurance company president (Richard Gaines) in *Double Indemnity* are only slightly more unsympathetic than the slick methods of the lawyer (Hume Cronyn) in *Postman*. Both characters demonstrate the distance between their cynical way of thinking and the public perceptions that they constantly seek to manipulate. Their masculine positions of administrative authority are particularly distinguishable from the economically marginal viewpoint of the young couple, whose murderous escapades appear so hopelessly desperate and obviously larcenous in motivation. A too narrow focus on the woman's subversive sexual agency, therefore, can overlook the fact that her goals reflect mainstream capitalist aspirations, which often do not encourage love and trust but objectification and distrust. The capitalist overtones of greed, envy, and intimidation prevail with a vengeance in noir and are reflected throughout its history, whatever the specific signification of the femme fatale in each cinematic era.

In classic noir but less true later, the deadly siren's cultural significance takes on a curious mix of moralistic and mythic elements. This is suggested in part by the representation of her restless ambition as a test not only of social law and her lack of access to it, but of fate. The woman's general exclusion from economic opportunity sets the stage for her limited choices and desperation. And the desire for an alternative kind of heterosexual teamwork (both sexual and economic) and reconciliation beyond crime is expressed by both Phyllis (Barbara Stanwyck) in *Double Indemnity* and Cora (Lana Turner) in *The Postman Always Rings Twice* at brief moments prior to their respective deaths. The aggressive Phyllis evokes slight sympathy after wounding but refusing to immediately kill her partner (ostensibly in the name of love) just before he kills her. Cora's doomed wish for a new life, meanwhile, is clarified just before she is inadvertently killed in a car wreck that leaves her lover unharmed. She is found to be pregnant in a scene preceding the auto accident, opening a momentary hope for a legitimate family life, but one that is never permitted to materialize. The seductress is thus made to suffer the more definitive comeuppance despite the fact that her partner is the actual henchman in the murder of her husband. She appears to be punished mainly for her adultery, which in these cases may be a greater threat to the economic and property arrangement in family patriarchy than simply killing her spouse on her own. Her knowing dependence on a man's help to complete the murder of her husband motivates her sexual involvement more than the other way around. It is the fulfillment of a frustrated mercenary desire and not the easier possibility of a sexual affair or deep animosity toward her spouse that compels her. Absent the acceptance of her legitimate business skills under masculinist patronage, she designates her sexual wiles to profiteering. Individuals, families, businesses, and communities appear to be threatened alike not by the greed-tainted sex of the seductress, but rather by her sex-tainted greed.

Her ritualized death also reveals her status as a mirror of deep fears that extend beyond economic and legal problematics. This dread is associated with the unabated lust and greed that lurk within the shadows of the capitalist impulse and forever beyond the limits of formal social law. As an inevitable part of the motivational rubric that binds personal desire to social status and authority, its feminized incarnation in the seductive figure of woman requires purgation rather than merely punishment. The seductress thus appears in the end to bow to a higher moral justice, which is implied in the one case by Cora's "accidental" death, and in the other by the emotional ambivalence of Phyllis at the moment she fires her gun but does not kill her lover/accomplice. Fate appears to step in where jurisprudence has failed or left off. It also appears to assume the form of a patriarchal authority at a moralistic, metaphysical level. Ideologically, then, the fatal femme both threatens and is used to reaffirm postwar America's highest sense of moral righteousness, which is a mythic and religious justification of its actual legal and economic codes. This authority appears to follow a Judeo-Christian tradition that asserts the sanctity of the male-dominated household through the breadwinning provider. In defying her husband with her ambitious sexuality, the seductress of the 1940s does more than threaten a socioeconomic structure. Her sexual license and murder in the name of insurance fraud is finally judged at the level of a generalized mythic consensus or poetic justice. These narratives have some sympathy with her desire for class mobility, but profit-driven spousal sabotage apparently requires recuperation through a sacrificial rite.

The femme fatale's use of illicit entrepreneurial scams in classic noir becomes a stereotype by the 1960s and 1970s and thus a platform for further generic transformation. This takes the form of a sympathetic narrative investigation into the causes of the siren's inability to think in terms of independent, legitimate business motivation at all. In both Hitchcock's claustrophobic thriller *Marnie* (1964) and the historically reflective neonoir *Chinatown* (1974), the duplicitous woman of mystery is revealed to be more the object than subject of family dysfunction. She becomes the focus of an inquiry that leads back to her youthful experience with economically tainted familial forces that continue to haunt her. Whether or not she is eventually raped or killed, her suffering and/or sacrifice reveal the "pound of flesh" demanded by the overlords of political economic exchange. The New Hollywood femme fatale thus appeals as a victim of circumstances controlled and created by the forces of patriarchal capitalism. Rather than formulating a lethal plot and money scam with a marginal male character as in earlier films, she finds herself already trapped by her own past and in need of someone who can help her disentangle her troubled history. She rather unwillingly becomes the object of a rescue effort by a man of intelligence, social standing, and business sense, who helps her deconstruct her problem and uncover not only parental abuse but also larger, related regimes of corporate and government corruption along the way.

Both Marnie (Tippi Hedren) and *Chinatown*'s Evelyn Mulwray (Faye Dunaway) suffer sex-related aggression in childhood, which is laden with economic overtones. Their victimization is narratively structured as a gradual revelation from out of the past, which now requires a sufficient therapeutic understanding. As discussed in Chapter 2, the adult Marnie sees herself as a subversive actor and interloper in the world of mainstream commerce and family, owing to an obsession for serial theft that she neither understands nor can control. Her personal sub-

3.4   *Chinatown* (1974).
Hired by Evelyn Mulwray (Faye Dunaway), investigator Jake Gittes (Jack Nicholson) gets a true but legally useless business scam and murder confession out of Evelyn's incestuous father, Noah Cross (John Huston).

terfuge, lying, and troubled relationship with her unfeeling mother, not to mention her struggles first with her employer and then with her big business husband, all point in the direction of the need for personal revelation and cure, a necessary preliminary step to legitimate economic contributions.[19] In *Chinatown,* Evelyn is killed in the end because of a similar inability to arrest or control her fate, to free herself from a life thoroughly inscribed from the beginning by the insidious methods of her tycoon paterfamilias (John Huston). In a film where the title becomes the ironic metaphor for the incestuous power of patriarchal capitalism, it is the city father and head of a wealthy family who is the ultimate seducer and destroyer of family and social trust.[20] Evelyn's father wants to drive farmers from the valley outside Los Angeles so that he can take the land and irrigate it with a new dam and city water at great profit to himself. The fact that he killed hundreds of people with a shoddy dam that was part of a similar scheme some 30 years previous is further testimony to the relentlessness of his powermongering in a phallic business environment. Against such a ruthless force, the wealthy Evelyn's occupation is reduced to the care and protection of her incestuous and disturbed offspring, an unsuccessful attempt to save the next generation from her own enslavement within the personal contexts of a corrupted regime.

Major Hollywood films such as *Marnie* and *Chinatown* clearly articulate the dark lady's association with personal, familial, and cultural repression, although it is no longer her sexual aggression that mirrors the unconscious forces of cultural contradiction. She becomes instead the key to the signification of political economic patterns of violence, rejection, and abuse, of the family spoiled and women's economic potential misdirected. Therefore, the woman of sexual mystery who appears in important films of the 1960s and 1970s, while unable to challenge dominant signification through business enterprise, goes a long way toward unveiling its brutish aspects through the illumination of her personal disasters. She tends in these films to counteract the language and ideology in Western capitalist societies that would mask these kinds of negative socioeconomic effects. She continues to carry the marks of political economic oppression and repression, but now she becomes the conscious focus of this oppression, releasing the secrets of long-repressed experience.

In this transitional era of cinematic experimentation and social protest, entrepreneurial women in Hollywood films also consciously struggle to liberalize gender attitudes despite their marginal and oppressed business circumstances. The noir thriller *Klute* (1971) was criticized for its placement of the woman, Bree Daniels (Jane Fonda), in the role of a helpless call girl as sex object. But seen as a neo–femme fatale, she is sympathetic as a struggling victim much as are Marnie and Evelyn, insofar as this text also exposes the pattern of her persecution by a larger economic imperialism. Her pursuer and assailant is clearly marked as a privileged corporate figure who uses his high-rise business office as the media control center from which he harasses her. In a similar vein, the depressed, opium-addicted Mrs. Miller (Julie Christie), madam of the frontier bordello in *McCabe and Mrs. Miller* (1971, Robert Altman), is, like her male counterpart (Warren Beatty), unable to withstand the violent economic pressures imposed by much larger business interests from outside their little township. Hence, Marnie, Evelyn, Bree, and Mrs. Miller are all suffering, damaged women whose negative experience insists upon greater freedom in women's economic and heterosexual lives.[21] And latent here as well is a new recognition of their wider potential usefulness in the career domain. The neonoir seductress as victim may be seen implicitly as a failed contributor in business and nurture who may otherwise have helped to counterbalance the forces of economic objectification.

After appearing largely as a victim in the neonoir 1970s, the Hollywood femme fatale of the 1980s regains phallic significance, and in a new way that suggests a late, postnoir stage of development. Consistent with the fact that more women were moving into positions of authority in the world of work, she is more likely to be an intimidating character of sophistication, wealth, and power. Dressed out in a successful corporate career or with the benefits of entrepreneurial economic independence, the contemporary (or postnoir) seductress is generally smarter and more sexually demonstrative than her classic and neonoir prototypes. She no longer needs the man for violence as she is fully capable of it, nor as a means to profit, since she is already rich (or at least fully equipped for business and career success). Her presence in two films from the early 1980s provides the first evidence for this trend.

Bob Rafelson's 1981 remake of *The Postman Always Rings Twice* looks back to the 1930s merchant-class setting of the original novel, while Lawrence Kasdan's *Body Heat* looks forward to contemporary professionalism. The *Postman* remake modernizes the psychic anxiety of its main characters, as well as increasing the seductress figure's economic initiative and abilities. After the murder trial has failed to convict the guilty couple but has given them notoriety, Cora (Jessica Lange) successfully expands her deceased husband's roadside restaurant to the point that her coconspirator (Jack Nicholson) feels superfluous. Women's increasing parity with men in careers and economic power in the early 1980s shifts her perceived threat in Hollywood film to more conscious forms of legal and business competition. She continues to reflect a forbidden sexuality. But under the liberalized sexual standards of the time, her greatest intimidation increasingly occurs in the realm of careers and professions.

In *Body Heat,* the careless lawyer Ned (William Hurt) pursues Matty Walker (Kathleen Turner), the sexy wife of a wealthy man. So thoroughly does she seduce the protagonist Ned, however, that he is shocked to learn that he will have no cut of Matty's inheritance and will instead take the entire rap for her husband's murder. Matty's role combines torrid sex with an elaborate legal strategy, which becomes fully apparent to Ned and the film spectator only in the closing scenes. The last shot features Matty enjoying her private wealth at some foreign resort where men cater to her every wish. Her intellectual and performance skills demonstrate a confident, leisure-class command of her turf that director Kasdan probably intended to rattle the foundations of complacent Middle America. In the Reagan years of business laissez-faire, the nation became attuned to an atmosphere of assertive self-interest and of image over substance.[22] In this setting, the Hollywood seductress appears driven to extremes simply because the very habit of success and privilege has elevated her appetites rather than absolving them. The entrepreneurial femme fatale continues, then, to measure the contribution of gender difference to the larger, changing cultural perspectives of economic desire and success.

In the late 1980s, the femme fatale's phallic potency becomes even more pronounced as the country begins to awaken from its Reaganite reverie to a huge national debt and a growing rich-poor gap. Understandably, the nation grew uneasy, and Hollywood was quick to seize the mood. In the professional-class thriller *Fatal Attraction* (1987), Alex (Glenn Close), a successful associate editor for a book publisher, pursues the protagonist Dan (Michael Douglas), a married and successful lawyer. She aspires to the bourgeois family model of ownership and possession in a way that has nothing to do with lower-class restlessness and everything to do with professional expectations and "family values" idealism. She represents an inversion of heterosexual plotting in classic noir because she enacts the "outsider" role, taking the initiative to terrorize and destroy her lover's innocent wife. In this scenario, the woman invader jeopardizes the entire patriarchal family, which has the effect of exacerbating the need for its paternal protection and rule. Alex is the aggressor in part because, at 35, she remains unsuccessful at becoming married with children. A vengeful woman, she finally wields a big knife because she wants control in the home as well as in the workplace. Her competitive will apes phallocentric mastery and creates a new variety of scapegoating whereby ambitious, single career women now become potential rogues, and married men with families become vulnerable to their aggressive familial rather than monetary demands.

First test-screened as a domestic drama that falsely placed Dan in prison at the end for Alex's supposed murder, the reshot thriller version of *Fatal Attraction* responded to the public's desire to see Dan successfully defend his family against the seductress invader. Just how much audiences wanted to demonize Alex is demonstrated by director Adrian

Lyne's decision to go for a horrific, slasher conclusion.[23] The crazed viciousness of Alex's attack in the released version pinpoints the level of anxiety attached to the preservation of the yuppie family and its constant pursuit of material security. The slasher/thriller ending also provides a vivid example of how commercial cinema modifies its scenarios to suit the box office, in this case altering character roles to fit pre-tested social fears. More than that, Alex's obsession with Dan and his preconstituted family strongly insinuates how woman's career success is insufficient to her sense of fulfillment without the family component. She doesn't seek to kill Dan so much as to replace his wife.

The mammoth public response to the film did reveal the audience's angst over the fragility of the young family in the face of urban decay, financial uncertainty, commercial encroachment, and new threats such as AIDS.[24] It is out of a desire for relief from Alex's manic assaults that Dan futilely moves his New York City family to a quiet Connecticut village. But Alex's outrageous demands on Dan might also be recognized as an overreaction vivifying postmodern culture's highly overextended consumer expectations, as if a husband and family could be acquired and attached to oneself like a new set of living room furniture.[25] The metaphoric role of the careerist femme fatale reflects more and more directly on contemporary marketplace dynamics. Because of the respective professional legal and publishing worlds that Dan and Alex inhabit, Alex's attempts to tantalize and intimidate Dan and his nuclear unit may be read as an assault on the family synonymous with the increasing pressures of the privatized commercial arena. In this sense, Alex articulates careerist/professional fears of downward mobility and ultimate separation from the American Dream. *Fatal Attraction* is not only a testament to the potential subversion of family security and the devastation that can accompany it; the slashing monster that Alex becomes in the end also signals a new sense of the inadequacy of career success to the assurance of the complete family package. Her hysteria is directed at the very conflation of the family ideal with career success, particularly for women.[26]

EROTICIZED SUCCESS MASTERY AND REPETITION COMPULSION

The conflation of romance, sex and work, and the production of women's work
as sexual performance (through the different configurations of prostitute/career
girl/professional woman in, that is, the image of the "working girl"), simulta-
neously conceals and reveals the complex interdependence of gender and class within
popular discourse.

—YVONNE TASKER, *Working Girls* (47)

In the postnoir thrillers of the 1990s, the femme fatale's drive for economic betterment usually takes the form of a sexualized careerist excess. These scenarios have their origins in narratives of the woman who
sleeps her way to the top, such as Barbara Stanwyck's role in *Baby Face*
(1933), or Joan Crawford's in *The Damned Don't Cry* (1950). Free to pursue most careers today, the contemporary sexual predator represents
a slightly different agenda. The aggressive sexual siren as pathological career ladder climber appears in a corporate setting in *The Temp*
(1993), and in a (journalistically challenged) news reader setting in *To
Die For* (1995).[27] But it is her antagonistic presence in the entrepreneurial
framework of *Basic Instinct* (1992), *The Last Seduction* (1994), and *Disclosure*
(1995) that most clearly illuminates her new identity not only as domi-
natrix of the gender wars, but also as a representative figure of the eroticized and complete exploitation by marketplace power itself. These
apparently self-driven, independent figures spring full-blown from the
boiling pot of exploitational capitalism rather than from any localized
sociological history. They are also sociopathic in their single-minded
determination to dominate in a success game long since detached from
any socially responsible order of meaning. In addition to their looks and
audacity, their appeal owes also to the already corrupted individuals
and/or institutions they challenge, which usually appear deserving of
such treatment. Their attitude and conduct in these films of the 1990s
mimics the in-your-face extremes of political economic hostility and
sexual exhibitionism already commonplace in today's promotional culture. Their obsessive need not only to exploit erotically but to exhibit
superiority in the pleasure of sheer power points to the new extremes
of an alienated fetishism of success. Winning economic advantage in
the sexual tryst of the moment is no longer sufficient for this contemporary figure, since her sexual partner must also be made to recognize
his competitive inadequacy and defeat, much like a highly personalized
loss in business and career.

The "erotic" thriller *Basic Instinct* does reveal character background on Catherine Trammell (Sharon Stone)—who probably commits a series of murders, beginning with the suspicious demise of her parents that results in her large inheritance—although the origins of her homicidal inclinations appear to be imbedded in cultural pathology. Currently, she exploits men for experiences that can be included in her best-selling novels. Suspected of killing her lovers with an ice pick just at the point of their orgasm, Catherine is taken in for questioning by the police investigator Nick (Michael Douglas), which results in the now famous, vulva-exposing leg-crossing scene. Nick knows the pattern of her probable in-the-act crimes and shares her bed anyway, presumably to catch her in attempted murder. And in this he mimics Catherine's exploitative careerism. Nick also has the reputation of being a quick trigger in police enforcement, which has earned him the nickname "Shooter" (the double entendre is also appropriate). His overaggressive tendencies have landed him on probation and also infect his sexual relationship with the policewoman (Jeanne Triplehorn) assigned to monitor his behavior, and who seems to love him. After nearly raping her, he later mistakenly kills her in a paranoid rage at the location where his sidekick has just been murdered.[28] The pattern developed here of deception, human objectification, and violence thus spreads from self-absorbed careerism into interpersonal intimacy. The alcohol- and drug-addled Nick is no closer to being a model of justice than Catherine is to being a model writer, and they prey on one another out of career-related motivations and without love or shame. Hence, selfish characters and their sexually intensified violence enact a plot that is less about the current state of heterosexual relations than about the vicious deterioration in the basic ingredients of a humane culture.

There is something of both the sadistic and the masochistic in the spoiled demand for immediate satisfaction in consumption, to be followed by a disaffection that requires further satiation. This environment creates serial killers who become best-selling authors, and bad cops with lots of attitude and itchy trigger fingers who enforce the law by sleeping with their suspects. Their self-interest finally has less to do with advancing their careers than with the act of intimate dominance itself, the insistence on the superior position—the being on top sexually—that controls the pacing of pleasure and orgasm at someone else's considerable expense.

Catherine's debased career trajectory here depends entirely on pleasure in exploitation, both at the moment her victim realizes his fate, and at the moment the circumstance is turned to further profit through extrapolation for public consumption. The text concludes with two interchangeable endings based on whether or not Catherine will kill Nick with the ice pick lying beneath the bed. This scenario further imitates the commercial exploitation of her novels as stories that may or may not have some autobiographical basis in fact. The realms of production and consumption become thoroughly corrupted in a circular frenzy of pleasure in the homicidal performance of exploitation itself. The pleasure derives from the fact that this gorgeous, thrill-seeking writer is so unruffled in her intimidating superiority: her sexual and cultural profiteering is engaging not only in its bold style but in its sophistication.[29] Catherine is ultimately more interested in the success of her thriller novels and their dangerous suggestions of her own possible guilt by implication than she is in her sexual "research" so lethal to her partners. And yet the one feeds on and necessitates the other. The American faith in self-initiative is turned here into a vicious cycle of destructive opportunism in which no one but Catherine ultimately profits. The abuse of eros both in and by the film also reveals how intimacy has been turned inside out for private gain. The final, perhaps unintended message of *Basic Instinct* is the displacement of professional careerism by an egomaniacal sadomasochism, where a semblance of joy is expressed only through homicidal and writerly provocation. Catherine's sexual body and mind become tools in Darwinian combat, which also leaves her nothing but the exhausted emptiness that necessitates a repeat performance. In this way Catherine's serial pattern of destruction evinces a repetition compulsion fully in step with the starvation and satiation dynamic of consumerist ideology. She has objectified herself into a destructive industry that perpetuates the glory of consumptive ecstasy. She is momentarily fulfilled but must constantly reiterate her entrepreneurship—to wit, the complete cycle and very image of exploitation.

Contemporary cinema's siren figure of high-tech business appears in *Disclosure,* Barry Levinson's screen adaptation of Michael Crichton's novel by the same name. Here, the career/gender wars are catalyzed by the temptress Meredith Johnson (Demi Moore), who is brought in from outside the young, high-tech DigiCom Company to fill a key executive position. She is a business schemer and sexual manipulator, who works within the internally loose ethical environment of conglomerate competition. On the surface, Crichton's novel and Levinson's film are about sexual harassment,[30] although the subject as presented strongly foregrounds two other significant and related themes. The most obvious of

3.5   *Disclosure* (1994).
Meredith Johnson (Demi Moore) has, for a while, the superior executive and insider position over Tom Sanders (Michael Douglas), who suddenly finds himself in a highly compromised role in more ways than one.

these is job insecurity, which topped the list of American anxieties at the close of the 1990s. Tom Sanders (Michael Douglas[31]) goes to work one day as a confident careerist and family man expecting a big promotion. But he returns home a scarred and shaken man, facing possible embarrassment, humiliation, and the loss of his job and possibly his marriage. In this contemporary setting of conglomerate merger mania, spin-offs, downsizing, outsourcing, the general dissolution of worker rights and privacy, and the decline of the nuclear family, nothing seems secure.[32] A society grounded in a belief in personal initiative and worker competence and creativity begins to grind to a halt in its own alienated, competitive fury.

The text indicts Meredith for allowing her relentless job-climbing, which is permissible, to spill over into sexual harassment on the fringes of work, which is not.[33] This suggests one standard of conduct for self-enclosed, self-administered corporate business, and another for "private" citizenship, which is vulnerable to all manner of personal and legal assault. Most importantly, Meredith's putative history of sexual dalliance with her male underlings posits a physical acting out of the same kind of power relationships encouraged by the predatory company system that employs her. DigiCom shows a tendency in certain circumstances to manipulate its employees and push its products in the same way that Meredith fucks her colleagues and promotes herself. Nor is product quality DigiCom's primary concern. Only the selling of the perceived potential of its virtual reality hardware is necessary to complete the highly profitable merger. In its will to advance, DigiCom, like Meredith, compromises employees and product to get ahead.

Not quite as extreme as the antagonistic women in *Fatal Attraction* and *Basic Instinct* who eventually fry cars in acid, boil pet rabbits, and swing ice picks in sexual climax, Meredith follows up her aborted office tryst with Tom by initiating a lawsuit over sexual harassment to destroy his career. The fact that Meredith is successfully countersued by Tom, however, does not end her power alliance with DigiCom's founder and CEO Garvin (Donald Sutherland). Garvin has little concern for sexual harassment but is obsessed with the company's public image, and thus incensed with Tom, whom he blames for endangering the lucrative, pending merger. The legalities of sexual harassment become almost irrelevant when Garvin allows Meredith to sabotage DigiCom's main production line so that he can fire Tom as a scapegoat. Tom learns of Meredith's ploy, however, and forces her out of the company instead. But Garvin remains untouched despite his cloakroom practices, and all the power invested in his corporate image system lives on.

Meredith has gotten away with sexual harassment in the pursuit of job advancement in the past, much as DigiCom is promoting its flawed hardware gizmos to accomplish an advantageous merger now. Company outsider Meredith was hired over Tom to fill a vacancy as product development administrator because of her strong "sales" persona, which seems to fit DigiCom's emphasis on image over substance. She becomes indistinguishable from Garvin's methods and marketing goals, which fully align her with his impersonal preoccupation with profitable appearances. Despite her ability to talk a good line, Meredith obviously does not understand the technical intricacies of advanced product development as Tom does, making her sexual advances to him an even more calculated ploy to neutralize any inherent power he may have to challenge her authority. When Tom decides to risk a lawsuit for sexual harassment, he knows the losses he is likely to sustain include his wife as well as his job. Tom's wife tries to overcome her distress over the incident, but though a practicing lawyer herself, she is unable to contribute to his ethical struggle at work. In the formal public hearing, Meredith quickly shows her willingness to go to any extremes for vic-

tory while appearing all along to represent the company's best interests. Meredith's individual demonization at this stage of the narrative
actually functions to distract attention from Garvin's increasingly cutthroat tactics, which point to the film's indictment of corrupt individual
and business practices generally.

Elizabeth Traube perceives the role of the seductress and related
women figures in films of the 1980s as scapegoats for new forms of conservative revisionism:

*Conservative rhetoric and the tradition from which it derives were reworked in the
pursuit of contemporary mass audiences. Instead of celebrating the values of work,
self-denial . . . the films that struck a responsive chord concentrate on attacking the
negative forces of excess projected onto women. Once women are constructed as the
source of social problems, their expulsion offers an imaginary solution.*[34]

But Traube's gender take on films of the 1980s seems not altogether
applicable to the final power relations established in 1995's *Disclosure*,
where Meredith's function ends before the film's closing section. Garvin
is the surviving tyrant, and the deposed Meredith remains the voracious
but failed executive in training. Meredith is no victim of patriarchal
capitalism, but one who mirrors the full co-optation of feminine sexuality by phallocentric corporate interests, which have long since colonized masculinity.[35] The glass-enclosed offices of the struggling workers
in this film clearly demarcate the dissolution not only of privacy but of
any personal autonomy whatsoever.

The hidden contradiction in *Disclosure* results from the way Tom's
victory over Meredith is also made to appear as a victory for his middle-
class family and its continued stability. This wishful logic is clearly
countered by Garvin's corporate mentality, which has no more use for
family per se than it does for Meredith once she becomes a possible
detriment to company profits. DigiCom's politics seem to enslave and
degrade its employees and to drive and be driven by the consumer market in ways that are opposed to the faint nurturant goals barely visible
in Tom's domestic milieu. But despite the text's conclusion of faith in
family survival, *Disclosure* reveals just how vulnerable and fearful the
contemporary employee and family have become. Research has shown
that most employees cite the way they are treated as the primary reason for leaving their positions.[36] Tom may preserve his job, and a good
senior woman administrator may assume the leadership of DigiCom's
subsidiary under Garvin (demonstrating the minimal relevance of the

gender difference factor), but the company will obviously continue to prioritize positive public images over more unpleasant realities such as the foreign labor sweatshops on which it depends. This ambitious film seems accurate enough in its overall perception that cybertech has become the hottest competitive tool in the Darwinian struggle of international conglomerates. But its representation of a dominant commercial regime of the sign creates a self-fulfilling and regenerative cycle of surplus production and consumption, and one in which Tom and his family remain entrapped. Garvin's final success reaffirms the fact that Tom and Meredith are so many undifferentiated pixels on his company's computer network screen, which recognizes differences in gender, class, race, and nationality only as a matter of political convenience in the bigger game of high-tech oligarchy.

Greed takes a decidedly independent form for the entrepreneurial femme fatale Bridget/Wendy Gregory (Linda Fiorentino) in director John Dahl's *The Last Seduction*. The audacious Bridget is an unredeemably cold and lethal seductress, who induces her husband to acquire and sell $700,000 worth of pharmaceutical cocaine and then absconds with the money. She takes a job in a small town and takes a new lover, Mike (Peter Berg), for both the heft of his penis and the weightlessness of his brain. When her husband sends a detective to capture her, she crashes his vehicle and kills him while he has his penis exposed, which allows her to blame the detective for sexual assault while she recovers from minor injuries. She is prompted to enlist Mike to kill her husband back in New York City. When Mike fails to kill him as she expected he might, she is there to stroll in and do the job herself. Immediately thereafter, she provokes the shocked Mike into virtually raping her as she dials 911. She sets him up to take the rap for both the murder and sexual assault. Bridget's cash-obsessed libido makes the trade-off sexuality of classical femmes fatales appear demure in comparison. Her sexual skills are world class, her mental capacities diabolical, and her capacity for violence worthy of the Terminator. In the end, she is driven off in her prearranged limousine, wealthy and apparently free of criminal charges. Her success depends in part on her anonymity, as she lives on in the dark underbelly of capitalism's idealized domain of entrepreneur.

Bridget Gregory and her aggressive career in sales and theft—accented by her reversible handwriting—signify a futility of hope in any possible entrepreneurial counterculture. Her sparsely furnished work and living spaces, and her numerous car scenes lend an indelible sense of job and domestic transience. Her creative style of sexual aggression

3.6   *The Last Seduction* (1994).

Bridget Gregory (Linda Fiorentino) captivates the overmatched Mike (Peter Berg) in ongoing scams, which include her final betrayal of him. A thoroughly unscrupulous businesswoman, she also represents more than gender domination.

trounces all of the men who try to deal with her. Bridget also knows that fat profits are built on mass marketing. She applies her criminal mind to uncover a voluminous list of names of husbands whose secret credit card accounts can mean they are cheating on their wives. These men are potential targets for vengeful spouses who might consider Bridget's services as an assassin. Her computer retrieval techniques make it possible to expand the individual spousal murder/life insurance scam of classic *femmes noir* into a full-scale murder-for-hire business network. And while she uses this scheme merely as a front to trick Mike, her methods suggest the expansion of sexual-economic abuse into an impersonal system.

Through Bridget, *The Last Seduction* implies a very late stage in the overall devolution of sign culture into political economic hegemony, where no space outside the realm of commercial seduction is long permitted to exist. At first, Bridget works as a manager for an office full of telephone "cold-callers," pumping them with cash when they succeed at selling virtually useless special coinage. Her next job, taken under an assumed identity, is in a related area of high-pressure sales management. Image promotion is essential in her employment and in her private schemes. While at work, she once warns her baffled playmate Mike not to "fuck with her image," which at this point is a front for theft. She is a consummate performer in a world of sexual/commercial exploitation, and she is therefore infinitely effective. Her kissing tongue in her husband's surprised mouth opens the way to a deadly injection of Mace down his windpipe. This climactic scene is comparable to the one in *The Grifters,* where Lillian (Anjelica Huston) smashes a water glass through her son's jugular vein and leaves him to bleed to death. Such excessive violations of family bonds for a valise of cash provide unmistakable commentaries on the current dominance of commercial over all other romantic, family, and community values. In the 1990s, Bridget and Lillian, like Meredith Johnson and Catherine Trammel, all signify a seductively willful, egocentric, and greedy force in mainstream society that has become one of its most defining characteristics.

The postnoir and contemporary femme fatale, therefore, whether she is killed, fired from her job, or simply escapes, has increasingly come to embody the overindividualized dynamic of the obsessive careerist, and the overladen, oversexualized sign of commodity fetishism. The male fear of the economically ambitious woman in classic noir, who grew up to the realization of women's political economic victimization in the neonoir era, now begins to recognize the full fruition and lethal power of women's commodification in the postmodern age. The history of the femme fatale's representation signals the increasing assertion of willful objectification in the form of sexualized greed, which has less and less to do with the personal body, subjective self, and inherent needs. The contemporary representation of her obsessions points to the alienated expression of a commodified body and mind as well, which enacts lust in terms largely defined by dominant commercial signification. Gender antagonism is thus not a sufficient description of this contemporary icon's function, if it ever was, because her current incarnation symbolizes an encroachment relevant to both sexes. The femme fatale has increasingly mirrored not so much the sexual angst of each American decade since World War II, but the growing exorbitance of phallic economic values that make a mockery of eros, much less nurture. In psychoanalytic terms, she also ceases to be the monstrous Other as a repressed ("feminine") libido, and has become instead the furious idolized beauty of the image reification process itself. In the 1990s, she apes the simulational, commercial spectacle in all its seductive and reductive power, thus reminding us of its increasing authority in the hearts and minds and bodies of the population at large. The contemporary entrepreneurial femme fatale represents not only the personally exploitative tendencies of business and consumer desire, but how personal eroticism has itself already become driven to self-objectification, fragmentation, and public performance. This figure provides the ultimate commentary on the commodification and embodiment of personal drives into commercial forms. Both Meredith and Bridget simply walk away at each film's end. Bridget is rich and anonymous, and Meredith assures the gloating Tom that she will make a comeback with an even bigger new company and eventually buy him out. These invasively aggressive women figures are unstoppable because they stand for the most dominant trends that thrive in the current marketplace of political economic reality.

Disclosure is preoccupied with new technology, and its setting is packed with all the latest digital equipment, including the undependable virtual reality system that is the reason DigiCom is being sought for merger in the first place. Meredith's secretive actions leave a trail of residue in the technical systems that Tom discovers and uses to trip her up. Tom stands for real technical understanding, which has a relative business value here, while Meredith was hired to make the merger work because of her ability to sell, to promote an image of technical invincibility. Tom's victory over Meredith in technical competence, however, is constrained by the perpetuation of the sales image perspective held by Garvin. He will continue to ensure that DigiCom's technical image remains unstained, whatever the internal reality of the company's production procedures and results. Garvin is confident in his assumption that emerging technology is essential to keep the production and consumer cycle running at a full and delirious speed. In the end, however, he doesn't assign Tom to an administrative position of authority because, to elaborate from the text, the specific function of equipment remains secondary to its sale and unquestioned consumption. The technological revolution in practice remains secondary to the selling of its empowering significance. This is the job that remains primarily in the hands of promoters backed by business sponsors such as Garvin, all of whom have a vested interest in seeing that the message gets through. Just how this has been and continues to be done is the subject of the next chapter on the all-important promotion industry.

Advertising is an important factor in the way people attempt to satisfy their needs through the consumption of products. In fact . . . "it is not that the world of true needs has been subordinated to the world of false needs, but that the realm of needing has become a function of the field of communication." An understanding of the communication industry that mediates needs is also a vital element in the understanding of the social role of advertising.

—SUT JHALLY, *The Codes of Advertising*[1]

CHAPTER 4
HUCKSTER FOREPLAY
THE PROMOTION INDUSTRY

Having considered the two general categories of corporate versus entrepreneurial enterprise in film, as well as important issues of gender, class, and racial and ethnic identity, I wish to turn in these two closing chapters to films that address the two most significant trends impacting career and life in this age. The first is the promotional dimension of consumer capitalism, which is essential to it, and the second is communication technology, which is closely related to the first and increasingly determinative of every aspect of contemporary work experience and personal and cultural identity. No discussion of the success mystique in American business and career cinema would be complete without a close look at the arena that is the driving force of consumerism and most responsible for determining the cultural understanding of success — advertising and public relations. Those who work in this regime are closest to the kinds of thinking meant to arrest public attention, not only for products and companies, but for social attitudes, styles, and finally political economic and ideological orientations. Media advertising and entertainment have also had a long and symbiotic relationship. Motion picture entertainment, for example, which once supplied boundless resources to the dull techniques of early advertising, can be seen in recent decades to have adopted some of the styles and flavor of advertising. In contemporary media generally, the relationship of promotions to information as well as entertainment programming has become symbiotic. This chapter looks at the cinema world in which promoters ply their trade, with specific attention to the social forces and contradictions that create them and that they create.

From the beginning, Hollywood cinema has represented the advertising and public relations industry with conventional protagonists, plots, and themes, but also largely with mistrust and sometimes ridicule. Only recently, however, has it touched upon this industry's massive impact on society. The historical predominance of ad/PR comedies may suggest a general cultural unwillingness to take the industry's economic and cultural impact seriously. Early silent comedies set the tone for this business film subcategory, which was followed in the classical period with more of the same. It is mainly in the extension of comedy into edgy satires stretching from *Putney Swope* (1969) to *Wag the Dog* (1997) that American cinema has suggested the greater cultural and ideological influence of promotional culture. For Sut Jhally, it is advertising more than any other single industry that most influences and defines American business and culture. Modern and late capitalism has required a huge investment in promotions and sales — $175 billion in the United States in 1996 — in order constantly to reinforce and magnify consumer demand.[2] And it is this gargantuan expenditure that supports the high costs of media outreach. Advertising in particular pays for the distribution of almost all of the cultural and informational data that reaches the public through the media. This means that contemporary capitalism would be unthinkable without it. More than the constant advances in technology, advertising is the linchpin of what has been called the information age, which should really be called the Age of Promotional Sign Culture. In this contemporary cultural setting, the media sign or simulacrum is continuously imbued with market connotations influencing its very existence, content, and form.

To understand contemporary capitalist culture is to understand advertising's full range of impact on cultural production and content as well as distribution and consumption. The specific effect of particular ads on particular audiences is only a small part of advertising's overall influence. It has become a central, assumed, and therefore almost unconscious part of everyday life through the way it conditions, among other things, the scheduling, organization, and design of the media. More importantly, it imposes itself as a part of the stories and myths that constitute national ideology by encouraging a certain kind of outer-directed "individual" identity, which requires perpetual confirmation through constant expenditure and consumption. As suggested, advertising's overall influence goes beyond specific commodities and creates a surplus expectation or reification effect, which sets the tone for the notion of a material "good life" in America and, indirectly, for the globe. Commodity fetishism also pushes marketplace values to the center of cultural ritual and meaning in the absence of alternative forces of comparable power.[3]

Postwar economic and consumer growth, following the rationing and sacrifice that accompanied World War II, saw not only a radical expansion in the promotional industry but an increasing awareness of it. Certain Hollywood films have all along contributed to the growing public recognition of this industry, as well as in some cases its critical assessment. The advertising/PR film, however, has tended like the corporate executive film to have a limited perspective on industry realities. The gradual professionalization and separation of the advertising and PR industry prior to the 1940s, for example, is not made apparent in Hollywood cinema until the 1950s. In my overall discussion of how Hollywood films have encoded the persuasion industry and those who have made a career of it, I will look particularly at how promotional strategies developed by the main characters in these texts are related to historical trends in advertising, and thus to the processes by which a personal and national success mystique are realized and sustained.

FROM EARLY CINEMA HUCKSTERS TO CORPORATE MEDIA DEMAGOGUES

In August 1916 the Associated Motion Picture Advertisers [AMPA] incorporated. . . . Advertising as a discourse created standards and exploited innovations. It estab-lished the grounds on which competition would occur and set up prescriptive values which became requirements for film practice in the United States.

—DAVID BORDWELL, JANET STAIGER, AND KRISTIN THOMPSON, *The Classical Hollywood Cinema* (103, 102)

While this study is devoted to films released after 1944, very early Hollywood cinema directed at the subject of advertising and media "publicity" is so highly informative as to require an exception to the be-ginning postwar time frame of this investigation. Certain silent come-dies reveal the confused beginnings of what was to become modern advertising and PR. These early films also set the stage for the devel-opment of the kinds of protagonists and attitudes that have long char-acterized these texts. In the early twentieth century, advertising and public relations were ill-defined as a calling, and were viewed with considerably more skepticism and controversy than today. And this skepticism also accompanied the shift in promotional logic from a general product use-value orientation associated with the industrial era, to a product sign-value orientation common to modernity. This change has its parallel in early Hollywood film, when protagonists began to be recognized as acting stars, and audiences began to pay as much attention to specific actors as they did to the films in which they performed. While advertising was slow to recognize the advantages of giving pleasure in visual ads, as opposed to simply showing products and listing their characteristics, it did finally awaken to the power of entertaining audio-visual images, which had always been the goal of commercial cinema. Cinema has served both as a general model for evocative images in audio-visual advertising, as well as a platform for all manner of product display, whether freely loaned by manufacturers, or donated with a publicity payment included (payola). Shooting on film has also provided the primary medium for major national ads, which continue mainly to be shot on film before being exhibited mainly through television. Hollywood's feature film industry has many carryovers from the production and performance side of film/video advertising, and many employees work simultaneously in both. The highly concentrated atmosphere and special effects produced in many major ads has been a training ground for directors such as Ridley Scott, who made the successful leap from commercial to feature film production. An important characteristic of contemporary sign culture in general is the interchangeability of images across commercial advertising and cultural production, especially where the advertising for cultural products like movies is extracted from their content as trailers, or transposed into graphic and pictorial signifiers in a widening pool of intertextuality. It is not enough that the stories of business films suggest the quest for success, but that the individual human and commodity models meant to signify success begin to run together, to collapse into evocations of character types, behavioral and dress styles, work and home and transportation scenarios, and finally to seepage into public attitudes, buying patterns, and values.

The first Hollywood film of significant length entirely devoted to industrial publicity, *His Picture in the Papers,* was produced by D. W. Griffith's Triangle Company in 1916 (the same year the AMPA was incorporated). It starred a new personality named Douglas Fairbanks and was directed by John Emerson and written by Anita Loos. A comic spoof lasting 68 minutes, the story plays on the therapeutic claims so frequently made for products by their makers. The film's introductory title sets the tone: "Publicity has become the predominant passion of the American people. May we introduce to you as a shining disciple of this modern art of '3 sheeting' Proteus Prindle, producer of Prindle's 27 Vegetarian Varieties."[4] This introductory jab at publicity and its "disciple" Proteus is confirmed by the ensuing plot, but not without fundamental contradictions in the film's enunciation.

Proteus wants to train his son Pete (Fairbanks) in his food business and asks Pete to go out and create some free publicity for the firm. Pete responds to his father only after his girlfriend's dad insists that Pete is not worthy of her unless he has an executive position in the Prindle Company. Now motivated by romantic desire, Pete pulls a series of publicity stunts only to learn that merely being newsworthy isn't necessarily *positive* publicity for his dad's company. At last, by chance, he has the opportunity to make a dramatic rescue of his girl's father from murderers. The press arrives and Pete attributes his athletic daring-do to the eating of Prindle's vegetarian products, which in actuality he has all along refused to consume. This public misrepresentation pleases his corpulent parent, a buffoon who has sought to instruct his son in the art of creating free publicity. Because the narrative largely holds Proteus responsible for encouraging his son toward false testimony, Pete escapes culpability and will gain not only promotion in the Prindle Company but the girl as well. Since his primary motivation stems from his desire to wed the girl rather than to boost Prindle's fortunes, his lying is largely excused in the comedy narrative. Hollywood protagonists are typically allowed a certain ethical leeway when fighting for their lovers, whether that entails advancing their employment or not. By film's end, Pete has learned to practice the more flexible consciousness of a promotional business administrator, a director of perceptions. Henceforth, presumably, it will be Pete's concerns for his wife and children that will justify his search for profit, power, and advancement.

The melodramatic and often comic tendency to highlight the protagonist's romantic life as a distraction from ethical problems in the economic arena is typical of early and classical Hollywood film generally, but it is particularly relevant for the male hero in advertising and PR settings, where some public resistance to the nature of his calling clearly exists. Pete is sympathetically portrayed as a free spirit trapped in the new industrial bureaucracy. He is easily distinguishable from all the other clock-punching desk jockeys who slave for his father. And he enjoys the special opportunity his father provides for him. Doing "pub-

licity" gets him out of the office and tests his resourcefulness. His energetic diligence must have appeared as a bromide to the drudgery experienced by most workers in the factories and offices of the time. And
because Pete's final prevarication to the press serves a purely romantic
rather than commercial goal, Griffith's studio could also sell his charm
as an irrepressibly romantic star of comedy. Therefore, while *His Picture* at first satirizes publicity, it also finally endorses it in the name of
family and heroic action. Pete's experience suggests that under certain
personal circumstances, lying to the public may be acceptable as well
as beneficial. The film ends on a note of reassurance that publicity can
be benign, even as the narrative provides a workshop in the manipulation of public forums for private business ends that, in the case of the
Prindle Company, do not serve the public.

The expression of public disinformation, while softened by the comedic tone of this text, is nevertheless at the core of the ethical dilemmas surrounding capitalist promotions generally. And these dilemmas
have several implications, some of which were matters of concern at
the time and some of which were not. Obviously, from a contemporary perspective, the journalistic press fails to question Pete's vested
interests in his allusion to the efficacy of his father's food products. The
gullibility of the press for newsworthy stories as well as its highly in-
terpretive function in news coverage and presentation is implied. But
Pete's wily claim also confirms Proteus's belief that the media can be
set up with promotions that will appear as factual news, which is an
important strategy of public relations. Hence, despite the film's unsympathetic portrait of his father's hucksterish attitudes, Pete as well
as Proteus do finally get exactly what they desire through misleading
public relations. And Pete begins to see the new value in image thinking. At best, then, *His Picture* pokes light fun at the deceptive side of
publicity by downplaying its potential public impact.

His Picture in the Papers also sets the stage for Hollywood's ad/PR
films up through the classical era, which create one very loose standard
of truth for commerce, and a much stricter one for personal behavior.
Once Pete's romance is legitimated through marriage and he becomes
a company manager, will his concern for the poor quality of Prindle's
food products at least equal his concerns for the company's publicity
and sales? Through its mild comedy, the film encourages a perception of
the publicity agent's vaguely defined role at the time that is consistent
with the founders of this industry. They were far more interested in
proving its impact as an effective business tool than in considering how

manipulated events, half-truths, or false claims might have an insidious effect on society.

Hollywood took an interest in the promotional industry early in the twentieth century because it was already a controversial subject at that time. For example, the original theorist and father of public relations, Edward Bernays, unabashedly made claims for "the engineering of consent."[5] On the other hand, culture critics such as Thorstein Veblen addressed the negative outcomes of advertising and press agency and coined the term "conspicuous consumption." Veblen's articles in 1918 and 1919 on "Vested Interests" and "The Engineers and the Price System" distinguish between *useful* industry and business sales *promotions,* which he condemns as wasteful. Veblen places this useless consumerism stimulated by advertising in the same category as "saloons, gambling houses, and houses of prostitution."[6] Dishonest promotions came under popular attack by the "truth in advertising" movement that developed by the 1920s. Veblen's critical thought was absorbed by the younger Stuart Chase, who saw advertising in the 1920s as an institution that was guilty of more than frivolous deception. According to Chase, consumer appeals were luring masses of people into debt to spend beyond their means on products as well as stock market speculation, creating a debt spiral that would eventually encourage conditions leading to a market crash. In his book *Your Money's Worth* (1927), he describes the manipulative impact of advertising on blundering consumers, those "Alices in the Wonderland of salesmanship," who "buy not what they freely want, but what they are made to want. . . . [T]his Wonderland . . . is stimulating, colorful, romantic . . . the next best thing to going to the movies."[7] Chase was especially sensitive to advertising's larger fantasy world projections surrounding commodities, those accoutrements of status deemed necessary to fulfill the latest version of the success mystique.[8]

Advertisers in Chase's time began to pay less attention to specific product characteristics and more attention to appealing social associations for their products. As Stuart Ewen explains in *Captains of Consciousness,* advertisements in the 1920s begin to project images of people who "take on life's problems through the benefit of commodities."[9] The new publicist and advertiser, then, direct attention to the carefully constructed image rather than the fact of the person, company, or product. Advertising further promises liberation from all manner of social problems and tedious work through focused consumer behavior. This in effect is what Pete Prindle encourages in the film when he attributes his new, hard-won celebrity status to his father's foods, although the film spectator knows better. The point is that Pete's education in publicity requires not only ironic distancing but a willingness to overstate or mislead. And this would seem to encourage the viewer toward the same kind of ironic, modernist skepticism, but also toward more devious ways of attaining success. Pete's shift from hourly wages to image-oriented contract service is presented as a step up in both worker sophistication and income. Ewen relates this shift in worker attitude and image consciousness to the new promises of consumerism, where the "consumption habits of the leisure class were now propagated as a democratic ideal within mass advertising. In order to sell the commodity culture, it was necessary to confront people with a vision of that culture from which the class bases of dis-satisfaction had been removed."[10] That is to say, advertising provided its audience a shortcut through fantasy to an otherwise difficult social mobility. "His Picture in the Papers" does much the same thing, while remaining within the framework of American ideals of a freewheeling private initiative as the way to class mobility and success.

With the passage of time, the male types who represent the promotional business in comedy also change. Douglas Fairbanks played Pete Prindle with an athleticism that evoked traditional masculinity and rural adventure. But this profile was beginning to be modified by 1923 into a more urbane profile in the bespectacled figure of Harold Lloyd. His starring role in the silent comedy *Safety Last* offers a more studious and witty version of the itinerant publicist. The central irony of *Safety Last,* in fact, is that the hero's gymnastic friend, whom he has enrolled for a building-climbing publicity stunt, cannot perform, forcing the lowly department store salesman (Lloyd) to do it himself. Less obviously robust than the Fairbanks character image, it is precisely Lloyd's physical skills that must be proven if he is to earn a promotion and be worthy of his girl. His class ambitions and ethical license—he deceives his boss and provokes the police—are similarly attributed to pure romantic desires. And the fact that Lloyd plays the role of a social underdog here (much as did Charlie Chaplin's tramp character) only adds to his appeal as one who is unwilling to accept traditional authority at face value. Because Fairbanks's and Lloyd's personal motivations are noble and their haphazard schemes are endearing in courage and skill, both films encourage a certain public expediency for the sake of private gain. And despite the fact that Lloyd's film is more socially progressive as to class status, both texts also underwrite the manipulation of surface appearances as a sign of social sophistication. This more aggressive characteristic of the promotional business must be distinguished from the two silent films' broader and more useful implication that class mobility requires a greater attention to sign systems generally.

The shift in the promotional business hero type from raw energy and robustness to a more sly, urbane wit also reflects the movie industry's own use of publicity, and specifically, as I mentioned, its competitive flexibility in developing the star system to meet changing market demands. The big studios, including the ultimate star contract writer and Metro-Goldwyn-Mayer boss, Louis B. Mayer, quickly learned to sell their films with star publicity the way corporate advertisers in general developed consumer recognition of their brand names and logo images to boost their commodity sales and services. The studios also learned to seek public recognition for their stars and individual films rather than for the studio, which became satisfied with simply including its logo on publicity at the beginning of its films. Janet Staiger found that the Hollywood industry had already made important discoveries by 1915: "Distribution would be predictably benefiting advertising; feature films would be differentiated and stressed; brand [studio] names would be submerged to product features (genre, stars, plots, spectacle, or realism)."[11] Studio Hollywood's dependency on the public's acceptance of its cinema products continued to enforce a conservative treatment of its stars and genre approaches as well as its own publicity apparatus. In the 1930s, for example, Hollywood did not seek to make films about advertising because—except for the gangster and horror film cycles of the time—its output was heavily oriented toward optimism and escapism, a typical PR approach in response to the serious economic troubles of the time. The last thing audiences of the 1930s apparently wanted was wily ad/PR men beating the drums for more commodity consumption. The classical male type for the ad/PR film, therefore, does not appear to be fully realized until the late 1940s, when the promotional industry underwent its explosive expansion.

As mentioned, the promotional industry advocates not only commodities but institutions, personalities, sociopolitical viewpoints and consumerism generally. Specific advertisements by organized lobby groups or political parties, as John Sinclair writes, can be and "are much more directly 'ideological' than product advertising,"[12] although this does not mean that the cumulative effect of the promotion industry is nonideological. Scholars of popular culture in the tradition of Veblen and the Frankfurt school have gone considerably further to note ad/PR's ability to mediate consciousness by reordering the forms and nature of personal and social communication. Writing in *Culture of Consumption* (1983), Richard Fox claims that advertising was partly responsible for the transition from a nineteenth-century "producer ethic" of work and saving to a twentieth-century ethic of consumerism and the "corrosive impact of the market on familiar values."[13] Technological advance, mobile lifestyles, and the cash flow of urban employment increased demand for quickly obsolescing mass commodities. These consumer goods and the media and advertising systems that sold them created or enhanced new social patterns as well as forms of legitimization. The old moral life of sacrifice and toil was giving way to a crisis in purpose as advertising helped to shift public concerns from the moral precepts of religion, which were oriented toward rewards in the afterlife, to private interests of immediate personal gratification.

The new profit-managerial core appeared with a . . . new morality subordinating transcendence to new ideals of self-fulfillment and immediate gratification. . . . While 19th century elites ruled through ethical precepts that they encouraged people to internalize, 20th century elites rule through subtler promises of personal fulfillment. The old idiom was individualistic and moralistic; the newer is corporate and therapeutic.[14]

The road to individual happiness was to be lined with fat incomes and commodities, the concrete signatures of the contemporary American success mystique. The secular environment of ad/PR was not only transforming interpersonal communication in the direction of purely commercial discourses, but organizing those discourses into a competitive hierarchy. The greater the variety of particular goods offered, the more advertising was called upon to appeal to stylistic rather than use-value concerns on the part of the consumer. Ad/PR was also increasing its influence on cultural attitudes surrounding group identity relative to success and mobility. This is the overshooting quality of reification in commercial promotions, the vibrant ideal of a pleasure beyond mere product consumption. Because Hollywood's entertainment films have no specific product to advertise so much as themselves, genre films in particular form an even more direct and comprehensive cultural discourse laden with the heroes and mythical stories meant to gel with the audience's concerns and hopes, as well as to bridge cultural contradictions. More directly than do other film genres, it is the ad/PR business film that highlights the specific processes of promotion meant to guide the public's understanding of self-improvement and upward mobility.

Because the Great Depression in America and Europe challenged the viability of capitalist economies (see William Wellman's 1993 film *Heroes for Sale*) and precipitated international political unrest, public interest in product advertising was shoved into the background as nationalistic propaganda and political demagoguery seized the world's stage. Hollywood films began to pay more attention to the private and/or political ownership of media generally, and to the particular interests of those authorities who controlled it. These themes are investigated in two major films from 1941. Orson Welles's *Citizen Kane* provides backhanded references to conservative media mogul William Randolph Hearst in an epic warning of media control by individuals with strong ideological agendas. Frank Capra's populist approach to the publicity industry in *Meet John Doe* again savages the fat-cat business and media mogul for an even more explicitly political form of exploitation. Here, the wealthy industrialist (Edward Arnold) commandeers a publicity ploy by a writer (Barbara Stanwyck) at one of his newspapers, and surreptitiously builds it into his own party campaign for president. Only at the last minute do the populist idealists who are the spokespeople for the campaign realize that they do not control the "John Doe" movement. Their concerns are to be swallowed up by the capitalist owners and sponsors of mediation who are the real determining forces in the economy and government. In contrast, then, to the comedic experience of the young business clerks played by Fairbanks and Lloyd, who learn how to use publicity to advance their jobs and status with women, directors Welles and Capra instead offer egotistic business moguls whose ambitions lead them to use their media empires as platforms for their personal and political power quests. These texts demonstrate the dangerous marriage of corporate capitalism and political expediency on a grand scale by accentuating individual pathologies of overambition in the context of potent new levels of media outreach. Following the end of World War II in the United States, as the films in this section suggest, promotionalism was established not only as central to business and consumer practice, but as the necessary foundation to the entire regime of consumer culture and its dependency on mediated signification.

DIRECTING DESIRE IN THE POSTWAR CLASSICAL FILM

The torrents of fresh business energy which open new opportunities for big profits also carry away with them much of the terrain of social conscience. In this sense it is not the periods of business decay but the periods of business expansion and vitality which play havoc with moral principles, because they fix men's aims at the attainable goals of the Big Money.

—MAX LERNER IN *America as a Civilization* (1957)

Instead of being identified with what they produce, people are made to identify with what they consume.

—JUDITH WILLIAMSON, *Decoding Advertising* (1988)[15]

If the advertising and publicity industry was pushed into the background of public attention by the depression of the 1930s, and then into the war effort[16] in the world conflict that followed, it quickly came into its own when America's pent-up consumer demand began to be released after the war. Helped by the massive introduction of television into private homes in the early 1950s, the American advertising and public relations industry grew exponentially at the cutting edge of a booming consumer economy. William Manchester writes in *The Glory and the Dream:* "In 1948, when the Public Relations Society of America was founded, there were about one hundred PR firms in the country. In Manhattan alone this number quickly shot up to a thousand . . . by the time the fifties were under way."[17] The situation in advertising was even more dramatic, where the gross total of advertising expenditures doubled between 1945 and 1950, and went up another 75 percent during the fifties.[18] John Kenneth Galbraith and other economists became aware that as production gradually outran consumption in an affluent society, more and more advertising would be required to keep the new "oversupply" of commodities flowing off the shelves. Large companies increasingly looked to special advertising and PR advisers and agencies to help them take advantage of the very latest market conditions and methods.[19] All this merchandising activity after the war sparked public interest in the field once again and thus alerted Hollywood to its renewed potential for story development.

Studio forays into the promotional business as an acceptable subject for major films after the war were specifically driven by proven bestsellers. Frederick Wakeman's 1947 novel, *The Hucksters,* was rushed to the big screen that same year by MGM, starring Clark Gable as Vic Norman. The book and film refer to the broadcast system of the time, when American corporations (outside the media) not only sponsored and owned entire radio and/or TV programs, but often produced them as well. This practice waned in the late 1950s because advertising on TV in particular became too expensive, and because advertisers wanted more diversity in how they reached their markets. As mentioned in Chapter 1, Sloan Wilson's important 1955 novel, *The Man in the Gray Flannel Suit,* was adapted into a Hollywood film a year later by 20th Century Fox. This novel and film put their stamp on the entire era, and also marked a new interest in media careers related to promotions. Both of these novels and motion picture adaptations play on the revelations of returning war veterans, who thought they were fighting for the widely held idealism common to the war years, only to find themselves in a postwar world of bureaucratized business methods and increased ethical ambiguity. Their war-weary independence and worldly experience permit Vic and Tom a certain critical distance from their media careers, and help them find ways to counteract their enslavement to big ad accounts or corporate pecking orders. This resistance, furthermore, seems to reflect the moviegoing public's own need to feel that it too could resist the calculated influence of advertising and PR. Each film thus reinforces a rather negative perception of the bureaucratic corporate domain and the role of promotions as a reflection of it.

Frank Wakeman's existentialist novel *The Hucksters* is a fictional exposé of the ad industry, and it pinpoints both sexual and socioeconomic controversy. In Wakeman's book, ad exec Vic Norman tries to carry on an affair with a woman who is married to an American soldier still serving overseas. Meanwhile, his agency's biggest client expects him to go to any length to assure the success of the industrialist's Beautee soap product. The novel's central irony is that Vic is finally trapped by his inability to reconcile either his principled success goals with his actual business experience or his private longings with society's ethics. His truest instincts lead him both to reject his obsequious role as an account exec for Beautee, and to discontinue his troubled love affair. By severing these ties he is finally left free, though he also recognizes that he has become a refugee from corporate society. He has grown weary of its endless procedural forms and deadlines, which grind one down even as gradations of advancement and wealth are held out as incentive. His crisis is clearly a form of spiritual alienation from society's dominant economic values.

In contrast to Wakeman's novel, the screen version of *The Huck-sters* (directed by Jack Conway) lightens the plot and turns the novel's Hemingwayesque hero into a slickly genteel ad exec (Gable) more typical of Hollywood romantic comedy. Vic's forbidden love interest in the novel is transformed on film to a conservative romance with an American general's widow, Mrs. Kay Dorrance (Deborah Kerr), who has two young children. The passionate and conflicted Kay of the novel becomes on celluloid a genteel British mother figure. If the wholesome image of MGM along with the Breen Code prevented it from recognizing illicit sexual affairs in 1947, one might also wonder why the studio found it necessary to change significantly the history of the Kimberly Ad Agency featured in Wakeman's book. The novel tells the story of an agency founder's downfall and of a judge's suicide, which resulted when that same judge accepted a bribe from the soap magnate, who wanted to stop a $20 million lawsuit against his company. The film version white-washes this criminal past between client and agency and refers instead to a mild power-grabbing intrigue that placed the agency in the hands of Vic's immediate boss Kimberly (Adolphe Menjou), who has been left guilty, cynical, and alcoholic from that former betrayal. The real story, however, remains the individual contest between Vic and the bombastic industrialist Evan Evans (Sydney Greenstreet), who demeans his employees *and* the hirelings in his ad agency of choice.

Debonair Vic Norman stands up to soap magnate Evans and his $10 million Beautee soap account by proposing a more aristocratic approach to Evans's obnoxious brand of advertising. Vic casts his new flame Kay Dorrance and her two perfect children as formal, aristocratic models in his print campaign. Their dignified, upscale pose in Vic's photo layout succeeds, proving that advertising need not confine its message to Evans's browbeating repetitions of brand name, much less his initial intent to display Kay as a single woman robed in a sheer nightgown. Vic's morally proper family approach also has the advantage of being equated with class mobility and sophistication. Furthermore, in place of Evans's supercilious onslaughts for the masses, Vic offers a softer "love that soap" pitch that addresses a more individualized and diversified audience. In its appeal to a cross section of consumer groups, Vic's radio ad reflects an actual historical change in advertising's approach toward its customers. Moving away from one-note mass marketing for all, the newer style tailored messages to a more individualized demographics, while further shifting the merchandising emphasis from a product's characteristics to its placement in lifestyle contexts.

4.1   *The Hucksters* (1947).
Beautee Soap manufacturer Evan Evans (Sydney Greenstreet) shows his idea of a promotional campaign to his own fawning executives. His approach is soon boldly rejected by his ad agency's account executive, Vic Norman (Clark Gable), who successfully pushes a softer family approach.

Boosted by the success of his campaign in the film, Vic decides to marry Kay and provide for her children. This occurs just prior to his being humiliated and then complimented by Evans. When Evans finally bestows the mantle of his lucrative soap account upon him, Vic is so disgusted at being toyed with that he finally revolts. He dumps water on Evans's head as he says, "For a man like you to control so much of what goes out over the air into the homes of America is all wet." The film is full of such obvious verbal/visual tropes. Vic's emotional commitment to Kay and her children has increased his concern for advertising's impact on the family. But his effort to purify himself through the love of the pristine mother/wife figure seems qualified by the fact that Kay believes he can shed the taint of hucksterism without sacrificing his advertising career. Kay admonishes him simply to "sell good things and sell them with dignity and taste. That's a career for a man."

With Kay's devoted help, any moral duplicity in Vic's job is to be resolved by dumping despotic clients and bland products in favor of more sophisticated ones. Such elitist reasoning in a transitional postwar era when the middle class was just beginning to locate hope for economic security helps explain why this film did not do well with audiences.[20]

Another reason for the public's tepid response could be that the most vibrant female character in the film is a young nightclub singer of little consequence in the novel, Jean Ogilvie (Ava Gardner). She helps Vic bid low on a deal for cheap radio talent. In return Vic helps her gain a fat singing contract doing Beautee soap ads for radio. But Vic also pushes her singing style to conform to Evans's lockstep rhythms of martial music, thus neutralizing her artistic credibility. Her sacrifice to profitmaking is used to reinforce Vic's resentment of Evans's demagoguery, although Jean conveniently disappears from the last section of the film. She is the aspiring working woman and rejected suitor left in the shadow, while the regal Kay (who lives on a general's army pension) provides Vic a prepackaged family with upper-class panache. Kay seems to float above the commercial hoi polloi, while Jean is left in its grip, more the object of advertising than the subject of her own music career.

Far from attributing significant negative cultural effects to the ad business, however, MGM's version of The Hucksters offers the same kind of plot payoffs in romance and upward mobility that are promised through advertising generally. At first, Vic does not hesitate to objectify Kay and her children for his own advancement and amusement. His ad photograph of them is a formal, pristine image that runs counter to his own initial sexual intentions with her. But the photo layout also invites the ideal man who will stand in and complete the family portrait. What Kay is made to signify in her Beautee photo, and what she comes to represent in the overall narrative, therefore, amounts to the same thing. The ad's idealization of family and class status is acted out in the promissory fulfillment stipulated by the film's romantic outcome. Despite the text's rejection of rude, bullying magnates like Evan Evans, Vic's growing attachment to family values with Kay proves the film's complicity with domestic consumer agendas identified with upper-class aspirations. Vic's willingness to reject Evans's fat salary offer at the time ($30,000) also comes *after* he bends his own ethics and delivers a successful radio show that Evans has demanded that he establish for Beautee soap's proprietary sponsorship. Vic's difficult experience with and final break from Evans's fiefdom can only point to a *potential* nobility in advertising and promotional culture, and only as it can be related to class ascension.

While *The Hucksters* and *The Man in the Gray Flannel Suit* want to insist that unethical, mean-spirited, or self-glorifying business promotions can be countered by honest romance and domestic virtue, this possibility is not convincingly resolved in the body of these texts. One might rather conclude from the former film that the cultural impact of hard-line corporate promotions is little more than a public irritant, or from the latter that corporate network television is mainly a socially benevolent institution of public service that happens to include the inconsequential clutter of ads.

But this was hardly the view of many cultural observers at the time. Writing in 1952, historian David Potter declared that "advertising now compares with such long-standing institutions as the school and the church in the magnitude of its social influence. . . . It dominates the media, it has vast power in the shaping of popular standards, and it is really one of the very limited group of institutions which exercise social control." [21] For Potter, the huge corporate expenditures that drive advertising make its influence so pervasive that it cannot help but impact the public's recognition of needs and the manner in which these may be fulfilled. Hence, the promotion industry is clearly central in the determination of sociocultural production as well as consumption. Promotionalism is the delivery engine that reaches out and invades every individual, home place, and public space with its messages. With its huge capitalization and direct or indirect underwriting of manifold media networks, it has also made mass consumption and the privatization of consumer culture possible. But for the aspiring promotional careerist, it has also seemed to offer something different from the corporate grind, perhaps a way to have a more direct impact on society at large. And while these films of the 1950s may be soft on the real cultural effects of big commercial promotionalism generally, they do nevertheless succeed in presenting some of the particular stress and contradictions involved in working in such a field.

The last important dramatic screen adaptation of the classical period is from Jeremy Kirk's 1951 novel, *The Build-Up Boys*. It is a fictional exposé of public relations and advertising that apparently was not judged suitable for mass-market cinema until 1962, when it was presented in a modified version by 20th Century Fox studios under the title *Madison Avenue*. Clint Lorimar (Dana Andrews) is not defined as a war vet-

eran, as are Vic Norman and Tom Rath, but he is, like them, a PR
genius. And he shares with them an optimism that highlights their faith
in democratic opportunity, despite the fact that all three are alienated
from their respective agencies and seek solace in their women. Clint
Lorimar must decide between a woman whom he has boosted into a
successful ad agency head, Anne Tremaine (Eleanor Parker), and one
Peggy Shanon (Jeanne Crain), who is independently building a successful PR career despite his personal inattention. The significant foregrounding of two career women as principal figures here does reflect
an important historical development that was changing the face of certain businesses. But Clint's choice of the warmer Peggy over the colder
Anne is clearly justified in the text. Peggy is long-suffering and obviously the more likely eventually to choose motherhood over career. In
the end, Clint does ask Peggy to marry him based on her position of
integrity and career strength, although their bond occurs in the context of joining the largest, most cutthroat ad agency in New York.
So once again the protagonist's romantic fulfillment displaces otherwise troubling signs of excessive corporate ad agency greed and cold-
bloodedness. The extremely insecure relationships between the adman
and his agency and/or clientele in all three of these texts are in fact
typical of the ad business to date, and they do not encourage the confidence and belief in independent choices that seem to prevail in the
personal and business lives of Vic, Tom, and Clint. In each case, the
protagonist decides how to balance his work and romance equation,
concentrating on the one or the other as he deems necessary, and thus
preserving the appearance of choice in and control over his personal and
economic fate, even where his financial circumstance may be insecure
in the end.

The protagonist of *Madison Avenue,* however, does begin a certain
break with the earlier hero formula. Clint sees the limitations in the industry he serves more sharply than do the admen in the 1950s films, and
he tries to do his image-making work honestly despite highly unstable,
competitive, and corrupting business influences. Early in the film, his
agency head, Brock (Howard St. John), fears Clint's success with a big
government defense account and with an important industrialist, so
he fires him from the agency before Clint might decide to start his
own agency with the lucrative accounts. Out of a job, Clint proves his
mettle by starting again from scratch and becoming successful in another agency he builds from the ground up but does not own. When
he refuses the agency owner Anne Tremaine's request to back an unde-

serving client (Eddie Albert) who wants a top national cabinet position, he gets fired again. But his professional ethics—which include resisting the temptation of personal vendettas against others—finally pays off. He is rehired by the man who fired him in the first place and gets the girl who best understands and admires him. Unlike Vic, Clint can only accept a mate who has already become a wizened but still ethical insider to the tough political competition of "the build-up boys." Hence, rather than family moralizing and class mobility, Clint's story points to a hardened professionalism, which also includes a higher threshold of tolerance for the petty vindictiveness of others. Clint's "Realpolitik" in business is based on tough experience and a certain cynicism toward middlebrow authority, an attitude that would become characteristic in films of the late 1960s. *Madison Avenue* is the most acute workplace film of the three discussed here because it most succinctly demonstrates the many pitfalls an active, honest promoter must avoid to be successful in the working jungle of boosterism.

Only the transitional text *Madison Avenue* touches on more significant public consequences of promotionalism both for the ad person and the typical consumer, as well as for the highest levels of government and business. Clint is initially fired by Brock because he is about to land a huge government defense contract, which Brock would rather not have because he assumes that Clint would then become a renegade and establish an immediately prestigious competitive agency. Clint's PR efforts after his job termination are dedicated to proving to himself and Brock not only that he can climb back on his feet, but that he can challenge Brock's agency power in open competition. Clint thus serves as an example of a highly conscious version of the need for identity self-construction in consumer society generally. He discovers his identity and power as a character through his comprehension of the dominant significance of the image, particularly where a small space is shown to exist from which to interrogate its validity. Exactly why Clint insists upon and is able to maintain professional ethics in his work is not explained in the text, but the very fact that he must struggle so hard in his career to preserve them (even to the point of compromising honest romance) is testimony to the growing pressures against the maintenance of such convictions. The promotional industry helps manufacturing to increase the rate of product obsolescence as quickly as it turns over its own employees. It also makes commodity and exchange values more abstract by heightening the role of consumer practices as an expression of identity. Clint seems to survive and represent a glimmer of hope in his chosen business because he keeps his professional standards of success separate from the consumer values he inevitably advances.

As I suggested earlier, some of the most perceptive films of the 1950s that deal with the media and its powerful reach are rise-and-fall over-reacher narratives, another subcategory of the business career text. The best of these are mainly exposé films involving promotional character types, from those in *The Big Carnival* (1951) and *The Bad and the Beautiful* (1952), to those in *Sweet Smell of Success, The Great Man,* and *A Face in the Crowd* (1956–57). All five of these films offer behind-the-scenes views, respectively, of journalism, moviemaking, newspaper column writing, and of course, television. And all of these texts warn of the media mogul's ability to control and distort his medium's messages, at least until a community standard reemerges to set things right again. The rise-and-fall overreacher film reveals a fundamental discrepancy between the optimistic attainment of business success and power—the idealized success dream—and its ability to corrupt. The American belief in individual initiative as a path to economic success becomes threatening when the individual turns, in a seemingly neurotic way, to overweening greed and demagoguery. The most grandiose examples of career success in the history of American film narratives have consistently reinforced the ironic notion that great success and power also corrupt. Material success, apparently, is more worthy as a goal than as an end result, which often leads to satiation and disillusionment. The mythical function of the overreacher plot is to confirm the quest for success as well as warn of the dangers of personal overinvestment in its material and power rewards. The promotional version of the capitalist success mystique, in other words, is highly suspicious of itself but reluctant to admit the tendency to corruption that exists in the ideology as well as in the system. In its Hollywood classical incarnations, the promotional overreacher plot really amounts, then, to a scapegoat narrative. It assigns the authority of hegemonic ownership/sponsorship to skewed individual personalities who, coincidentally, appear to be created by that very system. The misguided promoter who tries to rule the press or movies or television may be personally censured at story's end, but the promotional image system that makes his problematic rise to power possible is not. Overall, the spate of overreacher films in the 1950s testifies to public uneasiness with the growing power nexus of big business and promotional media, and of its growing potential to seduce and commercialize public consciousness on a mass level. These films seek to bridge the contradictions in capitalist consumer ideals.

Hollywood, desperately competing with television in the 1950s (and with little room to judge), often noted the electronic medium's blatant convergence of programming and sponsorship as a mark of its inferiority. This convergence, for Potter, reflects television's ability to "combine design and cultural symbolism with characterization, story line, and dialogue," in such a way that the "stylistics of imagery, patterns of attention, and programming format are bent to advertising purposes."[22] Advertising has always ruled American television, although advertisers and media owners have claimed that their ads and programs are benign because they simply give to the public what it demands. But the primary goals of America's commercial media are to emphasize information and images for mass entertainment and consumption in such a way that product and market demand is ceaselessly stimulated. This also has implications for the construction of career choices and goals among individuals. In any case, the main purpose of commercial TV, according to Raymond Williams and others, is mainly to deliver audiences to advertisers (measured in high viewer ratings).[23] And it is this entire commercial patronage regime, particularly as it applies to TV, that already conditions programming and co-opts any potential resistance among audiences or media critics who are dependent on that system. In this environment spearheaded by television, art/entertainment products are transformed into commodity status, creating what Adorno and Horkheimer identified as early as 1947 as a "culture industry." Furthermore, program and sponsor systems have an unrelenting appetite for new products and personality images to provide a constant flow of spectacle upon which to focus audience attention and buying power. To Williams, corporate sponsors were not only supplying the market with images but organizing it.[24]

Certain historians of advertising have called the period from 1945 to 1965 the era of "Personality"[25] because of the increased focus on, or exploitation of, individual personalities for promotional purposes. This is the central theme of *It Should Happen to You* (1954), featuring Judy Holliday as Gladys Glover, who becomes a wealthy celebrity by first simply advertising her name on Manhattan billboards. Her public persona as the outspoken and practical girl-next-door is soon commodified into a celebrity ad gimmick, which gradually becomes alienating and tiresome to her. She returns to her socially observant but impoverished filmmaker boyfriend (Jack Lemmon) in the end, suggesting that public success is not the utopia that it is made to appear to be. Her choice of the Jack Lemmon character over the slick and wealthy business owner-advertiser played by Peter Lawford also represents a further rejection of the artificial ad image, even as it is aimed, like Gladys's own ad work has been, to seduce the average girl. Gladys Glover's disillusionment with the artificiality of advertising and celebrity status was hardly a new theme for Hollywood, but Holliday's material does go further than anything Doris Day did in the early 1960s to establish the career woman's potential for career success through determined effort (see Chapter 2).

Certainly television and advertising did open new doors for women, although the emphasis remained on putting them in front of the camera rather than behind it where the other ad/media execs resided. Miss Glover's attempt to have her say and to control her own image in this comic text remains so mild that she hardly threatens anyone. Women's working image was still ruled by domestic concerns. Stuart Ewen points out that in regard to gendered media messages, women were said to have "directive powers over the home," but that these powers "were really invested in the hands of industry."[26] Similarly, Glover's empowerment as a celeb comes at the cost of having little control either over what she promotes or over her own life, which is largely in the hands of her agents.

The power of media promotions to isolate and exaggerate certain images while suppressing others is also the subtext of the two classical comedies cowritten and directed by Frank Tashlin in 1957 entitled *The Girl Can't Help It* and *Will Success Spoil Rock Hunter?* These texts spoof personal commodification by reducing it to the figure of the blond bombshell and her exaggerated sexual image. In each comedy it is the large breasts of the character played by Jayne Mansfield that achieve a virtually independent status as power icons. The mirth and excitement fixated around the constant imaging of her cleavage, her twitching hips, and her breathless squeals attest to her status as sexual commodity, which is catalyzed both by the male promoters in each plot and by the way each film is sold to the public. In Tashlin's texts, her hypersexual representation is meant as a joke on male lust rather than a commentary on depersonalized exchange value. As Sut Jhally and other scholars of advertising have been quick to point out, advertising does not promote real sexuality so much as the fragmented, disembodied, product-associated excitement of it.[27] Mansfield's parody of Marilyn Monroe's style constitutes a twice-removed extrapolation of the sex-commodity signifier. And it also demonstrates the way signs quickly take on a cross-

4.2   *Will Success Spoil Rock Hunter?* (1957).
"Lover boy" Rock (Tony Randall) literally hides behind a figure cutout of Rita Marlowe
(Jayne Mansfield). He has teamed up with the movie star to help sell lipstick for his
Stayput lipstick account. When they fake a love affair for mutually beneficial publicity,
Rock finds that he has suddenly lost control of his life in the celebrity spotlight.

referencing life of their own. The public image of the woman's sexuality
is displayed as something to be consumed, possessed, and therefore
"tamed."

Each narrative is at pains to point out how well-meaning and good
each Mansfield character is relative to the family status quo. As described in Chapter 2, the protagonist and title character Rock Hunter
is an ad account exec who promotes his lipstick line with the help of
a celebrity actress who needs the publicity. And *The Girl Can't Help It*
(reprising the plot dynamic of *Born Yesterday* [1950]), includes a press
agent (Tom Ewell) who is hired by a crook to give his voluptuous girlfriend a singing career. In both Tashlin films, the Mansfield characters'
problems and needs are resolved by a form of remarriage and redomes-
tication. Thus, her abstracted sexual image decenters both narratives
only long enough to invoke an equally artificial image of heterosexual
and domestic closure. Sexual exploitation, it seems, is finally as harm-

less as the lipstick and pop music peddled to the public in these texts. On the other hand, they do reflect an actual level of sexual obsession in culture that demonstrates just how thoroughly erotic impulses were being turned to commercial use.

In each movie, the male agent's service to his lovely client seems minimal from the beginning, since each woman character starts with so much raw sexual appeal that her promoter is barely able to coordinate it for her career ends. This constitutes an effective denial of the male agent's ability to manipulate women's sexuality for the purposes of promotion. The disruptive potential of his client's sexual power in each narrative appears to be something that only she can ultimately direct in the fulfillment of her personal desires. And her desires are of course directed toward a positive alternative romantic conclusion, thus contradicting the intent of the crook who hired the agent in the first place. No doubt the American public needed to believe that remarriage could resolve the erotic energies released from a previous bad marriage, and which were being commodified for marketing purposes. Exactly how the newly constituted family at each story's end might suddenly be an alternative haven from such exaggerated, body-alienating forces is not at all clear, however, since the wealth and sexual display of the two Mansfield characters has a life beyond the narrative scope of either film.

Her physical attributes in the diegetic marketplace of either cosmetic or music sales stand as literal comedic examples of a very essential commercial strategy. These films do not foster sensual eros any more than does advertising, but rather an objectification of their female characters meant to be recuperated through their sincere romantic intentions. The fetishized display of her body in the films, and the frantic overreactions of the male characters, also imply imitation by the movie audience as harmless, casual fun. But can laughter at the objectification of buxom stars and male lust find real closure in marriage so long as sexual titillation remains a dominant strategy of consumerism? Marriage cannot be expected suddenly to reverse a performative, commodified sexuality, much less secure for children healthy understandings of body and personal autonomy where promotional images are preoccupied with the commodification of sex and social identity generally. Because the actual effects of ad culture's sexual provocation go beyond product sales and cannot be contained by the idealism of family values, the tendency in a market-driven culture is toward the loss of more constructive, holistic forms of self-recognition and self-empowerment (which would also include the forces of eros). Instead, there is a frantic tendency toward external verification and satiation to substitute for inner loss, which further lends itself to obsessional and addictive behaviors so characteristic of American Life. Almost everything the diegetic public is led to believe within these Tashlin films is a lie meant to boost product sales and/or celebrity publicity. Yet the film viewer is asked to disregard this misrepresentation as if ultimately good-hearted intentions on the part of promotional players can be expected to prevail in the end over market mandates.

The widely noted breast fetish in male-dominated American media really began its sharp rise in popular culture during the 1950s, when slick magazines such as *Playboy* with its famous Marilyn Monroe layout, and well-known international films such as *And God Created Woman* (1956), starring Brigitte Bardot, liberalized pictorial standards for toplessness. The attention surrounding this phenomenon is notable because the emphasis was not simply on stretching acceptable degrees of female nudity, but on the objectification of a specifically large-breasted, slender body type presumably primed for leisure activities rather than childbearing. This objectified buxom body functions in the realm of commodities associated with leisure usage and, therefore, expendability.

The screen character who occupies this body image is typically (like Bardot's character) from nowhere in particular or an orphan, which suggests that she may be viewed as a grand metaphor for the loss of a more indigenous and nurturant family and community culture. The idealized woman's top-heavy, slim-hipped and flat-bellied body image reads succor without commitment, an active commodity loaded with possibilities for substitutional nurturance. Who would have predicted in the 1950s the explosion in breast enhancement and other surgical body molding already commonplace by the 1990s? Thus, the sexual come-on that is so frequently a part of product representation in advertising, and which is burlesqued in these Frank Tashlin comedies, becomes suspect when played out in plots that are resolved simply by marital bliss, however ironically represented. Tashlin's texts seem to want through comedy to reduce public anxiety about the very processes of sexual fetishization to which they in fact contribute. The extrapolation of the body and body parts into commercial image systems is obviously related to anxiety regarding placement of the self in society as well as in careers.

Growing contradictions between traditional family/community culture and the pressures of new pop culture influences in the 1950s
also prompted a generational crisis in America. The sudden arrival of
middle-class juvenile delinquency, more creative offshoots of rebellion
in Beat expressionism, and the hot new pulse of rock and roll also
expanded popular culture to new dimensions of both disillusionment
and creativity. Meanwhile, the conservative thrust of commerce was
pushing mainstream America further toward advanced consumerism
and class envy, which justified itself through a belief in capital and material development and expansion widely hailed as "progress." But the
growth of advertising clearly increased the transformation of goods and
people into reified images that short-circuited traditional structures of
personal, family, and community autonomy, which is traceable in the
ad/PR film as it is in cultural history generally.

Raymond Williams associates the Western world's historical change
in personal perspective with the influence of advertising's "organized
magic," which constantly addresses real human needs through commodities that cannot possibly answer to them.

*If the meanings and values generally operative in the society give no answers to,
no means of negotiating, problems of death, loneliness, frustration, the need for
identity and respect, then the magical system must come, mixing its charms and
expedients with reality in easily available forms, and binding the weakness to the
condition which has created it.*[28]

This radical redirection of essential needs into marketplace solutions
has been viewed similarly by Christopher Lasch, who finds that advertising "subordinates possession itself to appearance and measures exchange value as a commodity's capacity to confer prestige—the illusion
of prosperity and well-being."[29] For Lasch this means that "advertising
serves not so much to advertise products as to promote consumption
as a way of life."[30]

Will Success Spoil Rock Hunter? in particular, manages to personalize
for Mr. Hunter certain unfortunate effects caused by hypersexualization
and celebrity endorsements in advertising. The film creates an interesting metaphor in that the product endorsement game Mr. Hunter
plays with the celebrity actress keeps interfering with his real personal
desire, which is finally fulfilled when he returns thankfully to his original girl and a family life down on a rural chicken farm. True to comedic

form and like the false "lover boy" boosterism supplied by the actress, Rock Hunter isn't really seeking big money and power; he has just wanted the prestige of a key to the executive washroom so he can impress his fiancée. Tashlin's films promote themselves much as Cecil B. DeMille's big melodramatic films sold in the past: with scenes of lush, decadent overindulgence on the one hand, and church-school, good-girl-next-door moralizing on the other. They poke fun at the proven public power of advertising by making light of its effects on its principled and homegrown practitioners. They want to reassure us that while promotions may be a seduction that answers to the authority of corporate patronage, they cannot overrule individual desires. However, the fact that the male promoters in the two Tashlin films can hardly control their female subjects and the wider impact of their sexual display, much less its effects on themselves, may be the most valuable and obvious lesson of these 1950s spoofs on and participants in sexual commodification.

The promoters in the Hollywood dramas and comedies discussed here, in fact, do not ultimately define themselves through their work or through any social impact that it might have. Vic Norman, Tom Rath, Gladys Glover, the Mansfield characters, and Rock Hunter are all finally defined through their commitment to romance, which is idealized as beyond the reach of commerce. Despite their promotional abilities, these protagonists turn away from issues of their careers' social effects to the heterosexual coupling deemed most worthy of their attention. Success in ad/PR careers either cannot be taken seriously or appears inadequate as compared to personal desire realized through romance. This disregard and denigration of ad/PR thus marginalizes its increasing role in American culture. Promotionalism's expanding and deepening impact is denied in all of these films through a focus restricted either to cutthroat ad agency high jinks or nervous sexual comedy. The split between a less than fully endorsed but economically essential career form and reified true romance thus points to a deep cultural discontinuity. The problem that is increasingly apparent in the history of ad/PR films made since World War II is that the preservation of an acceptable success mystique in commercial promotions requires ever greater extremes of denial in relation to the real social effects of this growing enterprise.

EVIDENT RESISTANCE IN THE TRANSITIONAL ERA

*Ideologies cannot be known and undone, so much as engaged with — in a sort of
running battle, almost a race, since the rate at which all their forms, especially
advertising, reabsorb all cultural material is alarmingly fast.*

—JUDITH WILLIAMSON, *Decoding Advertising*

The transitional era of the 1960s and 1970s in Hollywood cinema meant,
among other things, increased experimentation and self-consciousness
in the rhetorical language of film, and an increased tendency in many
films toward a cultural critique. The ad/PR film that signaled the
change was *North by Northwest* (1959), a psychological thriller concerning
a disoriented ad exec. The British/American director Alfred Hitchcock
had already evolved the thriller form to the point where the reading of
carefully designed images could reverberate on several levels at once,
including particularly the psychological and political. And here, with
the help of screenwriter Ernest Lehman, Hitchcock's protagonist loses
his identity and begins to see and be seen in ways that he comprehends
only gradually. Clearly, his predicament in this existential thriller comedy does not follow the conventional career and family concerns of ad
execs found in earlier studio-era films. Furthermore, his crisis in subjectivity is woven into the mise-en-scène as well as the plot circumstance of mistaken identities.[31] This Hitchcock-Lehman project reveals
for its time an unusually telling grasp of America's commercial ideology, and of its impact on individual perception and development. Like
director Orson Welles in *Citizen Kane* (1941), Hitchcock was not only
expanding the stylistic language of cinema to accommodate a more re-
flexive form of signification; he was probing the American psyche and
its institutional and ideological assumptions.

As the successful head of his own advertising agency, Roger Thornhill (Cary Grant) is accustomed to setting seductive marketing ploys for
others. *North by Northwest*'s opening credit sequence offers a high-angle
view of the glassy exterior of a modern Manhattan high-rise, which
turns the enlarged reflections of the people and traffic below into so
many moving frames of abstraction. This shot suggests how the film will
compress and distort "normal" perspective into a narrative that will
challenge that reality. The choice of an adman for a story of deceptive
appearances is apropos, and made more significant in Hitchcock's lever-
aging of the theme of personal estrangement into an international, Cold

War intrigue. (Hitchcock always insisted that his films meant nothing in particular, but the care and sophistication of their construction clearly suggests otherwise.) The opening sequence continues down on street level, as Thornhill emerges in the rushing crowds, barks orders to his secretary, and grabs a cab away from someone else. He is on his way to a drink with agency clients before going to the theater with his overbearing mother. At the client meeting, he appears to respond to an announced phone call for one George Kaplan and is suddenly abducted by men he does not recognize. Thornhill quickly learns that his survival depends on understanding who or what Kaplan is.

In the process, he becomes involved first in a murder scenario at the United Nations, and then with a beautiful woman named "Eve" (Eva Marie Saint) on a train headed west. (The film's opening title graphic actually extends each "N" word into an arrow pointing first "north" and then "west" to indicate, presumably, a contradiction rather than a specificity of direction.) Thornhill has long since missed his connection with his mother, and because he is also now trying to avoid the train conductor because he has no ticket, he moves to the dining car and sits across from a flirtatious stranger, Eve, who has already helped him avoid his pursuers earlier. His disorientation intensifies as he finds himself on a middle ground between the sexual pull of this beautiful woman and the heated search of two groups of men who want his head. Eve's efforts putatively to protect him from his pursuers as well as to keep him intimately close are forms of involvement that make her a youthful substitute for his own mother, to whom he has remained closely attached through two previous marriages.

His identity crisis reaches a turning point in the film's extended central sequence set at an upscale formal auction. Thornhill has made an emotional/sexual connection with Eve at this point, but he has also nearly been killed by an aerial gunman in a setup to which Eve directed him. When he invades the auction scene to challenge Eve, however, he grows dizzy with jealousy at the sight of her being stroked by Philip Vandamm (James Mason), the leader of those apparently out to kill him. Roger accosts Eve under the paternal eye of Vandamm, who now appears to rule her behavior toward him. Vandamm's command over Eve is like that of a forbidding father figure, who actually threatens Thornhill in the present moment. The Oedipal overtones in the story (apparent in related Hitchcock films and widely noted by critics) help to reinforce the sense of Thornhill's childlike desperation, which results here from the combination of his perceived identity loss and his

4.3   *North by Northwest* (1959).
In an upscale hotel auction scene, Roger Thornhill (Cary Grant) catches up with Eve
(Eva Marie Saint) and asks why she nearly had him killed. But Philip Vandamm (James
Mason) has her in his thrall. Roger doesn't yet know who Vandamm is or why he or
Eve seem to want him dead.

betrayal by Eve. The psychological and the personal, it is now apparent
to Thornhill, are tied to a larger struggle that defines his very existence.

In addition to the Oedipal overtones and the Cold War intrigue,
Thornhill's intense exchange with Vandamm occurs right in the middle
of the developing sales auction activity. The relentless consumer context
of this posh affair is further presided over by an avuncular auctioneer
who could almost be mistaken in appearance for Dwight Eisenhower.
The auctioneer's authority, furthermore, is located in his promotion
and sale of goods to a largely preconditioned and passive buying audience. They simply await their chance to outbid their fellows during
the auctioneer's selected presentation of products over which they have
little control. It should be noted, too, that the auctioneer does not altogether run the proceedings, for when trouble arises, he turns to the
almost unnoticed figure beside him for help. This unidentified capitalist
overseer alerts the police to protect the sales process and the expensive estate goods on display, as well as the profits that he and perhaps

other unseen owners will reap. Thornhill, of course, does not share in the passivity of the auction audience, since he is as incensed with Eve's sabotage as he is anxious to preserve his own life. Stanley Cavell observes how Thornhill, to escape capture, "pretends not to know how to join in the bidding for things. The auctioneer at one stage says: 'Would the gentleman please get into the spirit of the proceedings?' that is, be decorous, be socialized; but society has been forcing an identity and guilt upon him that he does not recognize as his own."[32]

Hitchcock-Lehman present Thornhill as a representative of the promotional establishment who cannot now escape targeting by those very forces, which are shown here to be explicitly political as well as economic. While attempting to make sense of his crisis with his lover/ betrayer, Eve, he is compelled to play the bidding game enforced by a society that has, through an extended competition in the international marketplace, assigned him a false identity. Thus, Thornhill is recontextualized as a local and international victim. His subjective position as an ad agent has been inverted to the object position of one who is marginalized by economic and political discourse. His sudden identity trauma and marginalization create a breach that reveals the normally unseen oppressiveness encouraged by his ad/consumerist regime. In his effort to escape the auction scene, Thornhill makes a tongue-in-cheek challenge to the auctioneer's authority, which succeeds in getting him escorted out by the police and away from his homicidal pursuers.

The careful design of this complex sequence is also linked to other images that form a central motif in the narrative. Roger O. Thornhill's matchbook monogram and ad business trademark is "ROT," and when Eve asks him what it means, he says "nothing!" This confirms Hitchcock-Lehman's attitude toward the power of advertising/consumerism to skew perceptions. Early in the film and before his troubles begin, Thornhill explains superciliously to his secretary: "In the world of advertising, there is no such thing as a lie. There is only expedient exaggeration." But the text voices its view of the lie of promotional expediency in all that is presented thereafter. It does so dramatically by positioning the film audience in the same vulnerable state occupied by Thornhill. Set in such evocative national locations as the Washington offices of the CIA and Mount Rushmore, and under the explicit circumstances of the Cold War, the film not only places identity disruption in the context of advertising and personal commodification, but further suggests the conservative politicization that occurs in this socializing process. This is implied in the way Thornhill's romantic impulses are made to conform to the life-threatening forces of the international marketplace and its obsession with technological information. The airplane that buzzes Thornhill in the empty rural cornfield setting is the perfect image of a highly directive but little understood authority system intent on forcing him to accept his bogus identity. Similarly, when the CIA officer called notably "the Professor" (Leo J. Carroll) locks him in a hospital room after Roger helps the agency by playacting gunshot victim to preserve Eve's cover as a U.S. agent, he grows even more determined to assert his private interests over those of any government. At this point Thornhill makes a personal decision in the name of heterosexual love that appears to contradict the CIA's goals.

His subsequent efforts to rescue Eve, however, are generally in sync with the CIA's effort to stop the foreigners from stealing America's nuclear secrets. The plot's ultimate confluence of romantic and national security goals provides a convenient conclusion to this comedy-thriller. Yet the text also succeeds in introducing the dangers inherent in the political economic domination of individual identity. Hitchcock-Lehman investigate the commercial signifier from the perspective of a sophisticated but victimized American everyman. Roger Thornhill's conventional assumption of identity must be threatened with death and a lost lover before he turns to his innermost resources for self-restoration. He is forced to struggle beneath the weight of a massive enterprise of signification that has almost succeeded in controlling entirely who he has become. Notable too is the fact that his romantic union with Eve at film's end does not finally resolve either his career or his ideological dilemmas.

Initially ensconced in (maternal) dependency and surface truths, Thornhill quickly finds himself in a competitive marketplace of limited world resources that is irredeemably political and bordering on international conflict. He is made to experience the inequity and violence of market pressures lurking behind the facades of the grand auction that surrounds him. Only later, in a dramatic performance in which Eve appears to shoot him (reminiscent of Hamlet's play within a play), does he finally take the initiative and position himself to rescue her (with CIA help). Eve has already knowingly risked her life and Thornhill's in secret service to her country, but Thornhill has been slow to recognize either her commitment to ideology, or the political significance in his own commercial career as image maker. The story climaxes when he literally pulls Eve up from the precipice of granite heads on Mount Rushmore, those American icons who have fought for the dreams that have become hardened into Cold War dogma.[33] Figuratively at least, Thornhill gains a self-reliance that is less dependent on institutional and commercial assumptions. His identity breakdown and reconstruction points the way toward a hopeful but mythically inconclusive North by Northwest, which might offer some (perhaps artistic) alternative to that mainstream advertising orthodoxy that thrives on images of consumption as progress. One wonders if Thornhill, having once dangled over the faces of America's historic presidents, will once again return to his old life and his agency ROT?

In the early 1960s, Hollywood films about ad execs continued to emphasize comedy and romance. The decade begins with the fluffy Doris Day vehicles *Lover Come Back* (1961) and *The Thrill of It All* (1963), and with Jack Lemmon in a suburbanite farce entitled *Good Neighbor Sam* (1964). All three show the hilarious way promotional culture confuses the lives of the comedic characters who try to make a career of it. The image world again functions in these narratives mainly as a momentary obstacle to proper romantic closure. Advertising is represented as a man's white-collar game, where packaging reigns supreme in all its adolescent sexual hysteria. And it is in the face of such self-conscious sexual sparring, in fact, that traditional, family-oriented women are tested in these plots for the comic effect. An extension of the 1950s sexual comedies but not so narrowly obsessed with the blond bombshell, these films of the early 1960s show the increasingly active role of average middle-class women, including the confusion about the impact of their advertising careers on romance and marriage, not to mention sexual propriety. It is understandable why this conformist era's growing anxiety over public sexual imagery might prompt Hollywood to continue to address this subject through romantic comedies set in the context of advertising. In the conservative sex comedies starring Doris Day, her role as advertiser has competitive potency, but she remains at a very tame level of sexual appeal. As these films demonstrate, not only do the main characters' ad/PR careers disrupt their private lives; their careers seem to objectify and commodify their personal outlooks as well.[34] The great junk parts contraption that good neighbor Sam builds in his backyard is a testimonial to his own blocked creativity at his agency where paying clients rule. The stress on the comic impact of promotionalism in these films would seem to belie the fact that the American sexual revolution that began by the late 1960s was predicated in part on the very prominence over the last ten years of the sexual appeals imposed by modern advertising.

It is the Arthur Hiller film written by Paddy Chayevsky, *The American-ization of Emily* (1964), that first explicitly interrogates the ethical and ideological problem of publicity in an international as well as personal romantic context. Here, James Garner plays a cynical wartime navy "dog robber" who not only answers to his admiral's every material and sexual whim, but who protects his superior's authority image. When the admiral has a breakdown and the protagonist is forced into jeopardizing his own life in a navy publicity stunt on D-Day, he suddenly finds himself wounded and an undeserving war hero at the Normandy Landing. His noble new British wife, Emily (Julie Andrews), who earlier encouraged him to see the true sacrifices of war, now points out that it is better he serve a symbolic public function as a combat hero in the Allied cause by allowing a lie regarding his bravery to be perpetrated on the public. His position re-creates the contradiction between private truth and public posturing, ironically justified here by national allegiance to wartime morale (a dangerous precedent already entrenched in Nazi propaganda). Unlike the classical Hollywood cinema dealing with promotions, this film interrogates publicity as public deception before seeming to legitimate patriotic deception in its conclusion. The power of this text is the ethical seriousness with which it takes the corrupting influences of image-making and the tendency toward cynicism, as well as the way it recognizes promotionalism's potential, however ironically, for good. The noble Allied cause in war and the balancing of the romantic couple through their commitment to patriotism palliate the darker ethical issues. The myth is of greater value than the truth.

By 1969, the Western world's cultural upheaval can be felt in Elia Kazan's rambling study of emotional breakdown, *The Arrangement,* and in Robert Downey's fragmented and wildly insinuating *Putney Swope.* These films explicitly demonstrate how commercial production has encouraged a certain kind of well-paid image consciousness over substance, alienating individuals from themselves, and creating all sorts of additional class, racial, and ethnic tensions along the way. The American Dream of self-starting entrepreneurialism literally goes up in smoke in both films, but in slightly different ways. The protagonist of Kazan's text is ad exec Eddie Anderson (Kirk Douglas), who finally comes unglued because of the negative health effects of his successful tobacco campaign, which encourages the masses to smoke the Zephyr cigarette because "It's the clean one!" He tries to commit suicide, then neurotically latches on to an agency employee (Faye Dunaway), whom he drags back through his dysfunctional family history. This personal breakdown story traces the economic/emotional crises in his family and career that have brought him to his current impasse. The antihero Eddie, recognizing himself at the core of a promotional system he suddenly finds reprehensible, begins to unravel from the inside, much as Thornhill was threatened from the outside in *North by Northwest* 10 years before. Eddie rejects not only the duplicity in his work but the emptiness of his entire lifestyle, to which his advertising career has given credence. His alienation even more than Thornhill's mirrors the omnipresence of the commercial forces with which he must contend. Eddie's breakdown is shown to be a response to the proliferation of promotional thinking, whereby the public is constantly interpolated by the inflated and deceptive language of the commercial sign and the social relations it encourages. William Leiss and others have asked rhetorically, for example, "whether this [commodity] discourse in modern consumer societies is fully open to collective participation and therefore shaped by the public will, or whether it is too greatly dominated by advertising and thus under the sway of particular (corporate) interests." [35]

The sociopolitical import of the capitalist signifier is more broadly and bitingly focused in the low-budget *Putney Swope,* in which the white ad agency that suddenly becomes African American (and slightly Arabic) features a giant money hamper for stashing rapidly growing cash reserves. These profits are easily acquired from business, government, and foreign agents, and every other inventive crackpot in between. This satire demonstrates a vicious circle, where promotionalism is business and business promotionalism is politics, and where politics is money and money is more goods and power, all signifying nothing but the increased concentration of capital. In the end, the big hamper of cash is lit up in a great bonfire, confirming the absurdity of promotional culture generally. This chaotic takeoff on Madison Avenue is an ideological broadside that captures, as does *The Arrangement,* some of the satiric political flavor of the times.

But two films from the 1970s show how certain direct challenges against garish promotional campaigns can garner much larger movie audiences. *King Kong* (1975) and *The Electric Horseman* (1979) both feature grand outdoor ad spectacles in which captive, drugged animals — whether a giant gorilla or a sleek racehorse covered in flashing lights — are used as the central promotional attractions. In the first film the good romantic couple try to save Kong from destruction, and in the second they successfully kidnap the horse from further exploitation. Compared to the 1933 original, the remake of *King Kong* follows the efforts of one

Petrox Petroleum Company to wrest oil from Kong's remote island habitat, thus making the inclusion of the massive ape as the star in its commercial promotion back in Manhattan (complete with gargantuan blow-up gas pumps) almost incidental. The real ape shares the stage first with the huge facsimile Petrox pumps and then with the blond girl Dwan (Jessica Lange), with whom he absconds when the flashing media cameras all around her incite him. In *The Electric Horseman,* similarly, an aging rodeo star named Sonny Steele (Robert Redford) is promoted into a commercial celebrity by the conglomerate Ampco for its Ranch Breakfast Cereal product. After five years on the job and numerous ads and appearances as the featured cereal box cowboy, he has become rich but disillusioned and begins to drink too much. When a massive Las Vegas rally put on by Ampco pairs him with its new purchase, a $12 million racehorse named Rising Star, he revolts and runs off into the wilderness with his mount. Sonny and Rising Star are first followed but also protected by the TV spokeswoman Hallie Martin (Jane Fonda). They become a romantic couple, much as in the former film the giant beast and the beauty are pursued by Dwan's paramour Jack Prescott (Jeff Bridges), who like Hallie would rescue his love and the animal. Girl and ape become the sympathetic public victims of the overzealous Petrox promotion, while cowboy and horse become the appealing public victims of Ampco. The difference between Jack and Dwan's failed effort to save the ape and Sonny and Hallie's successful effort to save the horse is (other than the monstrous ape's destructive power) their use of counterpublicity. Hallie's TV coverage while accompanying Sonny on the lam generates positive publicity for his efforts to rescue the horse and places Ampco in a negative light, which compels the company to drop its charges and to endorse the cowboy's release of the animal into the wild. Small victories appear still to be possible through attention-getting seizures of media time. On the other hand, the TV journalist is successful only because Ampco can turn the increased publicity into the sale of tons more of the now famous new cereal brand. Nothing has changed, and the positive force of alternative forms of publicity is accomplished only through considerable personal sacrifice. Based here on preservationist logic outside the convenience of dominant commerce, it requires Sonny's breach of contract and theft of property, and a cold TV reporter's conversion to love and a willingness to risk her job. Their happy coupling, which evolves out on the desert, also points to a renewed sense of American longing for a moral Old West, an open space of possibility still free from the world of corporate media promotions,

4.4   *The Electric Horseman* (1979).
Former rodeo star Sonny Steele (Robert Redford) rides away from his cereal
promotion job with Ampco on the company's expensive and tranquilized horse,
Rising Star. Sonny is determined to rescue the stallion and himself from a
meaningless sales spectacle, which has left him disillusioned.

where a cowboy and a media-savvy city girl can get together and where
a horse can run free. If nothing else, both of these films demonstrate an
increased public awareness of massive corporate marketing and its encroachment on the last remaining spaces of autonomous, noncommercial experience. The giant gorilla from the verdant, uncharted island
and the sleek horse returned to the wild bespeak a growing nostalgia
for endangered forms of life, not to mention lifestyles. "Career" success
in these films thus becomes a question of locating meaningful resistant modes of promotion over against the demands of corporate ad/PR
schemes.

While identifying useful promotional work as that which counters
the corporate ecological threat, *King Kong* and *The Electric Horseman* are
also significant in the way they reveal the convergence of fantasy and
realism in their language and images. Each film produces the promotional mythic quality of TV reality that enthralls mass audiences and
has become a part of pop culture. In his study of celebrity and media,

Intimate Strangers, Richard Schickel explains how the language of news and of advertising have converged and become "a language that obfuscates through inflation." He notes, for example, how "television-driven" language, which evolved as a support system for imagistic communication, has taken on a life of its own.[36] The circulation of both audiovisual "news" and promotional media spectacles begin to run together in content and purpose. When the Ampco corporation receives bad publicity for its treatment of the horse, it simply tweaks the angle of its position regarding Sonny's horse-napping and makes itself the hero of Rising Star's release. The fluidity of Ampco's changing public stances appears to have little to do with the quality of its subsidiary's cereal product or the ownership status of its expensive horse. This is the kind of circumstance that reinforces Stuart Ewen's conclusion that "the cultural displacement affected by consumerism has provided a mode of perception that has both confronted the question of human need and at the same time resisted its possibilities."[37] These two transitional films want to believe that the right kind of local PR can at least momentarily counteract the mainstream promotional power of the biggest buyers. In promotional culture, however, winning the battle for the public's attention occurs mainly in relation to the degree of mass outreach. The protagonists here are not just fighting for ecological preservation through media signs, but preservation of their bodily identity instincts against a growing language and environment of media promotionalism they can hardly hope to overcome.

THE ENTREPRENEURIALIZATION OF EMPLOYMENT AND OTHER PROMOTIONAL REALITIES IN THE 1980S AND 1990S

In a world where oppressions of all kinds link with one another, nothing is felt to link with the self; the more acquisitiveness and consumerism take hold, the more the personality has to be sold rather than achieved, and the less is there any selfhood to return home to, when work is done.

—STEPHEN FROSH, *The Politics of Psychoanalysis*

Dramas and comedies of the 1980s and 1990s featuring salesmen, advertising and public relations agents, and media entertainment executives demonstrate a deteriorating environment of encrusted cynicism, distrust, and embittered rivalry. Because these employees are also isolated as individuals or placed in small groups in their work, their burden of individual performance in relation to fuzzy guidelines and often questionable promotional goals also leaves them pessimistic and defensive about their purpose and/or their institutional reward systems. Recent examples from all three areas of business are instructive, whether in the arena of direct sales (*Tin Men, Glengarry Glen Ross, The Boiler Room*), ad/PR and executive promotion (*Nothing in Common, What Women Want*), or big media entertainment and representation (*The Player, Jerry Maguire*). The atmosphere of the institutions represented in these movies can best be described as predatory and thoroughly antagonistic behind the managed facades they present to the public. The attempt to control the company image, to cover up individual and/or systemic corruption, is a theme running through all of them. The way the company presents itself guides the way the upwardly mobile promoter is to present him- or herself, whether the approach is to match or exceed the institution's tendency toward duplicity, or to call it to the attention of the public (as is the case with the whistle-blower film, to be discussed in Chapter 5). Ad/PR and sales involve the promotion of the institution as well as its product. But a corporation and its image are bigger than its particular products and its employees, who are frequently asked to be self-reliant and entrepreneurial in personal performance. The worker usually remains culpable and expendable within the larger system. This state of affairs is reiterated in all of the aforementioned films.

Most clearly vulnerable in the business hierarchy are those who carry the advertised product personally to the customer's doorstep: the direct salesperson. In this book's introduction, I alluded to the 1951 and 1984 versions of *Death of a Salesman,* where the split between the American Dream and its realization through an idealized career effort appears so hopeless. More contemporary treatments of the direct salesman in Barry Levinson's *Tin Men* (1987) and in James Foley's adaptation of David Mamet's stage play, *Glengarry Glen Ross* (1992), no longer show any belief in or shared commitment to a success dream, but only a restless perusal of options en route to the quick fix for competitive self-confirmation. The old-style pitch salesmen are dead because they cannot compete any longer with television, new technology, and the fragmented new working family at home. The tin siding sales teams in Levinson's film are already an anachronism in product and in approach, which pushes them to ever greater misrepresentations to their clients, and to the intimidation and sabotage of one another. The ongoing, self-defeating competition that becomes a war between two tin siding specialists (Richard Dreyfuss and Danny Devito) quickly devolves to an intimate personal seduction by one of the other's wife, which seems to have little more personal meaning for them (though it causes a divorce) than their smashing of each other's Cadillac. The personal associational fabric that once supported a fellowship of purpose among colleagues and in relation to clients appears to no longer exist.

Both of these films are also about personal disconnections among salesmen that have broader meanings. There is pressure exerted on them from authorities in each plot, whether from government over-sight in *Tin Men,* or from the corporation's main office in *Glengarry Glen Ross.* Because the real estate development company in Mamet's story knows it must motivate its sales force with something more than com-missions, it establishes a contest among the salesmen in which the top prize for sales volume is a Cadillac, and anything less is either second-prize steak knives or a firing. The contest reflects the do-or-die aspect of America's unforgiving success ethic, which drives the salesmen to extreme perceptions reminiscent of Willy Loman. But rather than in-ternalizing their pain and becoming self-destructive as Loman does in his conformist era, they conspire among themselves, not to steal money from the company but to steal the golden leads (the preselected client pool) that might result in possible sales. The premier huckster, the oili-est confidence man (Al Pacino), gets the best leads owing to his sales record. The others in the group are allowed either to fail or to go to jail for heisting the golden leads. The text is a dark parody of a Dar-winian business world, where for each winner in a sales promotion sweepstakes there are all the others who lose and fall by the wayside, beaten psychologically as well as financially by the heavy odds stacked against them. Glengarry Glen Ross is the name of the almost worth-less but superficially esteemed desert property "development" that the sales force is asked to market, meaning that career success here is to the detriment of the gullible customer. Because the real estate promo-tions misrepresent the property being sold, only disappointment and vexation can result. In this, the salesman career film in general offers a microcosm of the false promises of consumerism, where the promoter and the buyer both lose in a pathological substitutional pattern involv-ing codependency that no product can resolve. Meanwhile, the sales-men continue to chase the golden leads, those potentially, personally profitable tokens of their own career survival that will result in virtually worthless consumer purchases.

Boiler Room (2000) is written and directed by Ben Younger. It con-cerns a 19-year-old, Seth Davis (Giovanni Ribisi), whose father demands he give up his lucrative, illegal little private gambling enterprise and get a real job with a firm. Seth ends up at the J. T. Martin Company, a brokerage house for new recruits who are trained to do hard-nosed phone sales of stocks and IPOs that are eventually revealed to be bogus. His sales manager boss, Jim (Ben Affleck), mentions *Glengarry Glen Ross* as a model of toughness in his obscenity-laced pep talk to the young initiates, who seem so dazzled by his aggressive style and promise of millionaire status that they are unwilling to inquire further about what they are being asked to sell. J. T. Martin's "boiler," as the phone-calling war room is called, is crowded with suited men who similarly fast-talk flash to their "marks," and flash and trash (personally demeaning racist, ethnic, and gender slurs) to one another. The brokers in this macho men's club also know all the brassy lines from *Wall Street* and can recite on cue while watching the film in their off time. This self-conscious referencing of business films in Younger's text is nevertheless offset by a high-energy, realistic visual style. The viewer sees how a sharp recruit like Seth could for a while be seduced by such a hard-sell company allegiance and attitude. So devoted are the J. T. Martin brokers to their tough image that while out on the town together they stir up a fistfight with a group of young turks from another company. The culture within a company such as this, and the frantic fealty of its members, again insinuates a wider reading of the promotional and consumer landscape. The company creates an atmosphere of greedy personal expectations based in publicly proclaimed teamwork yet vicious individual competition, where the personal goal is to make as much as quickly as possible. The pleasure is less in the profits of one's labor than in the sales victory in which the client becomes the loser and the salesman proves his machismo. The consumerism of hard sales is in the sale itself, which yields a winner and a loser. The more useless the sales product, the greater the satisfaction in the sales scheme. In this enclosed factory of attitude and hype, outsiders are viewed with suspicion and a code of silence prevails, much like the code so violently enforced within Mafia operations. In the salesman film, the promotional business culture comes to believe in its own lies and proceeds to spread the disease among its uninitiated clients, resulting in victimization and bitterness all around.

The clannish insider groupthink of these backward-looking, conspiratorial sales forces is contrasted by recent films that highlight the individualistic ad/PR executive. Gary Marshall's uneven but thoughtful comedy-drama *Nothing in Common* (1986) features a boyish but successful advertising man, David Basner (Tom Hanks). David soon finds himself trapped between a demanding account at work and his divorcing parents. Suddenly his now single father (Jackie Gleason) is also fired from his sales job of 34 years and becomes extremely diabetic and dependent on his son. David mounts a strong ad campaign for Colonial Air Lines based on family cohesion and love, but he also feels compelled to reject Colonial's owner's demand that he travel to support the campaign. David wants to be available to his father, who is about to undergo major surgery. As a result, the airline owner takes his account and walks out on David, as does his daughter (Bess Armstrong). She helped him land the account and has served as David's able colleague as well as lover, but she now believes he lacks commitment to her father's company and other big-time accounts. So much for family cohesion and love. David must also tell his agency head that because of his dad's condition, he doesn't know when he will be able to return to the office. David's reluctant care for his obnoxious but long-neglected dad also leads him to a more mature reconnection with an old flame from high school, who recognizes his effort to grow up. His boss also makes the offer to restore his job when he is ready to return to the agency. Hollywood comedies such as this one thus want it both ways, seeming to fly in the face of poet W. B. Yeats's dictum: "An artist can perfect his life or his work. But not both." More importantly for David Basner, his return to his father's side represents a reconciliation with his past and with an identity search he had postponed in order to prove his independence and value as a creative talent. Mr. Basner is in part rescued by fate from an immersion in promotions that had seized control of his life.

The entrepreneurial adman's creative effort in the advertising/PR business film serves as an interesting metaphor for a tendency that social researcher and theorist Paul du Gay finds otherwise troubling in the world of contemporary business generally. The pervasive effects of promotionalism in society as a dominant economic and cultural discourse have contributed, according to du Gay, to an atmosphere that demands personal self-promotion in the conduct of career work. This has even taken the form of a motivating technique by employers in the private and public sector who have sought to isolate the worker as an individually responsible producer on the job. In his essay "Organizing Identity," published the same year as his complete book *Consumption and Identity at Work,* du Gay writes convincingly about recent, widely adopted managerial procedures aimed at creating what he calls "entrepreneurial organizational governance," where institutions socialize employees into personal commitment to a psychology of striving for the common purpose of the institution.[38] Citing many sources, du Gay observes the need for meaning in a globalizing world of fragmentation, which inclines the employee to be willing to sacrifice for an institution that would provide that meaning and purpose. Nor is it any longer enough in an image-based economy for the individual career worker simply to accomplish the expected results through tactical devotion to the company socius and its goals. It is now also essential to constantly package these accomplishments and make them known in order that they may be adequately recognized, much as a child seeks love and reward from the parent. Promotionalism has become a way of life in the contemporary consumerist environment, a methodology not only for selling commodities and company images, but for making one's personal goals, one's products and finally oneself into an industry of fealty, a success ideal realized through complete personal identification with company policy and the reigning attitudes of office culture. The pattern of recent entrepreneurial governance in business management, compared to the older Human Relations tradition, aims to create a careerism of business culture where the individual finds total meaning in the firm's work.[39] The self-governing and self-promoting employee (in a mixture of individual autonomy and centralized control) becomes the job.

Du Gay and Stuart Hall's argument against jettisoning all bureaucratic models and regulations of management in favor of entrepreneurial governance further notes the tendency for individuated, market-driven thinking to invade what remains of the public sector as it has the world of private enterprise. Du Gay describes his concern for forms of "private moral absolutism" overwhelming "liberal pluralist 'ethics of responsibility.'"[40] He sees value rather in the continued separation of the administration of public life from the private moral absolutisms that can characterize private business. He supports public oversight of businesses aimed at greater efficiency and lower costs. He is wary of both entrepreneurial governance within companies and the tendency toward the privatization of government functions by business generally.

An excellent example of the dangers of the privatization phenomenon in public life and of the entrepreneurial individuation of the worker as producer in business is provided in the powerful action satire *Robocop* (1987). Here, a corporation, OCP, has been hired to run Detroit's police department, a privatization of traditional government function intended to solve the inefficiency of state/city bureaucracy. But OCP is as riddled with corruption as the city streets, where drugs and weapons and violence exist in abundance. This leaves little room for honest cops, promoters, or corporate heads, who spend much of their time dodging bullets and rockets in a mode of duck and cover. For the sake of promoting its image as a responsible city leader, OCP puts its two highest-ranking and infighting vice presidents to the task of formulating and assembling an unstoppable police robot. Naturally, they create two versions: the new Ed 209 machine is placed competitively for development against the new cyborg experiment called Robocop. These are not merely law-enforcement tools, but promotional emblems of company power and authority. They are military as well as PR agents in OCP's effort to convince the public that it holds the answer to Detroit's crime nightmare. Because part human and not entirely instrumentation, Robocop is able to outduel Ed 209, further prompting Ed 209's executive sponsor, Dick Jones (Ronnie Cox), to order Robocop destroyed by the company's privately owned police force. After Robocop's escape and recognition that his human past involved the loss of his family, and that his own prior death was caused by OCP exec Jones and his criminal agents, the cyborg develops a personal motivation to punish his primary tormentors. Robocop has more to fear from the corrupted corporate executives warring for promotion than from the city's street criminals, whom Jones also provides with assault weapons for the continued purpose of annihilating Robocop. Individualized entrepreneurialism in the form of internal corporate executive competition, in other words, becomes self-destructive to the company and to its high-tech products (also seen in *Disclosure*). Both *Nothing in Common* and *Robocop* warn that purely self-promotional marketplace agendas in business and/or government create a loss of alternative meaning, and a need to recover some residue of a past that was not yet overwhelmed by career compulsions ruled by appearances.[41] Both films also convey a sense of longing for a collective purpose in the family and in the public sector that counteracts the forces of privatization in the individual's career commitment, in industry, and increasingly, in public service institutions.[42]

Another film about advertising that again demonstrates metaphorically how corporate and institutional employment has become more invested in the self-promotional commodification of the individual career worker is Nancy Meyer's *What Women Want* (2000). Here, the male ad executive (Mel Gibson) loses his expected promotion to a woman (Helen Hunt) brought in from the outside, but later manages to gain the promotion. During his effort to recover and further his job status, the divorced ad exec, through an accident of electrical magic, suddenly acquires the ability to overhear the thoughts of women — whether he wants to or not. This gives him an unfair advantage with his new boss and with those other women he seeks out for romantic conquest. In other words, he cannot avoid being any longer separate from self-promotional thinking either at work or in his private life. This ability to take on a foreign consciousness for business, and in this case also romantic, advantage is a further figuration of what du Gay has in mind regarding the trend toward the entrepreneurialization of employment, a self-promotional state of mind that gradually takes over the individual's perception. Individualized self-promotion as a form of identity displaces whatever residue of the self might still survive at the margins of indigenous consciousness. The promotional industry's advancement of a commodity environment based in an economy of loss and substitution. The objectified worker or producer/consumer is expected not only to take on an individualized competitive mind-set, but also to become a social participant in the instrumental consciousness of objectification.

The downside of excessive, self-selective promotionalism is apparent in a perceptive satire concerning the creative business elite of mass culture production. Robert Altman's *The Player* (1992) traces the compulsive drive of a self-centered Hollywood studio producer, Griffin Mill (Tim Robbins). Based on a novel by Michael Tolkin, the film concentrates on Mill's interior, paranoid perspective despite his power and income. The greater concern of his defensive and calculating little psychological world is to preserve his position of authority rather than to produce good movies. Griffin knows that the few projects in which he might risk the studio's investment are not required to be great films, but only successful at the box office. Given this nature of studio politics, Griffin tries to protect his tenuous job status by sticking a competitive new producer (Peter Gallagher) with what he thinks will be a bad movie development deal. In the studio environment of rapid turnover at the highest levels, strange forms of aberrant behavior might be expected, and with equally strange results.

The plot turns on Mill's partly spontaneous murder of a bitter writer who, he believes, has been sending him threatening post cards. Mill dodges the homicide investigation at the same time that he begins an affair with the writer's live-in girlfriend. He also drops his current romance with a supportive colleague, whose lone ethical voice in studio productions is now one he is less interested in hearing. Mill takes greater pleasure from his "political" coups that bump him up the Hollywood success ladder than from his intimate relationships, which may at any point change from being useful to being cumbersome to his advancement. From the beginning, Mill has to cover his back because so

many covet his position. Although the homicide brings him no sympathy, the film also makes apparent why he is lonely and desperate and
might be capable of a paranoid overreaction. The viewer is meant to
identify with his fear of disclosure in an apparent sea of sharks, where
money and appearance rule, and the box office is a notoriously unreli-
able résumé builder. Narratively, *The Player* mimes the thriller format
but for the fact that the protagonist is guilty rather than falsely accused. The head police investigator (Whoopi Goldberg) is convinced
Mill committed the crime, but she has both insufficient proof and the
power of Mill's position to contend with. She is also dazzled by his domain's culture power and the glitz of its movies and movie stars. What
is made apparent from Mill's dominant perspective in the film, however,
is a highly unstable studio world of constantly changing administrators
and endlessly negotiated projects that usually come to nothing. Of the
thousands of movie ideas and scripts Mill must wade through and consider, only a couple will get the nod from him in a year's time. They
must appeal to the broadest audience possible to be hit material.

The movies that do eventually get made and distributed are often
like the project proposed to Mill, which he personally disrespects but
helps to develop anyway. Initially intended to be a bold new social commentary with no stars, the project called *Habeas Corpus* is altered by the
studio to include big stars and a melodramatic, last-minute rescue from
a gas chamber. Of course, it becomes a big success. As original negotia-
tor and consultant on the project, Mill benefits from the studio's success. In the closing sequence, he drives his new car to his new home and
already pregnant new wife, who is seen standing behind a white picket
fence and near an American flag. His car phone has just provided him
with a pitch about a movie producer who kills a writer and gets away
with murder, which Mill is safely convinced will make a hit movie and
further enlarge his success. The crime that is incubated in free-market
consumerism can itself be exploited in the cultural reverberations of
the simulacra.

The Player's personalized but ironic portrait of Mill is both intense
and chilling. Robert Altman moves between Mill's calculating mind
and his unsettled surroundings with an array of cinematic techniques,
including a masterful, single-take opening dolly shot over and around
the studio grounds. This self-consciously observational shot movement,
further attributed to earlier moviemaking technique in the film's over-
heard dialogue, is briefly reiterated toward the end when Mill's former
girlfriend crosses the studio lot to plead her case with him. She has just

4.5   *The Player* (1992).
Griffin Mill (Tim Robbins) and June Gudmundsdottir (Greta Scacchi) look at Polaroids she has taken of him in her home studio. She doesn't know that her growing relationship with this wealthy and powerful Hollywood producer may also be with the man who just killed her boyfriend.

been fired for questioning the many audience-pandering compromises in *Habeas Corpus,* but Mill refuses to help or even speak to her. Earlier romantic scenes between Mill and his new paramour June Gudmundsdottir (Greta Scacchi) are also bracketed for distancing effect with wide shots in public spaces, tighter shots of Mill's face behind a plastic curtain, or with the two characters in separate full-body mud baths. Because Mill is continually isolated in his restless solitude and fear, despite being surrounded by others, he is a walking example of the extremes of entrepreneurial self-promotion in employment. He can never take a break from the image burden his employment forces upon him. A private scene of heated sexual intercourse with June is also the moment Altman chooses to have Griffin mumble his confession of murder to her, which she either does not hear or does not want to understand. (Her social status stands to be far higher with Mr. Mill than it once was with her now deceased writer.) Altman's cultural commentary is also strengthened by the cameo appearances by stars playing themselves for background, which has the further effect of erasing the line between Hollywood fact and fiction, or image and reality. The sum total of these techniques creates a dynamic tension in the film that comments negatively on Mill's studio business perspective. Altman/Tolkin's version of a tinseltown kingdom offers a high-stakes world of dream marketing, where reality behind the screen as well as on it seems constantly corrupted by self-serving exploitation. Altman/Tolkin's clever satire renews a certain faith in the value of thoughtful cinema as a self-critical mental and emotional reflection of contemporary culture, including particularly the way in which the decisions of powerful authorities get made and represented to the public.

Altman's film also reveals how the fantasies formulated by profit-driven entertainment packaging tend to reflect the same values that prevail in the studio's socioeconomic organization. If movie culture can be defined as a space where a society can tell stories about itself, then the behavior of the studio producer seen here suggests a scam on honest cultural expression. Mill's first name is close to (D. W.) Griffith, the father of narrative cinema who was also a sentimental practitioner. Griffin Mill's unusual full name suggests both mythic fantasy in griffin—the combination of a lion's body with an eagle's head and wings—and something contradictory in mill—a place where those fantasy images might be ground up to make something very different. He represents the location where the creative dreams of the cultural psyche are "milled" into a palatable meal for the diversion of the masses. Finally, *The Player* not only indicts movie studio politics, but offers a perceptive appraisal of the inner corporate workings of the culture industry generally. The film recognizes mainstream Hollywood's complicity with a corporate business system overinvested in image promotions rather than product quality. (The advertising budgets for theatrical movie releases sometimes match or exceed total production costs.)[43] Where movie production costs are so high and income returns so unpredictable, the big studio in this film appears to favor the advancement only of appearance-hardened executives such as Mill. Altman's motion picture specifically demonstrates how isolated career ambition can fester among jealous peers and lead to self-serving decision making that usually disfavors the film product. More importantly still, career competition here reflects all the negative traits of consumerism at large, including envy, obsessive longing, fear, and compulsive addictions. As a result, the cultural entertainment products that Mill's studio creates are recognizable by their exploitational spectacle in place of narrative depth, their pandering to stars, and their creative rigor mortis. *The Player* is finally interested in tracing the individual and systemic paranoia that exists at the heart of a capitalist promotional industry of entertainment, in which a corrupt producer preserves his job (despite his act of murder and creative abuse of almost everyone else), although he is also clearly controlled and victimized by it.

For Sut Jhally, the new media culture of promotional excess appears to have colonized the last vestiges of subjectivity with predefined experiential options as spectacle-laden as they are preoccupied with pop culture cross-referencing. Promotional culture has come to dominate the airwaves, the landscape, and the home and work environment, and naturally entertainment and leisure culture is saturated with it as well. Stuart and Elizabeth Ewen write in *Channels of Desire* of the "exponential growth of a modern media system," where "the shadows cast by the media grow more numerous, more authoritative, more alluring. . . . [T]hese shadows—with their distortions, assumptions, biases, and blind spots—*become* reality." [44] And so too do the practitioners of promotional business appear in films of the late twentieth century to be an increasingly ubiquitous and determinative force in daily contemporary life. These films accent the way the entrepreneurialization of work also gets managed in such a way as to create a psuedoindividuality in the images that get produced. The title of the studio's production, *Habeas Corpus,* self-reflexively implies not the absence of a corpse within that film, but the presence of that film's own corpse, which, like Mill, not only lacks a soul but represents a murderous lie.

Cameron Crowe's popular film *Jerry Maguire* (1996) is closer to *Nothing in Common* in its effort to trace the kinds of steps that might be necessary for career credibility and possible self-discovery in a promotional world full of too much money, too many egos, and almost no trust or authenticity. Jerry (Tom Cruise) works for a corporate agency for athlete representation, Sports Management International (SMI). He serves as a successful agent until he begins to recognize himself as "just another shark in a suit. . . . I hated myself . . . no, I hated my place in the world." In an effort to convince his huge corporate agency to correct its meat-market approach and recognize its human responsibilities to its agents and clients, he composes and submits a "Mission Statement" that is widely applauded for its truth and boldness, but which gets him fired. Criticism of one's employer is a risky proposition. In his dramatic departure he loses all but one of his clients and a corporate bookkeeper, Dorothy Boyd (Renee Zellweger). She is a widow with a young son who believes in his cause and helps him establish his own independent business. Jerry continues to shed his former corporate identity when

4.6   *Jerry Maguire* (1996).
Just after being fired for his "Mission Statement" against his corporate employer,
Sports Management International (SMI), agent Jerry (Tom Cruise) leaves his big office
building with a small fish and a staff employee, Dorothy Boyd (Renee Zellweger),
intent on starting his own agency.

he perceives his now irreconcilable differences with his fiancée, Avery
(Kelly Preston), a corporate events specialist. Avery, addicted to the
mainstream logic of the appearance of success as a couple, refuses to accept their breakup because it has the taint of failure. She punches Jerry
in the face. At about the same time, Jerry's one-man agency also hits
a low point, and he and Dorothy decide to marry and converge their
meager resources. The film thus articulates the way career necessity
can dominate and define personal agendas and identity.

Jerry's marriage begins to grow stale even as his one remaining
client, Rod Tidwell (Cuba Gooding), an African American pro football
player with a family, complains about the low level of endorsements
Jerry arranges for him on the side. Jerry presses Rod in return to give
heart to his game instead of to the money and prestige. And Rod, taking

a cue from his own happy marital state, encourages Jerry to be honest about his failing marriage with Dorothy. The film's truest scene has the white couple facing the idealism, career disappointment, and loneliness that brought them to marry but can no longer sustain them. Jerry eventually rediscovers Dorothy through their tenacious efforts to preserve his fragile business. And wide receiver Rod, taking Jerry's advice, adjusts his game attitude and becomes a star. It is Rod's fat new pro contract that rescues Jerry's dying agency and helps preserve Jerry's marriage.

But several story elements also remain as unsettling aftereffects to the film's highly exaggerated scene of Rod's football victory as well as Jerry's reconciliation with Dorothy. These include the traces of inequality that continue to exist between Jerry's status and his employee Dorothy's; Dorothy's low-paid nurse sister with her disillusioned women's group; and Rod's "unsuccessful" brother and his resentment over Rod's success. The film wants to make a case for interracial and family communication and the bridging of class and situational differences, and it is largely convincing in this worthy approach. Yet Rod Tidwell's marriage seems overly perfect just as Dorothy's son is overly cute. And the film thus overloads sympathy on the side of the independent-minded entrepreneurs. In the future, Jerry's single client base must be expanded if he is to continue butting heads with giant SMI and its bottomless resources. Against such an edifice Jerry has only his buoyant personality, idealism, and newfound credibility. Furthermore, the value assigned to TV performances that generate sports contracts, sell goods and images, broaden audiences, and increase demands will eventually spit Rod out just as it momentarily embraces him. The film appears to enhance the personal, family, and entrepreneurial discourse as a viable alternative to hollow mainstream corporate promotionalism, although Jerry's business options at the end remain limited. Jerry's entrepreneurial survival on the fringes of agency representation hardly offers a significant alternative to the prevailing pattern in the sports entertainment industry, however accurately the film registers disillusionment with it.

Crowe's film is appropriately remembered for wide receiver Tidwell's famous line to his agent Jerry, "Show me the money!" This motto is equally well applied to the world of promoters and promotional culture generally, where sponsorship increasingly determines the entertainment media reality, and where athletes are converted into promotional celebrities. In a highly fragmented consumerist society where individual and community autonomy has been under constant siege since the 1950s, sporting events, like genre films, have had a modest unifying influence for common group identity and ritual. But the exact character of those products as affected by promotion clearly also affects their reception and the nature of public ritual surrounding them. As Jerry Maguire's impassioned "Mission Statement" suggests, the lure of "winning" the mass audience and big profits soon has an impact on all those who produce and consume sports and genre films, drowning out much of individual identity and community voices on both sides of the media entertainment machine. Recent business films of cultural production such as *The Player* and *Jerry Maguire* ultimately point to the regime of corporate sponsorship and commercial media as the responsible party in career displeasure and alienation rather than primarily to the individual protagonists such as Mill and Maguire, who are either active participants or marginalized survivors in their troubled promotional domain.

Even those who confirm the flexibility of pluralist culture such as John Tomlinson admit that "capitalism changes the cultural practices of those who come into its orbit."[45] Hollywood has played a central role in media culture, not only in its focus on the middle-class conventions of mainstream genre films, but in its constant reassurance of salvation through romantic idealism, which is a characteristic of ad/PR and Hollywood films generally. This romantic myth has also been central in the promotional industry's transformation of the desiring subject into a tool of consumerism. In *Jerry Maguire,* it is already obvious that the young entrepreneur is squarely up against an economic hierarchy that feeds on corporate image and promotions to secure and hold its many market audiences. The huge world of contemporary sports entertainment in which Jerry struggles is a central aspect of a spectator culture of substitutional experience. And in this sense it provides a microcosm also of the increasing corporatization of the American worker and consumer experience. The promotion of big-contract stars and product endorsements are largely driven by media market domains that are also entirely self-promoting.[46] The history of Hollywood's business films concerning the ad/PR industry overall also reveal important stages in the long winding road to the present, where career and promotionalism become interchangeable terms in a narrowed, corporatized field of identity as a status image. For as Sut Jhally suggests in his thoughts on advertising as religion, "The ultimate power of advertising does not rest on its creative ingenuity or its ability to manipulate . . . but on its ability to mediate the dialectic of emptying and needing."[47] And this is a value-laden enterprise, which leaves a Griffin Mill shaken and guilty at the end, but also at the very top of the game.

It's not worth doing if it's not on TV.

—ASPIRING TV NEWS ANCHOR (NICOLE KIDMAN) IN
To Die For (1995)

As Truman grew up, we were forced to manufacture ways to keep him on the island. . . . Seahaven is the way the world should be.

—THE TRUMAN SHOW'S ONSCREEN PRODUCER/DIRECTOR
(ED HARRIS) IN *The Truman Show (1998)*

CHAPTER 5
WORKING IN AMERICAN TELEVIRTUALITY

It is the revolution in televisual and other communications technologies that most defines the contemporary age and, in conjunction with the promotion industry, sets the tone of everyday experience in American work and leisure. In addition to the central cultural position of television, both the specific work roles and career tracks of today's businessperson are increasingly impacted, like the marketplace, by the new hardware, software, and networking systems of the information age. When the constant demands of new communications technologies are coupled with the managerial trend toward the isolation of the individual as an entrepreneurial unit, the contemporary worker appears to have become an increasingly uprooted functionary of the mediated economy, however seductive and sometimes profitable that economy may be. This chapter is therefore devoted primarily to films that trace television and new media technology's imprint on avocational and cultural identity. For the sake of brevity, this chapter investigates those films most directly engaged with the business and culture of television and the televisual, where the powers of technoculture are currently most in evidence. For the benefit of perspective, one need only consider the recent history of television career films. In the 1970s, *Network* and *The China Syndrome* offer a cinema that is representative of significant social protests in TV contexts. *Broadcast News* and *Switching Channels* in the 1980s offer a cinema of accommodation to TV careerists and their medium. And in the 1990s, *Wag the Dog* and *The Truman Show* offer a cinema of the power and threat of the new televisual reality. Each film decade demonstrates changes in TV career experience as well as alterations in the business and cultural role of the televisual, including its increasing sovereignty as part of an expanded and converging digital media environment.

Television workspace is tied to leading-edge communications technology and serves, through advertising, those political economic forces that most directly shape national policy and cultural attitudes. Television is also the imaging system that continues to be the main switch-point of today's basic culture and reality sense. As the electronic family member in the home that we still watch and listen to the most, it is the working person's evening escape mechanism and the cultural guidepost for young and old alike. Its massive cultural outreach, saturation of daily leisure schedules, and ability to set the momentary tone and content of public discussion and awareness is undeniable. This pervasive mediation of everyday reality, and increasingly of the past and the future, is the predominating consciousness and memory of public events, and increasingly of private ones, lending itself to the concept of a "televisuality." The public reliance on TV reality that is joined in the 1990s by rapidly increasing attention to Internet/Web access and virtual effects has created convergent systems of interactivity that have the further potential of complete simulational experience, or "virtuality."[1] But this term alone fails to give television its due as the continuing cultural power center, the dominant cultural and economic industry that continues to supply the bulk of the most expensive advertising and full-motion news and entertainment, and which has yet to be unseated in its daily levels of influence by the Internet and the virtual reality of cyberspace. A term that preserves both televisuality and virtuality, therefore, would be "televirtuality." This nomenclature has the advantage of reflecting the greater scope of the total televisual, digital and online communicational world that now exists. Writing in 1995, Sherry Turkle observes that we are standing "on the boundary between the real and the virtual," that moment of liminality and "passage when new cultural symbols and meanings can emerge," and when "we are flooded with predictions of doom and predictions of imminent utopia."[2]

When the rapid expansion of the World Wide Web, e-commerce, and all of the related electronic business and commercial communications systems are added to the televisual mix, they infinitely extend the hegemony of the televirtual loop. Ellen Seiter observes how television and Internet connections are increasing so that "resemblances between websites and television programming"[3] are on the rise. TV fans have also become a "a formidable presence on the internet."[4] She adds that "connections between television and computer firms are proliferating. The association between television and the internet has been heavily promoted at the corporate level by access providers eager to lure as sponsors companies that invest heavily in television advertising, and by others seeking sources and inspiration for the new internet 'programming.'"[5] It is in televirtuality as a whole, then, that the domain of work is increasingly becoming absorbed, right along with the traditionally more private arenas of leisure experience. This distanced and yet simultaneously immediate and pressing mediational reality helps explain why characters in media business films at the close of the twentieth century—particularly those in the forefront of TV production and programming—struggle simply to locate themselves in their increasingly wired or wireless artificial environments, much less in their longer-range career goals.

The electronic age has in many ways invigorated the economies of countries already in possession of advanced technology, although a "digital divide" exists internationally as well as among workers within the class structure of the United States. The new digital age has compressed distances and intensified the speed of information exchange, and it has also altered the old barriers between material and symbolic orders and values. It is obvious that the industrial sector has declined in economic importance, while the information-processing activities of the communications sector have advanced. Image and imaging power in the marketplace, and particularly in the new high-tech industries that represent today's cutting-edge businesses, have also changed the traditional rules of economics. Information societies tend to be more reliant on electronic data, promotionalism, and delivery speeds than on qualitative substance. The emphasis in business has shifted wherever possible to close electronic company monitoring and rapid response, which may enable companies quickly to recognize the need for reorganization or merging. New and emerging televisual-related technology has also increased the role and power of images in a way that requires added resources and attention to the preservation of product and company appearances. (Consider the DigiCom firm in *Disclosure*.) As M. Carnoy notes, there is a tendency "to favour economic activities that focus on symbolic manipulation in the organization of production and in the enhancement of productivity."[6] High-tech businesses tied to new media and television promotions are not simply a recent fad, but part of an immense economic and cultural change that has rapidly been restructuring all businesses and major institutions, and therefore necessarily transforming work and career experience generally.

The constant demand for new technology and newly trained personnel may enhance but also continually unsettles the work place and current employees. In the online environment, workers pressurized by the latest tools gain outreach even as they also become more exposed, constantly accessible, and constantly traceable in every operation. Expanded outreach potential and access to high-end computing has been accompanied by greater individual job and market uncertainty, as well as new problems such as defining institutional e-mail or Internet protocols, avoiding system viruses and shutdowns, and protecting individual and institutional privacy, which is vulnerable at a level never before possible. *Sneakers* (1992), starring Robert Redford, is about the creative and sometimes clannish world of "techie" specialists or "geeks," who in this case come together to form an offbeat, high-tech security business intended to protect their client businesses against "hacker" invasions. The film is a reminder that the traditional social spaces of the typical workplace are giving way to workspaces organized around and dependent upon electronic communication, and thus the entire dimension of cyberspace.

Economic and political competition in this new business landscape has become more rapidly changeable as well as more dependent on electronic systems management and security. Technology can be as ideological in usage as it is expensive and intriguing. As *Sneakers* suggests, technical communications systems dictate their own forms of use and come complete with their own bundles of practical and ethical complications. The personal computer permits a greater and wider flow of information and personal communication, but can also, like television, limit time and opportunity for direct interpersonal exchange. Individuals in the workplace are becoming more like modular units, complete with all manner of electronic gear, who ride in gear-laden vehicles, and commute to homes complete with another layer of gear. The bases for identity for working men and women, therefore, are shifting from localized physical-interpersonal spaces to shared yet more amorphous, potentially disorienting, and less private communicational fields with vague borders and shifting interfaces. Obviously, the greater the volume of communication across career and home life, the greater the need for individual processing time. Humans, like computers, can crash from overload. The sheer multiplication of options in the televirtual domain can lead to fragmentation and/or isolation anxiety, the fear of missing something important or of becoming lost in the signal density and rapid change of postmodern life. New demands on individual identity flexibility and image management in the workplace challenge in-depth personal development as well as the related preservation of career ethics and worthy goals. In Robert Putnam's convincing study of the decline of civic engagement and the loss of social capital in the United States, *Bowling Alone,* he attributes the problem mainly to the isolating and desensitizing effects of television and the new digital mass media, which have supplanted "place-based, face-to-face, enduring social networks."[7]

In addition to several films that represent the history of the working arena of television since the 1970s, including particularly *Network, Videodrome,* and *Quiz Show,* there are no fewer than five important, interrelated American films of the late 1990s that address the new condition of televirtuality in the millennial era: *Wag the Dog, Ed TV, The Truman Show, Pleasantville,* and *The Insider.* All released between 1997 and 2000, this cycle of texts reflects the extent to which televirtuality has colonized contemporary experience. All traditional distinctions between subjective and objective, inner and outer, physical and mental, and public and private have become more blurred. Televirtuality becomes both a literal experience for the characters in these films (who work and live in front of the cameras or behind them) and a metaphoric representation of the new reality of media-dominant experience. An advanced form of sign culture, televirtuality prevails in these films, even as it is largely problematized from different perspectives. In redefining space and time, for example, the new image-driven culture has created new kinds of technological heroes and victims (combined into one in 1987's *Robocop*), and new kinds of antagonists (the shape-shifting alternately hard and liquid form of the futuristic adversary in 1991's *Terminator 2: Judgment Day*). Along with increasing the complexity and vulnerability of career life, televirtuality also calls forth momentary offshoots of spontaneous, nurturing, and/or artistic impulses that signal independence and resistance, however incompletely realized. Tracing particularly desperate although surprisingly domesticated narrative paths in character development in certain business/career films of the 1990s is an important focus of this closing chapter. I will begin with a brief history of major films about televisual careerists, their success quests, and the industry they inhabit, gradually expanding the discussion to include issues of reception and disassociation in televirtuality as a larger cultural metaphor.

FROM NETWORK TV TO CULTIC SPACE AND CULTURAL METAPHOR

Filmmakers who had been raised on television began to look through *television for their audiences.*

—JOHN BELTON, *Movies and Mass Culture*

We offer a community, a community we program an experience for.

—WENDY GOLDBERG, AMERICA ONLINE SPOKESWOMAN

Television remains the single most ubiquitous and influential source of "news" and "culture" in America. In the formation of individual identity, its impact arguably exceeds that of parents, schools, churches, and all other social institutions. So thoroughly has the television empire colonized American culture that it is hard to remember a time when it did not dominate the family focus and schedule at home, and its programming tends to define the local community and the national and international scene beyond. Douglas Kellner concludes that television leads the way in "mass-produced images [that] guide our presentation of the self in everyday life, our ways of relating to others, and the creation of our social values and goals."[8] Television has become something like the central mythic totem that once focused tribal systems into a meaningful coherence (the cosmic consciousness that preceded philosophy). Television—including its recent extension through broadband and the Internet and their potential for interactivity—has become the undisputed touchstone for information and mass meaning in contemporary reality.

Television today is intensive, ritualistic, and global in its outreach, but it continues to address the world primarily in an instrumental rather than in a sacred or philosophical manner. George Gerbner said that television is like religion, except for the fact that most people watch TV more religiously. The sense of personal time commitment and devotional openness to certain ways of seeing the world are simultaneously implied here. Television is a self-activating medium that lives in the home, where the set is typically turned on for more than seven hours daily in the United States. The average American now spends almost as many hours weekly watching television, 32, as at work or school. TV viewing has not only altered the basic way we physically interact with the world, but the way we think and use our language. Television has contributed to the transition from linear perception associated with print to a nonlinear audio-visual perception. TV's content also creates forms of shared, instantaneous experience that determine topics and positions of public dialogue. Because the development of the new broadband capacity delivered by digital wireless or cable systems also permits the convergence of computer, telephone, and TV functions with interactive capability, convergent technology is poised to become the most powerful cultural-economic tool of all time, dwarfing the impact of the printing press in its ability to inform, entertain, and inspire, but also mesmerize, sell, and dominate. American children (three out of five of whom have a TV in their room) now spend more time annually in front of electronic screens in their homes—TV, computer, and video games—than they spend in school.[9] The aggregate form of television and Internet media is quickly becoming the driving mechanism of the new society, transforming daily life[10] and the nation's political economy at an alarming rate. This televirtual domain also continues to alter the relationships between production, marketing, distribution, and consumption, as well as the career perceptions of individuals.

A historical overview of Hollywood films about television from the 1950s through the 1980s reveals some important texts and trends, as well as Hollywood's contribution to society's view of this medium.[11] The few examples of "TV films" from the 1950s reflect network television's most obvious new role as a corporate employer and programmer of entertainment, advertising, and news. Like classical corporate executive films generally, the plots of these films concerning the TV industry also feature executive competition and pressure on the private family.[12] Network television as a corporate employer in *The Man in the Gray Flannel Suit* (1956) is represented as a benevolent patriarchy in both its training of new executives and its attitude toward society. Like the newspaper and radio journalism films to which they are closely related, postwar films about TV figures such as the deceased one in Jose Ferrer's *The Great Man* (1956) emphasize their inflated, career egocentrism versus the public's trust in their media persona. Similarly, Elia Kazan's *A Face in the Crowd* (1957) features a populist huckster who works his way up from a radio "personality" to become an increasingly undeserving TV celebrity. His monstrous behavior behind the scenes—while partly learned from radio and TV promotional techniques—is associated primarily with his personal megalomania, which causes his fall. The film leaves a grim aftertaste of TV's ability to highlight and blend people and images in defined ways, promoting image over substance whether the subjects are politicians and political platforms, celebrity entertainers, or bed mattresses. Films such as Ferrer's and Kazan's helped alert the public to TV's commercial and ideological agendas, and to the impact of those agendas on programming, social movements, and political consensus. The huge success of the brash new gadget in the living room was thus not to be understood as some passing fad of the 1950s. With the help of media historians such as Marshall McLuhan and media scholars such as Raymond Williams, TV was quickly being recognized as a powerful new voice in political and cultural discourse.[13] It was in fact bringing those two worlds closer together in startling new ways, and setting the stage for the contemporary "culture wars," largely defined along the two political party lines, and molded in large part by the media's endless appetite for controversy. Prominent in these economically based culture wars has been the regulation-free "supply-siders" ranged against the socially conscious consumer rights advocates. Support for the promise of an advanced technoculture, however, has had mainstream support across party lines.

During the 1960s, films about the working world of television are directed toward the realm of advertising and treated mainly in the vein of light comedy,[14] at least until 1969, when they begin to take an even more generalized and alarmist view of what goes on behind the cameras in relation to what the TV viewer sees and believes. Films including *Medium Cool, Putney Swope,* and *The Arrangement* (all 1969) begin to define television work as a promotional and political kind of nightmare or insanity, where the news camera's impact on the events it covers or the selling of often harmful or falsely advertised goods flows right along with sitcoms, political promotions, and game shows. The central characters who work in the middle of these promotional media environments typically experience confusion or breakdown in their individual identification with the job and with its contradictions in social purpose and meaning. By the mid-1970s, progressive Hollywood films become even more comprehensive and overtly critical in their political economic assessments of television and the compromising roles of those who work in that field. In *Network* (1976), director Sidney Lumet and writer Paddy Chayevsky turn to black humor in their portrait of the TV industry in its most competitive and intimidating postures. Here, a longtime network newsman can be murdered with impunity while on the air simply for the sake of improved ratings. *Network* asserts broadcast TV's identity as a greedy corporation, whose creation of programming, including news, is entirely compromised by profit concerns. In Elia Kazan's other film about a television-related figure, *The Arrangement,* the central character as ad executive (Kirk Douglas) literally breaks down over the hypocrisy of having to provide his Big Tobacco clients with a nature-loving cigarette brand name and a series of TV commercials. His cynical work environment has already made him hostile and disrupted his marriage, and soon leads to his attempt at suicide. Director James Bridges's *The China Syndrome* (1979), on the other hand, features a TV journalist who successfully fights both her station manager and corruption in nuclear power plant construction to provide a public warning of a near plant meltdown, not unlike the Three Mile Island nuclear plant accident in Pennsylvania that occurred two weeks after the film's premiere. The film asserts that television's ability to create audience demand for public accountability (at least in fields other than its own) can exist, if only through heroic acts of investigative journalism. Lumet's and Bridges's films suggest a growing public recognition of network television's undeniable outreach, including its occasional benefits as well as public disillusionment with its overwhelming allegiance to, and fear of offending, its sponsors' agendas. Partly aided by the three films from 1969 mentioned here, television's cultural significance would no longer be so readily trivialized in major Hollywood cinema.

Examples of films from the 1980s such as *Broadcast News* (1987) and *Switching Channels* (1988) do include rather conventional critiques of TV journalistic careerism and insecurity. They continue to reveal the trend toward infotainment in news presentations already set forth in Lumet's *Network.* Sidney Lumet's *Power* (1986) also provides a first but very disjointed look at the new breed of political spin merchants. Most notably in the 1980s, however, *Poltergeist* (1982), *The King of Comedy* (1983), *Videodrome* (1983), *The Running Man* (1987), and *sex, lies, & videotape* (1989) begin to break the traditional careerist orientations of films about television and video. These latter five texts provide discomfitting TV/video spectacles that explore for the first time on a major scale television and video's encouragement of obsessional, cultist behavior as it relates to real social and psychological pathology. The centrality of TV experience in culture creates anxiety because of its uncontrollable externality, as well as its ability to make televisual viewing seem more exciting and real than fully embodied, direct personal experience.

Steven Spielberg and Tobe Hooper's *Poltergeist* (1982) — a mainstream

brother in horror to David Cronenberg's more pornographically suggestive *Videodrome*—presents the TV's cathode ray light waves as a conduit to other threatening dimensions, and thus as a catalyst to the destruction of the vulnerable TV viewer and homeplace. The protagonist
is a father who is employed as the real estate salesman of a housing
development where he also lives. The development is built by his boss
over an old American Indian and cultist burial ground, whose unsettled
forces return to haunt the family and destroy the housing project, and
thus avenge the developer's disregard for ethnic values and sacrosanct
space. The intensive, physical poltergeist intrusion into the salesman's
home appears to rush up through the fuzzy electronic TV screen in
ghostlike streams of light, which for a while holds the family's young-
est daughter hostage. The film's closing scene shows the father shoving
a TV set from the motel room where his family has been forced to seek
refuge. The dimensions of TV's effects on audiences, it is suggested,
far outdistance the mere content of its everyday programs. Televirtual
space—directly associated here with exploitative capitalism and the
forces of nature it denies and represses—becomes a domain of horror.
This domain has already begun to feed on the innermost workings of
consciousness.

Compared to films of the 1980s and their frequent evocation of psychic terrors in relation to teletransportation, films about TV in the
1990s are generally more realistically direct in their representations of
television's encroachment on everyday life, and in a way that is closer
to the open-ended and fluid powers of cyberculture. Robert Redford's
Quiz Show (1994) is important for its narrative shift from a focus on TV's
individual performer (still apparent in the rise-and-fall story in *To Die
For* [1995]), to a concern with a Justice Department investigator's probe
of an actual game show scandal that momentarily rocked the entire TV
industry in the 1950s. In the tradition of *Network, Quiz Show* explicitly
pinpoints for the movie audience subtle associations between sponsors
and network brass and their programming decisions, as well as television's rapidly expanding role in the performance of American politics
and government. The text first unravels the way in which TV sponsors
can insinuate themselves into the very content of programmatic production. But the Senate hearings that reviewed the scandal, as the film
makes clear, failed to blame either the NBC network responsible for the
phony quiz show called *Twenty-One* or the directives given by the spon-
soring authority Geritol, whose sales had skyrocketed from the show's
success. The collusion between the corporate network and its sponsor-

ing agent Geritol is so complete that NBC finally excuses itself in the congressional hearing with a significant policy statement that is a gem of public relations. It claimed that its business is not the production of truth, as in a court of law, but mainly entertainment. In the words of the Geritol sponsor (Martin Scorsese), "We give the public what it wants," which is not intellectual ability but the cash earnings: "They just wanted to watch the money." Less and less value, in other words, is attached by network TV or its sponsors to the credibility of information or intellectual skill presented. They are mainly concerned that the show's packaging continue to hold American audiences' fascination with spectacle and with special shortcuts to wealth and fame.

What Geritol does not say, but which is also revealed by history and the film, is the way the actual *Twenty-One* show contributed to American stereotyping of race, class, and religious preference through its "casting" of the contestants, and the length of time they are permitted to remain on the program. It is Herb Stempel (John Turturro) who initiates the first suspicion about the show in his protests about being beaten out as a contestant. The contestants are immediately made pawns of the network and sponsor, who are sworn to secrecy regarding their public deception. It is a credit to the text that rather than ending on romantic escapism, it concludes instead on the central issue of the role of network TV in the greater public trust. Can a system built on commercial sponsorship and dedicated only to audience approval be credible in game show programming or as a source of information? The so-called "dumbing-down" of American culture appears to result directly from this closed circularity of commercialism.

Through the *Twenty-One* show scandal that erupts over Van Doren (Ralph Fiennes), and indirectly his esteemed literary family, the film also recognizes the historical displacement of America's literary culture by a TV culture, including the loss of cultural depth and insight which that displacement has for the most part signified. This transformation is sharply evident at the Van Doren family birthday dinner for Charles's father, where a round of Shakespeare-quoting tête-à-tête is punctuated over dessert when the father is given a console TV on which he is now expected to watch his son's "intellectual" performance. The issue is not high culture versus popular culture, but refined truth versus public misrepresentation. The investigating Justice Department prosecutor Dick Goodwin (Rob Morrow) continues to observe and question Charles closely about the show despite their growing friendship, just as he questions other past contestants about receiving contest questions and an-

5.1   *Quiz Show* (1994).
Charles Van Doren (Ralph Fiennes) and the more ethnic-looking Herb Stempel (John
Turturro) appear as contestants on the rigged *Twenty-One* game show. Herb already
knows from the NBC network producers that he must fail to answer a question,
leaving the popular Van Doren to continue as the show's winning contestant.

swers in advance. His questions to the show's producer, Dan Enright,
result only in accusations against Stempel. Success for Mr. Goodwin
requires an effort much like that of the lone whistle-blower, who is also
typically up against the powers of big corporate and/or political resources. Goodwin's government position will be on the line should he
fail in this heavily politicized arena of prime-time American cultural
reality. While Goodwin is a fictional composite character not true to
the historical scandal, he does personify the Justice Department's partial success in exposing one network's hoax on the public. The film
successfully conveys the relevance of this historical event to American television's actual cultural role within a commercial entertainment
mind-set. The concluding and most poignant scene shows Dick Goodwin leaving the Justice buildings in Washington, D.C., alone, knowing
that the hearing has failed to damage the public influence of commercial TV and its version of reality, which seems impossible to pin down
in its sheer ubiquity.[15]

These films emphasize television's dominant advertising and promotional functions, and how they have created a circular reification of

informational, entertainment, and commodity images that constantly engage the public in the rhythms and values of the marketplace. Raymond Williams has described television as a "flow" of varying types and segments of images that constantly blur the lines between its programs and its sponsorship. The commercial industry that is television has had the further effect of expanding its viewers' audio-visual outreach while simultaneously altering the recorded event into TV space and time, further distancing the original recorded image from its referents.[16] As early as 1964, Herbert Marcuse observed how "mass communications blend together . . . art, politics, religion and philosophy with commercials," and hence "bring these realms of culture to their common denominator—the commodity form."[17] In this way, American television and its heavy viewership have provided a prime example of what Guy Debord means about mediation when he writes of "an immense accumulation of spectacles," where "everything that was directly lived has moved away into a representation."[18] From the cradle to the grave, Jean Baudrillard has further noted, individual psychology and social experience have been increasingly dominated by a culture of televisual "simulation," of Disneyesque "hyperreality" that is beyond mere representation, and which is driven in the United States almost exclusively by promotional consumerism. In this world of fetishized products and information, images take over, losing their referential base in a flurry of cross-referenced, recombinant signs or simulacra.[19]

More attuned to the feel of 1990s extremes than the historically oriented *Quiz Show* is Kathryn Bigelow's *Strange Days* (1995), which updates the TV as cult focus theme of the 1980s by evoking the millennium. It concerns an underground dealer (Ralph Fiennes again) in multisensory disk recordings, an entrepreneur in mostly sexual experiences with a marketplace that increasingly demands perversity and violence. The disks are part of a system called "Playback," which re-creates a full sensory experience at the time of recording. By fully simulating the emotional experience of another time and place and (usually) person, Playback takes the subject out of present consciousness and permits the complete sharing of another's sensory world, expanding the individual's awareness even as it threatens core identity by stretching the borders of the self to the breaking point. Like the virtual reality trips in the futuristic *Total Recall* (1990) and *Lawnmower Man* (1992), or the supposition of an everyday reality that is actually a matrix controlled by artificial intelligence in *The Matrix* (1999), the question of ever returning to a recognizable personal reality base becomes increasingly terrifying. The recent comedy *Nurse Betty* (2001) also stretches to the brink of disaster the protagonist's inability to distinguish her sitcom medical hero's television career from his real life. In *Strange Days,* the virtuality disk hustler's unintended associations with perpetrators of real crimes such as rape and murder also leads him into drug, racial, and political wars in the big city. His haphazard and opportunistic career identity (which also involves his own pleasure in the use of Playback) becomes thoroughly overwhelmed by these larger forces that rule his landscape. The full exploitational potential of electronic simulation via Playback is also specified, including the tendency toward sensory addiction and the brain-deadening dangers of signal overdose. Bigelow's film, much like the Wachowski brothers' *The Matrix,* warns that the recent directions of the technological revolution have a serious downside potential in the furthering of individual and social dependency, resulting in self-centered indulgence and social myopia on a massive scale. Television's performative encouragement of audience passivity coupled with self-indulgent consumerism, as these films suggest, has been imbibed to the point that it is the dominant internal as well as external experience of contemporary life. In the futuristic matrix of that film's title, even the possibility of escape only exists any longer in an electronic, coded form.

Televirtuality not only impacts the "reading," recording, reporting, and transfer of all data that reaches public recognition, but it also lends special weight to the roles of those involved directly in its production. This is the subject of the important cycle of five films of the late 1990s that address the realm of television. Each text focuses on different areas of this medium's production and reception, which is saturated in promotional concerns. Barry Levinson's *Wag the Dog* (1997) and Michael Mann's *The Insider* (1999) deserve the most extended discussion on the issue of television production, although Ron Howard's *Ed TV* is also worthy of brief mention at the outset. *Ed TV* is close to *The Truman Show* in its emphasis on a hypothetical situation of TV production which radically invades personal career circumstances as well as family life. The intent of the television producer characters in both films is obvious in the loop each production system forms with its audience, where almost no strategy appears too outrageous or unethical to keep the shows on air. In Howard's comedy of a reality TV show involving 24-hour live documentary coverage of Ed and his family, Ed is clearly more the object than the subject of the show's existence. He loses his privacy and

5.2   *Ed TV* (1999).
Ed Pekurny (Matthew McConaughey) discovers that Shari (Jenna Elfman) is unwilling
to pursue a relationship under the pressure of live TV camera surveillance. Now a
celebrity, Ed attracts new women but finds no solace in his loss of privacy and
self-determination.

experiences the disruption of his family and his romance, almost losing
control of his life altogether.

Ed Pekurny (Matthew McConaughey) is suddenly recruited for the
new cable-TV show because he is such an innocent joe-six-pack kind of
guy. Despite his big contract and his exploding celebrity status, certain
truths are forced on him and his broken family history that probably
would not have been otherwise revealed. Ed soon tires of the constant
presence of production crews and public audiences, and of his self-
alienating position as star of a show whose image he cannot control
or ever fully escape. He cannot direct his employment in the media
world but is rather directed by it. Ed's agreement to be employed as
the real-world subject of the show is a choice that he finds himself con-
tractually bound to. It is only through his on-camera status that he is
able to insult his producer and finally win his release. But the thematic
sense of a choice in the film between Ed's being the celebrity object of
TV cameras or merely another potential addicted viewer of TV seems
mainly a matter of degree. The diegetic TV audiences for Ed's show
are completely drawn into and become dependent on it, altering their

schedules en masse to catch the show at moments of high melodrama. The film suggests that like TV's colonization of Ed's psychic and physical space, so does the unsuspecting TV viewer in the real world (although far less dramatically) become a psychic participant in this seductive, cinema verité soap opera, which encourages substitutional fulfillment. In the final analysis, however, the comedy *Ed TV* seems to exploit its actual movie audience with tabloid spectacle in the same way that Ed's cable-TV station producers are blamed in the narrative for exploiting him. This problematic stance of the film goes along with its hackneyed lesson that big salaries and stardom may not be all they are cracked up to be.

Pleasantville and *The Truman Show* move from a concern with TV's image makers and producers to emphasize the condition of individuals enclosed in televirtuality at an early age. In both cases the main characters' lives are captured for an extended time within television's programming sphere. Because *The Truman Show* provides such a complete allegory of televirtual experience, however, I will give it the full discussion it deserves in the close of this chapter. *Pleasantville,* on the other hand, is a more tame satire in the way it turns televirtual experience inside-out by transporting its contemporary teenage protagonists into a nostalgic microcosm of a 1950s family TV series. It becomes both a coming-of-age story and a reflection on the modern social history of the nation through a self-consciously corny kind of magic reminiscent of the Pottersville fantasy section in *It's a Wonderful Life,* only more upbeat and less threatening. The role of the reality-altering angel in Frank Capra's film is taken by a comic wizard of a TV repairman (Don Knotts) in the latter film, written and directed by Gary Ross. In the aesthetically formalized TV-as-time-machine fable of *Pleasantville,* the young, clean-cut protagonists (Tobey Maguire and Reese Witherspoon) enjoy the advantages of a 1990s consciousness in a narrow little fictional town, where they are permitted a personally therapeutic form of wish-fulfillment. The plot traces Pleasantville's fall from black-and-white fictional innocence to colorful live experience, from frozen time and enclosed space to a contemporary openness of rich emotion, eroticism, and movement. Thematically, it also suggests the importance of defying generational, peer, and media pressure with emotional integrity and activism. Living in the 1950s TV program world finally reverses the siblings' previous contemporary identities as TV nerd and pretty girl. The girl becomes studious and wants to stay in the 1950s where she can go to college, and her brother returns to the 1990s where he now

5.3   *Pleasantville* (1998).
Two siblings from the 1990s (Reese Witherspoon and Tobey Maguire) suddenly
become reformers inside a 1950s family TV show called "Pleasantville." They cause so
much change within that programmed world that they are themselves transformed by
the experience.

rejects the escapist seduction of television and begins to take responsibility with his real mother and this community. It is his leadership
experience in the virtual but physically real Pleasantville that makes
possible his undertaking of responsibility and direction in the present.

Pleasantville offers a lesson in the history of community close-minded-
ness, and in the possibilities of growth when consciousness is thrown
open and one is able to break free from TV's surface-image culture to
a real life that might exist whenever direct physical and emotional engagement takes place. The irony that this engagement occurs in a TV
fantasy world, one that is badly in need of a radical injection of physical awareness and 1990s consciousness raising, also allows the film to
create a metaphoric national history. The film suggests the process of
changes since the 1950s in the nation's attitudes toward race, gender,
and artistic expression. It also tries to bridge the contradiction that we
can all learn through the fantasy process of media entertainment, but
that only escape and learning outside the box of a desensitizing contemporary televirtuality can provide the nurturant context for significant
leaps in consciousness and self-revelation.

All five of these recent TV reality films advance a sense of the absorption of career goals and identity within a media space that has already predetermined it, a centering of reality in a world dominated by corporate media culture. This televirtuality so contains and alters space and time in each film that even scenes of a possible existence beyond commercial mediation remain wishful fantasies. The next two sections of this chapter are devoted to a closer reading of *Wag the Dog, The Insider,* and *The Truman Show.* All three foreground televirtuality in relation to career objectives and personal life.

THE DRIVE TO VIRTUALITY IN PRODUCTION AND CONSUMPTION

TV is to news what bumper stickers are to philosophy.

—RICHARD M. NIXON

In a tortious interference lawsuit, the greater the truth, the greater the damage claim.

—A CBS LAWYER TO THE PRODUCER (AL PACINO) OF
60 Minutes IN *The Insider*

Wag the Dog (1997) features those engaged in the behind-the-scenes process of political spin, while *The Insider* (1999) features those engaged in publicly identifying and challenging the devastation of hazardous commercial products for consumers. In both narratives, television is the battleground where image producers and consumers either fall in line or go to war. The extended discussions that follow will first address Barry Levinson's hypothetical political film, and then Michael Mann's recent rendition of actual events surrounding acts of corruption by corporate Big Tobacco at the close of the twentieth century.

The plot and literary background of *Wag the Dog* may be briefly summarized. Just before an unnamed Democratic president's "firefly girl" sexual incident in the White House hits the news, Conrad Brean (Robert De Niro) is brought in for political damage control, who in turn hires an egotistic Hollywood producer, Stanley Motss (Dustin Hoffman). Working together to deflect public attention from the president's problem, they invent news of an American response to terrorist aggression and thus manage a convincing war story that dances barely one step ahead of credibility. "Politics is show business," Brean explains, and "War is show business. It doesn't have to prove out, it just has to distract them."

Fomenting international war to shore up one's national leadership status is the key idea adapted from the 1993 novel by Larry Beinhart, *American Hero,* upon which the film is very loosely based. The unusual editorial postscript to Beinhart's novel references articles and books on the Gulf War that consistently refer to it as the first true Videowar, "a tale manufactured for television from beginning to end."[20] Just how "manufactured" it might have been is indirectly suggested by Conrad Brean's comment in Levinson's film. He declares that the famous Gulf War image of the smart bomb going down an industrial chimney in Baghdad was a video fake. When his associate Motss asks if this is true, Brean responds, "How the fuck do we know?" Unlike the novel, the film's emphasis is no longer on an actual war (programmed for TV) to get a Republican president reelected, but on a virtual one to reelect a Democrat. Scripted by David Mamet and Hilary Henkin, Levinson's film significantly updates the novel and alters the story to the point that it rightfully carries its own title.

Using White House news releases sometimes backed by studio-produced footage, Brean and Motss build a brazen media claim of Albanian aggression and American troop involvement where none exists. When their stipulated hostilities are denied on TV news by Albania and the CIA, Brean feels beaten at his own game. But Motss says, "This is my picture, not the CIA's picture. . . . We are only at the end of Act I." In Act II of Motss's movielike creation of dramatic events, they will switch their attention to their TV war's presumed aftereffects and focus on the return of an American soldier left behind the lines in Albania.[21] An even larger publicity campaign with all the pop culture trimmings is mounted to support this specious claim, including sympathetic out-pourings for the "combat hero" through the production of fads, military parades, patriotic pop music, and merchandising tie-ins. Observing all of the expenditures and political spin in motion, the president's assistant (Anne Hecht) is finally moved to exclaim, "Television has destroyed the electoral process!"

Her comment reflects a growing popular awareness of the evaporating boundary between news journalism and sheer show business in the political domain. Media analysts have been saying for some time that where politicians once surrounded themselves with a reality-based "brain trust" of economists, intellectuals and engineers, they now have

5.4   *Wag the Dog* (1997).
Political spinmeister Conrad Brean (Robert De Niro) has the president's assistant
(Anne Heche) request particular words from the agent giving a live TV press
conference at the White House. Movie producer Stanley Motss (Dustin Hoffman)
watches it all, intrigued at the possibilities. Photo from Photofest.

an "inner circle made up of pollsters and image consultants. . . . Every-thing is broken down into market segments. You have no political pro-cess. As prime-time political promotionalism takes over . . . democracy is reduced to cynical spectatorship." [22] This is also what Neil Postman had in mind when he observed that in the United States "the fundamen-tal metaphor for political discourse is the television commercial." [23] The entire system of sponsored television has thus grown to dominate gov-ernment, since political leaders are chained to the need to project their image and party programs through costly TV airtime.[24] Televirtuality has forced politics into a particularly money-mad form of showmanship, displacing indigenous political activity with a grand media landscape that has become as potent as it is expensive. Hence, the covert spin doctors in *Wag the Dog* are paid to capture and hold their public's atten-tion with elaborate scenarios they coyly refer to as "pageants," which imitate movies and the fictional programming on TV. Every category of television's constant lumping together of news "reality," entertainment fantasy, and advertising are put to use by the promoters here to en-hance the loose, malleable, and constantly cross-referenced image flow that makes up television's particular reality sense. What distinguishes Levinson's film from other more dated examples of political campaign narratives such as the less successful Sidney Lumet film *Power* (1986)[25] is its assumption about promotion as a reality-making tool as well as a device for political propaganda. The new technology of television pro-duction offers the tempting gimmicks of seamless original creations indistinguishable from video recordings of real events.

Levinson's film succeeds in part because it is an exaggerated but consistent dramatization of the way political "image consultants" can wag the body of the entire nation-state. They no longer merely lead an electoral campaign; they begin to lead public policy by creating mock events in the name of the incumbent president. Levinson's narrative strategy is not invested in which of his characters gets elected or which myth is invoked by his media brokers; rather, it is intended to illu-minate the attitude and technical arsenal of the new breed of political image brokers. His pacing of the film, for example, is set to match TV's rendition of the rapidly changing political world, which his protago-nists are trying hard to control and direct. In his demonstration of the flagrant fabrication of spin, Levinson accents his story throughout with a comedic, self-reflexive style that provides the critical distance char-acteristic of satire. To maintain his perspective, he offers images that often include foreground-background visual inconsistency, cinematic mirroring devices such as reflective glass, and unusual camera angles and constant movement, all of which contribute to a dialectical and ironic depth of mise-en-scène. After a plane accident suddenly stops the helter-skelter spin group's leapfrogging around the country, Levinson frames them all packed tightly into a harvester machine, and rumbling tediously across a midwestern cornfield. The director also pokes almost as much fun at the Pavlovian public in his film as he does at those political manipulators who are hired to make it salivate. To show the public's gullibility for fads and their propagandistic function, Levinson has his media specialists successfully staging "spontaneous" and officially sanctioned events for public broadcast. The film's joke on the public's largely passive complicity with TV reality is made yet sharper by the lives that are lost in the spin process. Death is either explained away in so many sound bites, overturned in its importance by more pressing breaking news, or transformed into grandiose and carefully scripted public media rituals.

Public complicity is further elaborated in the blue-screen studio production scene, where Motss works with film compositors (and a young actress dressed as a peasant) to make digitally originated images appear to be location news footage. Here, Levinson not only calls attention to the constructed nature of both, but to the way explicitly political and demagogic purposes can be realized through the new technology. What distinguishes this contemporary political propaganda from older versions of more doctrinaire appeal is the precision of its apparent representational viability. Levinson's point is not that the president's victory is based on one particular phony war strategy, but rather that the entire process of mimetic representation in media is now suspect as a source. This is highlighted by the fact that the individual person of the president—he is never named or shown in frontal view—is downplayed in favor of a consistent focus on the spinmeisters' winning covert methods.[26] The president's visual identity is secondary to his directives given behind the scenes. And so focused is his political image team of two unmarried men and a single woman that this Hollywood script, much like All the President's Men before it, does not allow them even the possibility of romance, a physical-emotional immediacy that runs counter to their mentally reactive image cognition. The disorientation of image warriorism infects their personal space with the obsessional need constantly to tweak reality rather than to live within it. They play a form of image combat that has less and less to do even with political party propaganda as it takes on the unreal ambiance of a video game. The job of spin merchants is central in the land of televirtuality, where they create the best political version of reality money can buy.

Television sets and their images appear in almost every scene of *Wag the Dog* either to provide a running commentary on new developments or to spark character reactions. In content, these TV images include news commentators and their clips, White House press conferences, statements by the president's political opponent, and talk show rejoinders. All of the staged and unstaged "newsworthy" events shown on TV screens or heard over the sound track are woven seamlessly into the live-action plot so as to suggest television's central role as arbiter of reality. TV news is like the burning bush of the Old Testament that transports the message of divine authority. At one point following the crash of the small plane that left the White House spin crew unscathed but shaken, their Republican opponent's voice speaks up from a small portable TV lying in the smoldering wreckage. He reminds them of the political race they are on the verge of losing. Their media hoax of a foreign war must constantly be updated for new drama to make their television voice the loudest perpetual alarm for directing public opinion. They successfully build public consensus in the film with whatever they assign significance to, and woe to those insiders who do not abide by its rule.[27]

Most appropriately, *Wag the Dog*'s closing section is set up by a television gab show called "Talking Politics." Stanley Motss, just after he has raised a glass with Conrad Brean to toast their accomplishments, becomes engrossed in watching the TV gabfest. He is outraged by the television pundits' conclusions, which attribute the president's successful reelection entirely to a bland public ad campaign, the weakness of which they have surreptitiously been hired to overcome. Because he has failed to win an Academy Award for movie producing, Motss suddenly wants to bare the device of their spin, to get public recognition for *his* role in the president's victory. He would violate the main rule of anonymity applicable to all who work the control boards of political media service. Brean cannot dissuade him, and Motss marches off indignantly to begin his long trip home to the West Coast, with security men notably in tow. The film closes first on a shot of the funeral of Sergeant Schumann, and then on the exterior of Motss's California residence just as his death — which is attributed to heart failure! — is announced by a TV commentator's voice.[28] When a hearse arrives in front of the Motss mansion, a voiced-over TV news update suddenly alerts the nation to another uprising in Albania, which will necessitate further military activity. Once again, the covert operations of spin (now already the cause of two deaths), kick in with a flood of new, endlessly pressing events. Under these circumstances, the TV news broadcasts begin to look increasingly like hypnosis, relentlessly filling every waking moment with new claims for its distracted audience.

But more than that, the production of political spin in *Wag the Dog* appears tantamount to the production of the world of television generally. Douglas Kellner observes how media culture has come to "play key roles in the structuring of contemporary identity and [the] shaping [of] thought and behavior. . . . [T]elevision today assumes some of the functions traditionally ascribed to myth and ritual."[29] This public ritual function has been particularly prominent in the recent American legal fiascoes of the O. J. Simpson trial, the Clinton impeachment juggernaut, and the Elian Gonzales parental/national custody battle involving Cuba and the United States. All three incidents reveal TV's grandstanding power, which feeds off the racial, political, and/or nationalistic fears that haunt the country. Just as in *Wag the Dog,* television orients public experience into breaking "news" stories, and increasingly to the kind of spectacles that can lend themselves to extended disclosures that thrive best on scandal, partisan controversy, and acts of violence and war. Don Hewitt, the executive producer of *60 Minutes,* called the O. J. Simpson trial "TV's longest running entertainment special." Television's feeding frenzy atmosphere reached new heights when House Republicans almost succeeded in turning the Clinton-Lewinski sexual escapade into a constitutional crisis. Whether prompted by crime, scandals, partisan initiatives, or acts of war in Kosovo/Serbia/Albania, these actual long-running TV spectacles are so close to the ones in Levinson's film as to confuse the television news "reality" with the fictional world of the film. The film's domain of TV politics and news spin mocks Americans' increased reliance on sponsored television's worldview, including its inscription of effect.

As Levinson's film title suggests, television and its new extensions in computer convergent technologies are in the middle of the information superhighway and its rapidly growing material and data exchange, which has created a new world political economy. Carnoy and his fellow authors observe how this economy is "based less on the location of natural resources, cheap and abundant labour, or even capital stock, and more on the capacity to create new knowledge and to apply it rapidly, via information processing and telecommunications, to a wide range of human activities in ever broadening space and time."[30] And while there is certainly truth to this tendency toward the valuation of information over material resources, high-speed information exchange does not eliminate political economic realities; it merely changes their tenor and effect. Levinson's film foregrounds the strategies of covert image makers and demonstrates the extent to which certain tailored news images can be elevated to a life of their own at the level of cultural ritual. This entertainment news not only sells airtime but guides public opinion. Brean is clearly less interested in the commodification of "news" than in its specific shaping of political effect. The economic shift predicated on televirtuality's rapid image exchange appropriates workers and their products, data, and money on a global basis, constantly both isolating workers and throwing them together in configurations attuned to regional media sales sectors and subgroup identifications.

Because this satire warns literally of the ease with which reality can be invented or slanted by vested interests operating through both staged news and ad sponsorship, it also suggests how certain political economic voices do prevail. TV media analysts such as Dean Alger have demonstrated how the global marketplace and its consolidating and monopolizing hierarchy of conglomerates are increasingly invested in media ownership and control. This global consolidation of the media—whether it is CNN's "news" under Time-Warner and AOL, Fox system's showmanship under Rupert Murdoch's News Corporation, or MTV's exploitation of youth culture under Viacom—tends to absorb the cultural into the economic and political sphere, creating all the tendencies of inequality, homogenization, and marginalization in media that was once characteristic of colonialist military rule. Alger warns that the primary threat both to a free, open society is no longer the government, but the few monopolistic conglomerates that make up what he calls megamedia. "There are megamedia empires with stupendous size and resources, national and international spread, and control across types of mass media. . . . [I]t is in those media empires where the greatest danger to freedom of the press and democracy and . . . creative expression is to be found as we move into the new millennium." [31] It is not that a single conglomerate or even a small corporate group's particular viewpoint necessarily would hold global sway, but that the system of information and cultural production by virtue of its very forms would have enormous influence.

The personal consequence of Brean's job requires that he have no public existence outside of his secret function. Political spin doctors are infinitely expendable if they seek to have a life beyond their work, just as many in corporate organizational structures may find themselves either unable to fit demanding work schedules expected for promotion and success or rapidly outdated by the high speeds on the information superhighway. The economics and politics of sign culture place a certain extra burden on the individual to be media fluent in ways that usually lead away from personal and interpersonal rootedness. American politics today and its astronomical expenses — which have reached the $3 billion level in the national elections of 2000, already 50 percent more than in 1996 — are tied up in the media wars of televirtuality, which are themselves aligned with transnational conglomerate media empires and their service to the highest-paying commercial interests. *Wag the Dog* emphasizes this political news dimension of the televirtual world and the way it drives and is reflected back through the public's perceptions of reality. But it also reminds the viewer in a satiric way of what happens to those who dare to differ with the huge commercial and political interests that determine the current, greatly accelerated electronic reality.

This is also the primary subject of Michael Mann's *The Insider* (1999). As opposed to the hypothetical imagings of the televirtual world in *Wag the Dog,* Mann's film is a reality-oriented account of the actual experience of a recent whistle-blower, Jeffrey Wigand (Russell Crowe), who lives a kind of nightmare from the moment he decides to challenge internally the behavior of his employer, Brown & Williamson (B&W) Tobacco. Wigand's actual struggle, as represented in this film, is a testimonial to political economic workings of the televirtual reality. In content, Wigand's story demonstrates how even a company vice president with hard evidence will have extreme difficulty challenging massive corporate interests such as Big Tobacco in the public arena. While Mann's film resorts to a variety of formal devices, including visual effects such as slow motion and news video inserts, it also takes a few liberties with the character and story. But this is common in dramatic adaptations of true stories and does not alter this basic case history and its national significance. The brazen disregard of truth by Big Tobacco and its misrepresentation of the dangers of its products' contents are particularly grievous given the scientifically established correlation between tobacco usage and a variety of health hazards, including deadly cancers and heart disease. This makes Wigand an easy sell as public hero in principle, although as dramatic art Mann's film relies on a personal focus on Wigand and on the CBS *60 Minutes* producer Lowell Bergman (Al

5.5   *The Insider* (1999).
Lowell Bergman (Al Pacino), the CBS producer for *60 Minutes,* helps convince former tobacco industry insider, Dr. Jeffrey Wigand (Russell Crowe), to go on the air with the truth about the practices of tobacco companies. Meanwhile, Wigand considers the personal cost to himself and to his family.

Pacino). Bergman fights a corporate media insider battle of his own to get Wigand before his show's cameras and finally on the air nationally with his story.

The complex maneuverings of Big Tobacco to squelch Wigand at every turn begin when he is fired in 1993 from his job as vice president of research and development at B&W because he questions the use of a dangerous carcinogen (coumarin) in its Sir Walter Raleigh pipe product. At his firing he is also forced to sign a confidentiality agreement related to his B&W employ and severance package. Six months later B&W tries to sue Wigand for breach of contract, and under threats of losing medical benefits for his sick daughter, he is forced to sign a yet more strict confidentiality agreement. By 1994, Lowell Bergman anonymously received Philip Morris tobacco documents, which he asked Wigand to analyze. In April of that year, top executives from the seven largest tobacco companies in the United States, including B&W CEO Thomas Sandefur, testified before Congress that nicotine was not addictive. The actual video footage of this denial in the hearing is shown several times in the narrative to great effect.

Mann's film is stretched by the myriad unfolding details of the actual case, although it simplifies and compresses them to a considerable degree. Bergman does manage to get Wigand before the cameras for his interview with Mike Wallace (Christopher Plummer), but this is just before CBS goes on the block and "merges" with conglomerate Westinghouse (which owns a tobacco company of its own). CBS lawyers, mainly because sensitive to the merger as presented in the film, have Bergman's story killed due to a "tortious interference" lawsuit involving Wigand's aforementioned confidentiality agreements. Bergman momentarily gets around the problem of broadcasting the Wigand tape by having it reported on *60 Minutes* that they are *not* being allowed to show it. More importantly, although it moves the film away from Bergman for a while, there is an elaborate re-creation of the Mississippi lawsuit against the tobacco industry, which deposes Wigand and permits him an official hearing in which he testifies that B&W CEO Sandefur lied to Congress while under oath, and further conducted a large cover-up of research documents regarding the dangers of tobacco. At this point B&W hires a PR agent to throw dirt on Wigand and subpoenas him for violating his confidentiality agreements. The film shows Bergman effectively fighting B&W's smear campaign against Wigand through direct contacts with newspaper editors and reporters. Wigand's trauma is further elaborated in a scene where his wife receives an e-mail death threat followed by Wigand finding a bullet in his mailbox.

The film would have us believe that the turning point comes for Bergman and *60 Minutes* when the *Wall Street Journal* refutes the smear campaign B&W has conducted against Wigand, although it is the *Journal*'s publication of Wigand's leaked testimony from the Mississippi deposition that apparently cleared the way for CBS to feel sufficiently comfortable to air the Wigand interview. The film's reference to the *Wall Street Journal*'s February report on the personal allegations against Wigand, which are called mostly "unsubstantiated," does not mention that the article also adds that the allegations are a "chilling insight into how much a company can find out about a former employee and the lengths it may go to discredit a critic." From the standpoint of personal career ethics, it is this statement that most closely reflects the film's theme involving the personal sacrifice that Wigand is forced to make as a result of his decision to challenge his corporate employer. Yet more significant for my emphasis here, producer Lowell Bergman tells Mike Wallace that he feels compelled to quit CBS because he no longer believes he can in good conscience count on the network for a lack of bias in the selection of segments to appear on *60 Minutes.* Corporate CBS, à la conglomerate Westinghouse, cannot be trusted to support investigative journalism. At one point Bergman laments the drift toward TV infotainment and screams at his supervisor, "Are you a businessman or are you a newsman?" The film's ultimate theme is the difficulty of making corporate media responsive to serious and valid corporate criticism in a capitalist milieu ruled by constant conglomerate expansion and merging. Like the individual careerist who chooses to overlook company ethical problems to rise in rank and authority, corporate CBS wanted to avoid the controversy of the tobacco issue (even on its investigative journalism show) to insure *its* success in merger expansion. Again, profit concerns and political power brokerage become determinative of the public image systems, which only the most dedicated and brave seem capable of forcing to the public's attention and benefit.

RECEPTION AND SIMULATIONAL IDENTITY IN CYBERSPACE

Space is political and ideological. It is a product literally filled with ideologies.

—HENRI LEFEBVRE[32]

In contrast to *Wag the Dog* and *The Insider, The Truman Show* represents a shift in narrative focus from the staging of television news events to the construction and personal experience of a "live" entertainment program. It demonstrates in a literal way how the regime of televirtuality has overtaken individual life with one of artifice. The world of Truman Burbank (Jim Carrey) provides a grand metaphor of contemporary existence under the hegemony of a corporate media and consumer reality. For a while, Truman believes (like the average consumer) that he controls his world through his everyday decisions. But he slowly comes to see that his domain is circumscribed, and that it plays to him even as it arranges his world of options. The intentions of the actors closest to Truman are to keep his life choices within the parameters of acceptability set by the TV show's producer/director Christof (Ed Harris).[33] This makes it easier for the Show to surround him with all manner of commodities and promotions. The Omnicam Corporation, which produces this highly successful worldwide satellite broadcast, not only demands a certain level of everyday predictability in Truman's bourgeois lifestyle, but projects this same conservative message to its live TV audiences.

The constant bombardment of precautionary warnings that have

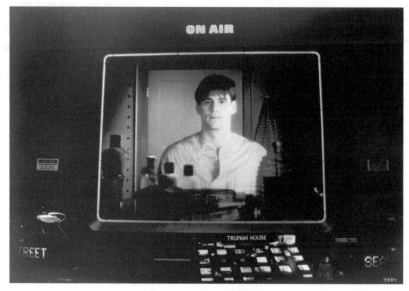

5.6   *The Truman Show* (1998).
Truman Burbank (Jim Carrey) is already alerted to the presence of probing camera eyes behind his bathroom mirror. He appears here on the huge studio monitor of the TV show's control room 221 floors above the staged community of Seahaven.

been scripted and directed at Truman throughout his youth, and now in his maturity at work and at home, are meant to distract him from doubt by undermining his self-confidence and will to resist. His insurance sales job in particular is a constant reminder of the need to avoid risk and to seek security. On one occasion when Truman appears to the Show's producer to be getting too bold and curious, he is given a job assignment that requires him to ride a ferry across open water. Due to a previous boating "accident" that "killed" his "father," however, he is unable to bring himself to board the ferry. Truman's TV show existence, then, is ultimately based on fear and intimidation. His will to independent thought and action threatens his televirtual overseers, who have heavily invested in the perpetuation of this high-security consumer utopia. The Truman Show's model village of Seahaven—a nostalgic, restricted, and fake community, where everything is catalogued and available for purchase—leaves Truman, once he grows suspicious of his artificial condition, only one real choice. He can keep everyone he knows happy by continuing to try to please them, or try to find a way out! Truman's final rejection of the charade that confines him raises the hopes of those in his TV audience who do not approve of Omnicam's secretive life programming, but it disappoints many other viewers who are avid fans and want to hold on to the Show's reassuring little world. Televirtual consumer logic, as it is served up 24 hours a day and 365 days a year on the corporate god-game called The Truman Show, is a great and comfortable kind of "reality" programming on which viewers can depend for entertainment.

TV critic Mark Crispin Miller has observed that the "inert, ironic watchfulness which TV reinforces in its audience is itself conducive to consumption. As we watch . . . we are already trying to live up, or down, to the same standard of acceptability that TV's ads and shows define collectively: the standard that requires the desperate use of all those goods and services that TV proffers." [34] But consumer TV culture is not just about products and sales and commodity image status. "TV also advertises incidentally an ideal of emotional self-management, which dictates that we purge ourselves of all 'bad feelings' through continual confession and by affecting the same geniality evinced by most of TV's characters." [35] Truman's personality is a prime example of this ebullience. There is an ease and confidence in Truman's manner that belies his unknowing status as captive. It also lulls his TV audience into passive acceptance of his circumstance and of the Show's constant incidental product-placement, which permits it to broadcast without ad breaks. Truman's wife often communicates with him in the lingo of product ads. He is moved, at these particularly artificial moments, to remember a young woman he was drawn to while in school. The young Lauren/Sylvia (Natascha McElhone) tried to warn him of his status only to be wrenched suddenly from his arms and from his town by a man claiming to be her father. The Seahaven sphere of commerce and apparent choice thus robs Truman even of this most natural of human attractions. It is the former actress Sylvia who eventually becomes a real voice of protest against Omnicam's show. Sylvia leads a "Free Truman" movement from the outside and is even permitted to question Christof on Omnicam's sister show called "True Talk." But her viewpoint is squelched as much by "True Talk's" commentator as by Christof, who views the Truman Show as a series of "episodes."

Otherwise, Truman's relationships have all been carefully scripted, since the actors are constantly prompted by the show's director over hidden radio microphones. Truman's "mother" is the spokesperson who vouches for the constructed history of his early life, including the sad loss of his "dad" to the dangerous sea. His family, best friend, and career are all a part of the phony apparatus. But there are mistakes on the giant TV stage. When Truman notices strange inconsistencies in his world—such as the sudden appearance of his "deceased" father, or an actor's break room where an elevator should be—his wife, his male friend, and/or the Seahaven media quickly find rationales for such "appearances." One turning point for Truman is when he overhears the Show's internal radio circuitry giving constant updates of his whereabouts. From this juncture on, Truman mistrusts his "reality." When his "spouse" Meryl (Laura Linney) does not want to take a long car trip, much less go abroad to Fiji, where Truman thinks Sylvia might be, she pleads with him to postpone a big vacation. She wants them to stick with their jobs (she putatively works as a nurse) so that they can pay off the mortgage and car and have children. Meryl also punctuates her plea to Truman with an invitation to bed, reminding the film viewer of her earlier comments in an interview external to the show where she notes the importance of her role in a "noble" public life. Truman finally forces the issue of Meryl's perpetual conventionality to the point that the actress panics, causing Truman's "friend," who works appropriately as a food automat vendor (a regimented system for feeding the masses), to step in and rescue her. Subsequently, she demands that her TV "marriage" to Truman be ended. In response, the Show quickly introduces to Truman a new romantic possibility at work in the form of a pretty new insurance sales associate. Again, the workplace becomes the location for a direct, public form of intervention, whether to create fear, or in this case to create a seductive romance that will lead to children (Christof wants to orchestrate "television's first on-air conception") and thus Truman's further containment. But like his TV audience and certainly by now the film's, Truman is already alerted to such controlling scenarios concocted on his behalf.

The film spectator has been given privileged glimpses of The Truman Show's director as well as its TV audience from the beginning. The Show's fans are shown in several locations including a middle-class hangout called the Truman Bar. Late in the story, it is revealed that the Show is broadcast worldwide by Omnicam's Truman satellite, and that its studio rivals the Great Wall of China in scale. It is also learned that Truman was given up for adoption at birth and is now legally *owned* by the Omnicam Corporation, which has all along staged him as an unprecedented form of living documentary. Omnicam and its director are clearly responsible for the Show's creative manipulation of their human subject, whom the director treats as his own child/creation. The film viewer is left, therefore, to identify fully with Truman's final, desperate attempt to leave the island and locate his youthful love. Truman is led emotionally by his early image of her bravery, in contrast to the increasingly defensive behavior of those who surround him. He notices how his inquiries and probes only seem to raise the level of their dissimulation.

Overcoming the fear of water with which he has been programmed, Truman briefly eludes the many TV cameras hidden all over Seahaven and seizes a sailboat (named the Santa Maria no less) to challenge his destiny alone. The show's director, meanwhile, quickly locates his wayward TV star and nearly drowns Truman in a heavy storm to prevent his escape. Most of the Show's television audience now take exception to this abuse. And wary of alienating its TV viewers, Omnicam pressures its director to stop the storm. (The trope of drowning in and on televirtuality seems especially apt.) In the final sequence, Truman's boat pierces the painted horizon of the Omnicam studio sphere and Truman climbs a stairway (to "heaven") and locates a doorway out. The Show's director suddenly speaks directly to him for the first time in a disembodied, godly voice from above. The director explains how much Truman, as a happy model citizen, has meant to millions, making their sick world better. Truman is expected to feel some obligation to the life Omnicam has gone to such trouble to create for him. But Truman doesn't buy this. And the film viewer too is left to reject the Seahaven environment and its safe but all too familiar realm of vested interests.

Truman is not one who has simply acted out the status quo of the American consumer Dream. He is one who has been turned unknowingly into a proponent of it through his effort simply to live. The program's TV viewers are mostly willing supporters who complete the loop between the live show's production and product placement, and their reception and consumer response. Weir's film establishes Truman as a sympathetic victim of the entire process of consumer TV. Virtually everything Truman does within his landscape is "developed" narratively in such a way as to increase entertainment and profit value for Omnicam's Show, which gains dramatic punch from the expression of Truman's actual if broadly scripted desires and activities. Within Seahaven's contexts, "True-man" becomes the ideal performing object of TV commerce, who reflects a captive subject position suggestive of all of America's TV audiences. Truman has been not only a consumer of goods and an entertaining conduit for sales, but a happy representative of a secure, conservative lifestyle who is at the center of his media zoo. The staff and actors on the Show share with its fans a paternalistic collusion, a colonialist patronage, which nevertheless evokes some fan resistance to the confines of Truman's life and support for his growing self-awareness. His final effort to escape is thus intended to point figuratively at the viewer's own need for escape from interpolation by an ersatz world of commercial image construction.

Given the allegorical leaning of the narrative, it is obvious why the 30-year-old Truman's unknown guide/controller and show director should be named Christof. His TV re-creation of the story of Adam (Truman) in the Garden of Eden (Seahaven) places him in the role of God the father, who further offers Truman as a Christ-like therapy to a suffering mankind. Christof thus serves as a debased worldly deity who offers up a life of pleasantly entertaining media fare and sales rather than of spiritual liberation. Christof is formally introduced to the movie viewer early on as the beret-wearing spokesman for the Show, who operates Truman's gargantuan studio world from a master control room on the 221st floor. He directs the 5,000 camera options that follow Truman as he remains the unknowing object of mass public scrutiny, just as most of his TV viewers are turned into problematic voyeurs. They have become followers of the "life" of a thoroughly commodified man whose fate speaks, perhaps unconsciously, to the direction in which they too are headed. The conservative expectations for Truman's life trajectory further suggest that his commercial world of images cannot be politically neutral. Omnicam wants his experience to enshrine a new kind of secular trinity that merges personal identity with a mediated "lifestyle" consistent with conglomerate marketing agendas—something like a true man's life according to Omnicam Inc.

Certain cultural observers have tied the alienating effects of living with and within commercial television not only to its reified commodity spectacles but to the totality of its effect on human perspective:

In postmodern culture, it's not TV as a mirror of society, but just the reverse: It's society as a mirror of television. *And it's not TV as a reflex of the commodity-form, but the commodity-form in its most advanced and exhausted expression living finally . . . as a pure image system, as a spectral television image . . . TV is, in a very literal sense, the real world."* [36]

In Weir's film, the domain of televirtuality is represented not only by Truman's microcosmic Seahaven, but by the entire global communications system in which Omnicam participates with its satellite broadcasts. To say that commercial TV is central to televirtuality, moreover, reflects on the position held by postmodern theorists such as Baudrillard, who finds that the society of late capitalism no longer simply consumes products, but all of media's associated signs and signifying practices. Media consumer culture is the way of life under televirtuality. Speaking of Truman, Christof tells his TV audience that he finds it comforting that we should "accept the reality of the world with which we are presented." These are the words of the corporate technocrat of human engineering which The Truman Show viewers seem to follow in their televisual addiction, even when they oppose him and cheer Truman's decision to escape in the end. As Anthony Giddens says of televisual experience, even "self-actualization is packaged and distributed according to market criteria."[37]

Baudrillard's sweeping interpretation of contemporary media's all-absorbing presence, its simulational "hyperreality," has been variously questioned and modified by the work of British cultural studies, which has placed more emphasis on the active audience.[38] In general, attention has been given to the receiver/consumer's ability to appropriate, rearticulate, and even transcode the programs of mass media. Television's mixed effects on culturally diverse audiences have also been hailed as contributors to a cosmopolitan ideal of multiculturalism. The receiver is seen to have autonomy or subcultural concerns outside or counter to media's dominant messages. But even if all such claims for variously counterhegemonic positions were possible, the very real move in the national and global media industry toward increased consolidation, conglomeration, and monopolization still proves highly problematic. Many media culture critics, including George Gerbner and Dean Alger, have pointed to the way American media conglomerates have used mostly free public air space—currently being multiplied sixfold on the American broadcast spectrum by broadband digital signals—to dominate the cultural and political economic environment.[39] Gerbner and Alger also make the undeniable claim that fewer and fewer monopolistic conglomerates are making critical media decisions for more and more of the world's populations. Their directions in programming, while mitigated by consumer response, also already assume an immense level of presold public participation in the mostly one-way information and entertainment televisual experience. The few cultural observers who have insisted that commercial television can stimulate diversity and perhaps even resistance through certain expressions of popular culture must continue to account for some of the political economic realities in which an increasingly global televirtuality operates.[40]

The frenetic attraction of televirtual experience cannot be underesti-mated. The meretricious roles of those actors who serve on Omnicam's Truman Show, or those who leap to become incidental performers in *Ed TV*, do furthermore call to mind the active participation of nonactors on shows already currently popular on American television. Those indi-viduals who seek to appear and act out on *The Jerry Springer Show*, for ex-ample, amply demonstrate that no coercion by television is any longer necessary to prompt them to conform to its programming and mes-sages. Endless numbers seek to exhibit their innermost fears and desires on the air, and thus to become some part of the prevailing reality of TV. Far from wishing to escape sponsored mediation, as Truman finds he wants to do, these individuals appear determined to do absolutely anything—including maiming each other—for the privilege of being before the cameras. Contemporary personal experience has apparently become so bland and washed-out for some, so lacking in authenticity, that the television stage provides the only remaining setting for substan-tiating their significance. Nor is this impulse limited to those desperate to perform on *Jerry Springer*. Gus Van Sant's film *To Die For* is based on a true story featuring a wanna-be television newscaster (Nicole Kid-man) who has her husband killed because he gets in the way of her TV career. That television career presence is the only reality she recog-nizes as having significance. Her career success fixation is both learned from television and interiorized as her personal mission, a conversion of her personal space and psyche to a success image already saturated in televirtuality and its particular kind of truth. The seductive force of television can hardly be more blatantly expressed than in these real-world obsessions to be a performer in the ritualistic glow of this seem-ingly transformative mass medium. The availability of everyday people as performers in television marathons is also shown by the recent prolif-eration and popularity of reality TV shows including *Reality TV, Survivor, Big Brother* (which was developed first in Belgium), *Survivor II,* and a con-tinuing host of others. Producers have found a variety of ways to make artificial and enclosed social circumstances interesting to large tele-vision audiences, who in some cases enjoy a limited say in what happens to participants on these shows. The recent film about Jerry Springer and his show (*Jerry Springer, Ringmaster,* 1998) paints him as a sympathetic spokesman and hero of poor and working-class people, who addresses rather than exploits their problems in a therapeutic way. In fact, all of these examples reflect the steady march toward avocation as a form of

televisual engagement or performance that only appears to be in the
service of personal development.[41]

Personal identity in the postmodern age has become at best a fragile
and changeable thing, increasingly subject to a rationalized, bureaucratized, and fragmented consumerist society dependent upon mass media
in all its variant forms. Lacking the roots for identity elsewhere, many
now seek legitimation in, or in relation to, the public domain of televirtual images they do recognize. Truman is an extreme case because he
lives unknowingly within a specific corporate televirtuality, and his life
direction continues largely to be constructed for him through his career
and domestic circumstances. He confronts a human-made regime constructed to limit his consciousness. Truman's obvious lack of choice
about his life makes his quest for freedom from the TV sphere that much
more decisive and poignant. Escape requires a risky process of trial and
error that is largely motivated by heterosexual love (much like Win-
ston Smith's experience in George Orwell's *1984*). In the terms posed
by Peter Weir's narrative, Truman's struggle constitutes a longing for
self-discovery that can only be realized beyond his given televirtual
world. This lends an existential dimension to his quest for authenticity.
The question finally posed by the claustrophobic world of The Truman
Show, then, is whether a fully mediated, transnational technocapitalism
has not already established the same kind of scenario for the average
citizen. Has contemporary media culture not already succeeded in con-
structing a substitutional world for the film viewer that is every day
more and more like Truman's?

Stuart Hall and Paul du Gay assert that subjectivity "is always inscribed within cultural codes of differences that organize subjects by
defining social identities."[42] Clearly, televirtuality specifically con-
strains the possibilities of experience by legitimating certain representations and discourses over others, or by melding oppositional stances
in such a way that differentiation becomes meaningless. This also applies to the domain of work related to production and consumption.
As du Gay has concluded:

*In effect, workers are encouraged to view work as consumers. . . . Through the image
of the "sovereign consumer", the relations between production and consumption,
between the "inside" and the "outside" of the corporation, and most importantly
perhaps between work-based and consumption-based identities, are progressively
blurred.*[43]

This blurring of worker and consumer identities takes on further significance in the larger context of cybertechnology, which is playing an increasing role in the televirtual domain. To this point I have identified the cultural emphasis and dominant socializing force in the United States as mainly consumerist in nature, although the latest configuration of televirtuality suggests an identity problematic that is yet more intimidating and personal. Marcuse wrote in 1960 of the contradiction posed by advanced media technology, where "technological reality . . . extends liberty while intensifying domination."[44] This paradox certainly characterizes the millennial era, in which the furious idealism of technoculture so fully embraces the latest virtual extremes of simulational experience. The promise of empowerment through data and shifting virtual identities also implies, however, an increasing relativity of personal identity. The current rise in technocultural absorption at work and at home, where televirtuality seduces with the promise of empowerment in a bodyless cyberspace of data flow, demands a certain identity flexibility or contingency in career and domestic life that is not only new but problematic from a humanistic standpoint. Is, for example, contingent identity not vulnerable and superficial identity, where increased spatial and bodily disorientation might lead to increased indifference toward or obsession with the ever-imperfect embodied self?

Some contemporary scholars have drawn very similar conclusions from this condition. For Julia Kristeva, writing in *New Maladies of the Soul,* the images of new media, like a drug, also increasingly distance our physical body networks from the kinds of experience that can enhance personal growth. The world of images merely covers over the surface of the emptiness we feel facing the loss of personal meaning.[45] If Kristeva is correct and the essential ground of contemporary psychic experience already suffers disconnection and fragmentation as a result of the growing hegemony of digital mediation, then no amount of reform in specific social problem areas will correct this widespread malady. The contemporary identity and autonomy crisis, therefore, takes on personal, regional, national, and global proportions under the innervating onslaught of advanced electronics. Arthur Kroker and Michael Weinstein recognize the new technoculture as a dangerously data-obsessive and empty "technotopia" where the substantive body has become appropriated by cybersystem interfaces. Instead of possessing information, the embodied person is read through with and possessed by it.[46] The crisis in contemporary media consciousness, then, is partly a crisis in disembodiment and body abstraction, assuming that subjectivity is even possible under the psychological pressures of identity contingency in a world of simulacra. Baudrillard has already answered this question in the negative. He asserts that a simulational, substitutional world (the environment of televirtuality) cannot produce coherent subject positions, whether in the realm of production (career work) or consumption.[47] Bill Nichols, writing in 1988, remains cautiously hopeful in his challenge: "The task is not to overthrow the prevailing cybernetic model but to transgress its predefined interdictions and limits, using the dynamite of the apperceptive powers it has itself brought into being."[48]

This chapter has considered how films such as *Wag the Dog* and *The Truman Show* reveal a breakdown of the old space and time and information constraints relative to production and consumption, as well as the growing mystique of technological empowerment and superiority as a whole. These films see America in the late 1990s on the verge of living in a political economic, hypermedia fantasy that is a kind of Truman Show, where the body as well as the mind are increasingly seduced in the direction of consumer and cyberspace images, and away from interpersonal realities conducive to self-determination and personal responsibility. In such an image world driven by an increasingly seductive electronic media, personal and career identity become destabilized and vulnerable. As progressive theorists of postmodern media culture and Hollywood's best films about televirtuality in the 1990s warn, traditionally resistant personal and social impulses that may have once grown and thrived on the margins of market-driven practices and ideology may be running out of space and time. We may not have the luxury of waiting for enlightenment, as Truman is compelled to do, until the day when the stage lights begin to fall from the skies.

Today we have good cause to understand texts as one part of a far broader cultural enterprise. Only by shifting attention from reception practices alone to the broader — and conflicting — usage patterns of all users can we escape the residual tyranny of the text king.

—RICK ALTMAN, *Film/Genre (113)*

CONCLUSION

This study of success ideology in the American business career film from 1945 to the present reveals several things. It demonstrates both how little the basic personal quality of individual initiative required for success has been altered over time, and how much the recently technologized business and work environment has changed. Career as a base for personal identity has, like the family, become less stable and more complex. Ubiquitous communications technology is tying the business office to commercialized workspace in the home, as well as merging domestic electronic entertainment, information, and consumer functions with the new social realm of e-mail, chat rooms, and so on. Looking back to a studio-era movie such as *Executive Suite,* therefore, corporate successorship is presented as a very different experience for characters than in the high-tech global environment of electronic industry apparent in *Disclosure.* And while this genre has continued to affirm the belief in vertical promotion as a sign of career attainment, it also reveals the continually rising expectations of the image necessary to represent public success. The myth of equal opportunity for all remains a strong assumption, even as the gap between rich and poor steadily widened in the United States during the latter half of the twentieth century. Films in this genre also mimic the historical trend, where the actual working experience and longevity of the corporate employee begins to imitate the rapid obsolescence of electronic equipment, while the survival rate of small businesses continues to flounder (*You've Got Mail,* 1998).

Add to this the cartel tendencies of transnational corporations, and the cutthroat tactics encouraged by contemporary capitalism's quick profit emphasis, and the individual success dream can quickly become lost in the compromises of dominant political economic mandates. This is shown to be the case in recent exposés of corporate corruption (*The Insider*), parodies of debilitating office tedium (*Office Space*, 1999), independent dramatic films of competitive sabotage (*In the Company of Men*, 1997), and satires of business and family life (*American Beauty*, 1999). These texts emphasize torturous career struggles, which can destroy the self-confidence of individuals and families, or turn workers into obsequious drudges for whom career success means little more than a small annual pay increment.

In screenwriter Allen Ball and director Sam Mendez's *American Beauty*, Lester Burnham (Kevin Spacey) suddenly awakens for the first time to recognize that he can do something about his stale career as an ad clerk and his degraded self-image. His initial rebellion, however, becomes an exaggerated version of the same inappropriate consumerist mind-set he has so passively shown earlier. He exults in a form of countermanipulation at work by blackmailing his employers into giving him a lucrative retirement package. He also lustfully pursues his teenage daughter's friend Angela (Mena Suvari), challenging his career- and commodity-obsessed wife and his body-obsessed daughter all the while. The family crisis that results forces him at last to see the consumer selfishness in his approach. It is the showers of red rose petals in his dream, and not explicitly Angela's nubile naked body that signal his opportunity for liberation and self-renewal. In Lester's fantasy, Angela is at first perceived as a reified image of erotic reawakening, which he knows only how to desire as a sexual conquest. But as he awakens, Angela too gives up her lies. He now recognizes her as a confused, insecure teenager already locked on the consumer image thinking of sexual self-objectification and competitiveness. This had also been the modus operandi for him and his wife Carolyn (Annette Bening), and the consequent undoing of their marriage and family.

Business-themed cinema like *American Beauty* thus provides an extreme model of self-revelation and resistance to rosy consumer success mythology. It is true to Hollywood form, however, in its tendency to find hope primarily in brave individual efforts at personal and career rehabilitation rather than through institutional reform. Another business-related satire of the time is *Panic* (2001), in which the protagonist Alex (William H. Macy) explains to his psychiatrist that he has two jobs:

CI   *American Beauty* (1999).
Lester Burnham (Kevin Spacey) is stuck in every aspect of his life, including career
and marriage, until his daughter's high school friend Angela (Mena Suvari) suddenly
startles him awake to the possibilities of major changes in his existence. The question
is, what kind of changes and to what end?

"I run a small mail-order business out of the house. Lawn ornaments, kitchen geegaws, sexual aids — things like that. And the rest of the time? I work for my father. I kill people." The story of Alex's weaning from the rather lucrative family business is a hopeful but comically bloody affair, and hence an ironic commentary not only on small business training in the family, but on the cynical trend in corporate business and political ethics in America generally, which is reminiscent of business satires the 1980s.

Corporate leaders are in a world apart from small business, particularly in the way they develop direct monetary and personal links with the primary figures of political power. A current example is the giant Enron Corporation scandal, which began with its filing for Chapter II bankruptcy in December 2001 — the largest corporation ever to do so in U.S. history. As recently as early 2001, Enron was the nation's seventh-largest company in revenue with an aggressive lobby on Capitol Hill. The Houston-based pipeline and energy corporation was on President George W. Bush's list of top campaign contributors in 2000, and it also donated large sums to many other Bush administration officials, including Attorney General John Ashcroft, who recused himself from the current investigation into Enron's affairs. Enron executives met six times in the past year with officials from the Bush administration's energy task force headed by Vice President Dick Cheney. News reports indicate that Enron hid its losses in off-balance-sheet partnerships to fraudulently mask its financial troubles and keep its credit rating healthy and its stock price high. While 29 Enron executives and directors began selling their shares near the top of the market from 1999 to mid-2001, most Enron employees were not informed of the company's financial problems. Some 20,000 employees were also not permitted to sell their 401(k) shares in the company during a critical time, and they and retired shareholders thus lost the value of their pension annuities. Nor were general investors informed of the problems. Approximately $30 billion in shareholder value has evaporated. Cabinet officials have claimed that it was not their responsibility to inform Enron employees or the public of the company's problems. And, too, what were the company auditors doing in all of this, since the SEC did not launch even an inquiry until late October 2001? Suddenly the fictional *Wall Street* story of the SEC busting little Bud Fox and his fast-talking mentor Gordon Gekko pales in comparison to the scale of the real Enron fraud. The Enron corporate treachery points up failures in the system of oversight in such a thoroughly politicized corporate economy. America's primary enemy appears to be the individualistic profiteering and political payoff system that represents the greedy extremes of its very own prescription for success.

Therefore, the very basis for judging individual career and business success in society and in the business genre film continues to remain stuck on the two-horned dilemma of sheer profitability versus social responsibility and the necessity for oversight. Once a character such as Bud Fox or Griffin Mill is initially seduced by his society's dominant commercial messages, and absent other mitigating forces, the outcome becomes predictable.

The business career goal of economic growth and power tends to continue to be in conflict with more personal forms of career fulfillment throughout this genre's history. The "take this job and shove it" attitude (expressed by Lester Burnham, for example) has remained a signal of personal liberation from oppressive work experience. But where most workers are on their own, most companies and institutions of any size have more expansive resources for their image promotion and survival. In some cases individual workers get blamed and fired or even killed for systemic company problems, while the firm may soon resume its questionable practices largely unscathed (*Disclosure*). In recent decades, the potential for positive, lasting social influence through career work appears to have decreased, as localized family and community autonomy has given way to commercially hegemonic rather than pluralistic economic forces. In the 1950s, even the more progressive business executive films such as *The Man in the Gray Flannel Suit* and *Patterns* suggest strong limitations to what the individual could do in the new managerial system, in its own way sometimes as baffling and degrading as was the previous rule of robber baron types, or the current pretensions of a politically established corporation such as the utility company in *Erin Brockovich* (2000). The politically correct working environment of recent decades has often meant only more grandiose political contributions and more convincing internal and external company PR, and the growing advertising and legal budgets to back it. Government oversight boards and criminal and civil courts remain the key to sorting out differences between corporate leadership and the public trust, company and employee, and manufacturer and consumer, which also explains the prominence of lawyers in business films of the recent past.

While the history of the business genre has confirmed that greater gender role diversity in work has gradually been won, economic uncertainty since the 1960s has nevertheless forced most dual-parent families — of which there are fewer and fewer — to have both parents employed. This has further stressed family viability despite all the political rhetoric of "family values" to the contrary. (In 1998, it was two-parent families with both parents employed that became the majority, just as the numbers of women returning to or finding work with a child "at home" younger than one year has nearly doubled since 1976.)[1]

The business and career film genre also indicates that women workers in particular have not escaped the burden of being viewed as potential mothers first, and as long-term committed employees second. More important still is the fact that the high expectations placed on women in the home regarding child rearing, meal preparation, and domestic management have been separated from the area of paid employment in society, and thus from direct economic and political leverage. The area of women's work in fiction film has been particularly revealing on this subject, because the undervaluation of personal nurturant functions, not only in the home but on the job and in the business marketplace, speaks to a variety of contemporary problems related to the cultural overemphasis on strictly commercial values and ideology.

Aggressive single working women characters in film are still more likely to be antagonists and femmes fatales than workers who represent family and community welfare. Entrepreneurs of both sexes, furthermore, find it almost impossible to separate their business from their domestic life. Resolving both simultaneously is uncommon, especially for women characters in either comedy or drama. Portraits of women's struggles in gainful employment, as in *Parenthood*, continue to be important because of their lasting associations with family life, and thus with the impact of business greed and consumer pressure on domestic well-being. Unregulated and exploitative laissez-faire capitalism is not generally shown to be a family or public value. A prime recent example is the woman-as-whistle-blower film *Erin Brockovich*, made in the tradition of *Silkwood* and *Marie* of the mid-1980s. Based on the "true story" of a divorced mother's campaign to challenge the lethal water pollution caused by a powerful utility company, it suggests some of the advantages of a working mother's personal connection to victimized families. With the sometimes reluctant support of her fair-minded boss (Albert Finney) in the legal office where she finds a job, she is able to make an aggressive response to injustice. Otherwise, lacking any authoritative government or community oversight, private enterprises such as the corporate utility here have insufficient incentive to monitor or remedy the negative public effects of their practices, including the mismanagement of their waste products.

Entrepreneurs from a variety of ethnic and racial groups continue to be shown as largely trapped, first by indigenous majority Caucasian models of success and prejudice, as well as by the singular, individualized profit mandate. This translates into strife within and among minorities, who also reflect the majority dichotomy in values. Ethnic small business films highlight in particular the way cultural differences among social groups influence the conduct of the minority individual's success quest. The struggle to realize the self is doubly difficult for the minority entrepreneur, who must locate identity within the minority, as well as in terms of the potent majority influence. While usually closer to the essential domain of family and local community survival, the entrepreneur in general is also more constrained in what he/she can do in the marketplace when compared to the corporate careerist, who can usually move about and redefine career goals more readily. As a high-tech-oriented business film like *Disclosure* suggests, individuals as well as companies have had to become leaner owing to the rapid changes in required skills, production techniques, and marketing methods. Further-

C2 *Erin Brockovich* (2000).
Erin (Julia Roberts), a twice-divorced high school dropout with two young children, and her employer, attorney Ed Masry (Albert Finney), take on a major public utility company with only meager resources and her determined guile.

more, problems unique to minority small business films can be a valuable cultural educator for otherwise limited mainstream perspectives. Business success for the minority entrepreneur character may simply reinforce the larger success mystique, but it can also delineate the degree of that character's struggle and thus serve as a reminder of how great the obstacles to success can be when inequality of opportunity, or a corporate leader's witch-hunt against an individual employee, is thrown in to the business success equation.

The discovery of career can be a lifelong pursuit, just as the discovery of self can be. And whether career success in social terms equals personal fulfillment or not, some individuals are defined more through their life course of refining their career through job changes, just as others (now less frequently) may find sufficient self-realization through the long-term refinement of a single business association. The lesson in *Cider House Rules* (1999) is that the discovery of the appropriate career and the discovery of self may not occur simultaneously. The protagonist Homer (Tobey Maguire) works his way into professional medical knowledge with what he is given as a young man, but also before he has an opportunity to mature in the world. Through his travel and confrontation with cider house work and romance and the personal maturation it brings, he learns to appreciate the unique, beneficial role that he formerly provided to distraught pregnant women and orphans at the institution for indigent children where he grew up. Romantic satisfaction is not presented as a substitute for career frustration here, but a helpful if painful reminder of the sacrifice that career recognition and choice can sometimes require. But *Cider House Rules* also looks back nostalgically to an age preceding advanced promotionalism and televirtuality, when medicine could still be practiced on a more personal and direct financial basis (despite, as in this case, certain legal restrictions regarding abortion).

The representation of advanced promotionalism in contemporary cinema is often found in romantic comedy. *You've Got Mail* (1998) and *What Women Want* (2000), for example, show the excessive measures taken by potential lovers to overcome competitive commercial environments, and to finally see one another in terms other than those defined by patriarchal business power and the assigning of career prestige. *What Women Want* emphasizes gender competition and requires unearthly jolts of electricity to help the male divorcé and ad exec see the errors of his macho assumptions. Nora Ephron's *You've Got Mail* is based on the premise that a partly blind e-mail correspondence, the benefits of new technology, can help bridge on the personal level an obviously tense business rivalry. True to Hollywood's romantic comedy tradition, real character growth occurs only at that point where emotional commitments are tested beyond considerations of economic and social advantage. But this does not mean that these narratives fail to "pay off" honest romantic commitment in the end. The final confirmation of a couple's true love in a business context usually shows the way also to career and/or economic success in the closing scenes. What is notable about these contemporary romantic comedies is again the lack of a supportive, normative grassroots community that might modify the impact of their personal and financial isolation in urban business environments.

As noted, too, the growing invasion of promotional images and the rapid merging of transnational conglomerates with media subsidiaries has further centralized and determined the avenues of media outreach, while at the same time imposing greater commercial market pressures on what remains of public-sector concerns. This has also tended to break down the separation between private business and public institutions (including government), as well as between work and domestic space. The career experience within advertising and PR production films, in fact, insinuates the growing preoccupation with defining career according to perceived consumer needs. Because success is culturally coded and increasingly based on widely advertised models of wealth, power, and esteem, promotionalism plays a very direct role in the perpetual reiteration of various models of success and the ideal lifestyle, as well as the worker's personal approach to career. The postmodern world, largely suspended in a constant flow of intertextual mediation, becomes for the career worker a less anchored and more ephemeral place, an arena of growing dependence on electronic tools that alter not only the forms of communication, but its very content and personal and social significance.

The contemporary hegemony of televirtuality, supported by the closing media loop of cultural stimulus and response, has turned traditional consumerism into a mind-altering landscape of self-absorption at every generational level. Films such as *The Truman Show, Ed TV,* and *The Insider* address the coercive trend in the mediated promotion of corporate political interests, and insinuate the question of whether televirtuality will be recognized on a mass scale for the addiction that it is and that it creates in its regime. In the current televirtual domain, where the career worker continues for better or worse to be at the mercy of these historical changes, reality has very simply become technological and market values ever more pervasive and forceful. The history of the most progressive films of the business and career genre, however, also continues to demonstrate how career protagonists who are compelled to compete against purely economic success models tend to resist such narrow values, frequently seeking alternative and fuller self-confirmations, even when these appear to come to fruition only through romance and/or financial impoverishment. The televirtual world, already growing at warp speed in the millennial era, presents certain potentials for career and social success as dynamic and multifaceted as they can be intimidating to personal and localized community space. If new communities exist only within commercially oriented mass media spaces rather than more interpersonal fields of exchange, then opportunities for alternative, more personable career and business methods and standards of service are diminished. Local communities, whatever their scattered identity base and varied reception to film genres, will nevertheless continue to have to struggle (mostly through the donation of private time) to find the wherewithal to control their own destiny. They will continue to have to confront large corporate and private political interests who possess superior resources for PR and legal muscle. The steady rise in consumer ambition and demand to the detriment of interpersonally nurturant family and community resources provides clear evidence of the new crisis of career desire within televirtuality. One uniquely comic example of this is provided in *Nurse Betty* (2000), where the waitress Betty (Renée Zellweger) loses the ability to distinguish her dream to become a real nurse from the TV soap opera about a doctor in a hospital setting. Even the working protagonist's dreams of community service and meaningful romance and family have become infected with televirtual distortion.

Meanwhile, the business career genre film continues to measure the changing conditions of work and work ethics and ideals, however narrow the windows for personal and organized resistance to dominant orientations. Rick Altman is certainly correct when he writes of the great need of "constellated" communities for the kind of sense of shared concerns and communication that film genres can offer.[2] In the case of the business career film, that sense of common problems and needs has particular meaning in relation to the setting of career goals, career ethics, and the relationship of both to the business/institution and its social role. Each era of this genre since World War II has presented a focus on a particular kind of theme or enterprise, whether dueling corporate execs in the 1950s and 1960s, or emerging businesswomen in the 1970s and 1980s. In the 1980s and 1990s, films about hard-nosed speculation and immigrant business are foregrounded, as are texts involving assertive and aggressive women aiming for quick profits, or simply to break through the glass ceiling. The promotional, televirtual landscape that dominates the best business and career films of the millennial era point to a form of media and information saturation where creative, localized, and socially useful work necessarily seems most often to be forced into highly marginal or resistant positions, as in *American Beauty* and *Erin Brockovich.* Lester Burnham finally gains a degree of personal retribution outside his work, while Erin finds purpose and meaning and even financial reward through her dedicated efforts of active social resistance in the name of those who have been victimized by corporate greed and deception.

The success mystique no longer involves merely the appearance of success through consumer images, but the guarantee of success through technical empowerment. Increasingly, televirtuality promises a virtual pleasure based in the cybernetic, where the individual is removed ever further from bodily and geographic reality. As the body loses substantive and subjective placement, so too does the mystique of success become increasingly depersonalized into an image form, an icon within virtuality. Televirtuality can only signify virtual success in a virtual business career. Ricky Fitts (Wes Bentley), the young man with the digital camera in *American Beauty,* strains to capture something worthy of attachment in a world already disconnecting him—like the floating plastic bag he records with his lens—from earthly gravity. Already removed from the continuity of a historical reality where his parents have already grown impaired, the forced, chameleon nature of his identity will continue to float on the data stream of cyberspace in search of meaning within or perhaps necessarily beyond televirtual existence. The futuristic dilemma of the machine-controlled 'normal' world in *The Matrix* is yet another example of the limiting force of televirtuality.

Advanced technologies, while more than supplying survival needs, have also enhanced the mechanism of envy for status and prestige, too often turning the best intentions of career logic into small-minded office politics, finally unseating the ground for personal self-revelation with substitute rewards of temporary self-fulfillment. The success of advanced consumerism speeds up the constant movement and volume of information and commodity flow even as it simultaneously creates gridlock and frustration. This has become not an "information age," but an age of late consumerism featuring indulgent greed that is rapidly depleting the globe's natural resources. Cultures of televirtuality have strengthened the tools of rapid and distant communication, but largely failed to respond to nurturant individual, family, and community needs, leaving income producers (like a Truman Burbank, Lester Burnham or his wife) trapped in workplace and homeplace consumer success mystiques over which they wield no real influence. As *The Insider* and *American Beauty* make clear, journalistic and cultural production must continually resist or at least remind us of the abuses of greedy capitalism and its consumer promotion barrage. Capitalism can create energy, opportunity, and worthy ambition in its encouragement of the ideal of career self-initiative and fulfillment. But the realities of high failure rates in start-up businesses, and the employee's toil in obsequious negotiations with labyrinthine corridors of institutional power can be devastating. The increasing global hegemony of capitalist televirtuality will continue to be shadowed by highly volatile markets, high rates of corporate greed, and all too willing government sponsorship.[3]

In view of such daunting historical tendencies, the fragile business career trajectory in all its potential economic and political significance continues to be imagined by the best of American cinema, as a key counter for individual identity and the possible establishment of social worth. The success mystique must not be allowed to be reduced to career image, consumer buying power, and technical prestige only, where it tends to be submerged in marketplace rhetoric and power politics. One would like, in the American cinema of business and elsewhere, to continue to find ways to reaffirm what is most significant and rewarding in private enterprise, and what personal and social purpose it can be made to serve in the end. The business career genre has so far provided memorable reflections on the success mystique. And while it has certainly not altered the larger trend toward televirtuality, it has at times suggested watersheds of personal resistance for the individual and community. This positive influence recalls the original purpose and democratic dream on which the country was founded, as well as the nation's necessary obligation as a progressive leader in, rather than primary consumer of, global destiny.

LIST OF FILM STILLS

NOTES

INTRODUCTION

1. Concerning the seduction of American youth by capitalist greed and class chauvinism, see my "*Wall Street:* The Commodification of Perception," *Journal of Popular Film and Television* 17, no. 3 (fall 1989), in *Cultural Power/Cultural Literacy,* ed. Bonnie Braendlin (Tallahassee: Florida State University Press, 1991). It also appears in *The Films of Oliver Stone,* ed. Don Kunz (Lanham, Md.: Scarecrow Press, 1997).

2. After World War II, legitimate corporate raiders were introduced to the public in the films *Cash McCall* (1959) and *Wheeler Dealers* (1963). Inspired by the Reaganomics era, problematic versions of the type reappear in *Trading Places* (1983), *Other People's Money* (1991), and *Barbarians at the Gate* (1993), though none have the alarmist quality of *Wall Street.*

3. David Bordwell, Janet Staiger, and Kristin Thompson, *The Classical Hollywood Cinema: Film Style and Mode of Production to 1960* (New York: Columbia University Press, 1985), 16.

4. Consider among others family melodramas, Westerns, and musicals, as well as war, science fiction, and gangster films.

5. See also Steve Neale's more recent *Genre and Hollywood* (London: Routledge, 2000), 2–3, where he explains: "the institutional role played by Hollywood and its 'inter-textual relay' (Lukow and Ricci 1984) in the generation of expectations, in the provision of evidence as to the existence of genres, as to their prevalence in Hollywood's output at any particular point in time, and as to the meaning, application and use of genre terms. The term 'inter-textual relay' refers to the discourses of publicity, promotion and reception that surround Hollywood's films, and includes both trade and press reviews."

6. Rick Altman, *Film/Genre* (London: British Film Institute, 1999).

7. Thomas Schatz, "The Structural Influence: New Directions in Film Genre Study," in *Film Genre Reader II*, ed. Barry Keith Grant, (Austin: University of Texas Press, 1995), 96.

8. *Atlanta Constitution,* August 17, 2000, A23.

CHAPTER 1

1. C. Wright Mills, *The Power Elite* (New York: Oxford University Press, 1956), 119.

2. Only the typical suffering of the mogul's wife and close friends might be seen in some cases as metaphoric of a wider exploitation. Journalistic and business-political manipulation of the public are blatant in Billy Wilder's dark tale *The Big Carnival* (1951). For further discussion on the rise-and-fall business film, see Chapter 4. Raoul Walsh's version of the Huey Long story, *A Lion in the Streets* (1953), following closely on Robert Rossen's film adaptation of Robert Penn Warren's famous novel, *All the King's Men* (1949), are close political cousins to the entrepreneur-turned-business-mogul story. *Citizen Kane* and *Meet John Doe* both provide big capitalists who seek to make the move over from business success into national political office.

3. C. Wright Mills, *White Collar* (New York: Oxford University Press, 1953), 106.

4. Mills, *Power Elite,* 141.

5. In *The Power Elite,* Mills explains how "the career of the business executive has become a movement within and between the corporate hierarchies," increasing "from 18 percent in 1870 to 68 percent in 1950" (132).

6. This phenomenon has also been called the triumph of managerialism. See Edward S. Mason, ed., *The Corporation in Modern America* (Cambridge: Harvard University Press, 1959), 5. "The one-hundred-and-thirty-odd largest manufacturing corporations account for half of manufacturing output in the United States. The five hundred largest business corporations in this country embrace nearly two thirds of all non-agricultural economic activity. . . . But by now we are all aware that we live not only in a corporate society but a society of large corporations. The management — that is, the control — of these corporations is in the hands of, at most, a few thousand men. Who selected these men . . . to exercise vast authority, and to whom are they responsible? The answer to the first question is quite clearly, they selected themselves. The answer to the second is, at best, nebulous."

7. This type of family dynasty melodrama became extremely popular when it moved over to broadcast television in the 1970s in serials such as *Dallas* and *Dynasty.* In these serials, Ellen Seiter observes how "the oil business is taken out of the impersonal, corporate world of Exxon and Mobil, and placed in the realm of family inheritance and personal fortunes." See "Men, Sex, and Money in Family Melodrama," *Jounral of Film and Video* 35, no. 1 (winter 1983): 19.

8. Thomas Elsaesser, "Tales of Sound and Fury: Observations on the Family

Melodrama," in *Film Theory and Criticism*, 4th ed., ed. Gerald Mast, Marshall Cohen, and Leo Braudy, 523 (New York: Oxford University Press, 1992).

9. Thomas Schatz, *Hollywood Genres* (New York: McGraw-Hill, 1981), 223. Schatz notes that "the prospect of a liberating marriage is actually quite rare in the '50s family melodrama, which usually depicts that social ritual as solidifying the couple's position within the community rather than providing them with an escape from it" (223).

10. See David N. Rodowick, "Madness, Authority, and Ideology: The Domestic Melodrama of the 1950s," in *Imitations of Life*, ed. Marcia Landy (Detroit: Wayne State University Press, 1991), 241.

11. Mills, *Power Elite*, 141.

12. Ibid., 118–46.

13. The inclination toward an exposé of corporate penthouse life rather than toward a realistic depiction of the problems of modern leadership is consistent with MGM's Pressbook on the film, which accentuates the personal and sexual intrigues that surround an industrial power center.

14. The product-based orientation of the corporation featured in *Executive Suite* changed during the 1950s, but not in the direction advised by efficiency experts, who continued to be looked down upon as late as 1957 in *Desk Set*. By the end of the decade, films such as *The Man in the Gray Flannel Suit* and *Cash McCall* (1959) signify the increasing importance of PR, advertising, and speculative concerns in the choice of industrial corporate leadership. Chief financial officers (CFOs) had to wait until the 1980s before they became the category of choice to fill the seats of chief executive officers.

15. See John Kenneth Galbraith, *The Affluent Society* (Boston: Houghton Mifflin, 1958), 84–92, and Richard Godden, *Fictions of Capital* (New York: Cambridge University Press, 1990), 179.

16. Peter Biskind, *Seeing Is Believing* (New York: Pantheon Books, 1983), 250.

17. David Riesman, *The Lonely Crowd* (New Haven: Yale University Press, 1950).

18. William H. Whyte, *The Organization Man* (New York: Simon and Schuster, 1956), 44. Whyte goes on to say that "the premise is, simply, that the goals of the individual and the goals of the organization will work out to be one and the same. The young men have no cynicism about the 'system,' and very little skepticism— they don't see it as something to be bucked, but as something to be cooperated with" (44).

19. Biskind, 309–11.

20. Whyte, 148.

21. The desire for advancement, including the willingness to relocate, have long been expected of employees. For many of those at IBM, for example, the company name came to mean "I've been moved."

22. Susan Van Horn, *Women, Work, and Fertility, 1900–1986* (New York: New York University Press, 1988), 208.

23. Barbara Ehrenreich and Deirdre English, *For Her Own Good: 150 Years of the Experts' Advice to Women* (New York: Anchor Press, 1978). See also Van Horn, 206.

24. Jackie Byars, *All That Hollywood Allows* (Chapel Hill: University of North Carolina Press, 1991), 99.

25. Heidi Hartmann, "The Family as the Locus of Gender, Class, and Political Struggle: The Example of Housework," *Signs,* 6, no. 3, (spring, 1981): 368.

26. Mills, *Power Elite,* 68–69.

27. John Kenneth Galbraith, *The New Industrial State* (Boston: Houghton Mifflin, 1971), 391–402.

28. Ibid., 74–83.

29. Richard H. Pells, *The Liberal Mind in a Conservative Age* (New York: Harper & Row, 1985), 55.

30. Galbraith, *New Industrial State,* 230. Defense outlays (excluding those for veterans and interest) were a little over a billion dollars in 1939. "In 1968, military expenditures in the administrative budget were an estimated $75 billion or about 56 percent of the total budget" (231).

See also Godden. "In 1919 the U.S. demobilized, whereas after the second world war it expanded militarily, with the result that by 1955 10% of the GNP was being spent on 'preparedness'. Percentiles cannot capture the enormity of the investment: between 1945 and 1970 the U.S. government expended $11.1 trillion for military purposes, an amount which exceeds the 1967 valuation of all the nation's business and residential structures. In effect the USA became 'a defense economy' through which the state, as chief purchaser, might regularize and direct accumulation" (175).

31. William Manchester, *The Glory and the Dream* (New York: Little, Brown, 1974), 877.

32. Mills, *Power Elite,* 168.

33. William M. Dugger, *Corporate Hegemony* (New York: Greenwood Press, 1989), 121–22. See also Edward S. Herman, *Corporate Control, Corporate Power* (Cambridge: Cambridge University Press, 1981), 106–7.

34. David A. Cook, *A History of Narrative Film* (New York: W. W. Norton, 1996), 533.

35. Michael Maccoby, *The Leader: A New Face for American Management* (New York: Ballantine Books, 1981), 37.

36. Corporate job security has not been as dependable in America as in other modern technocracies such as Japan. But from a contemporary perspective— where runaway mergers and "company downsizing" take such a heavy toll on individuals' financial and psychic security—job reliability in the 1950s looks idyllic.

37. See Marshall B. Clinard and Peter C. Yeager, *Corporate Crime* (New York: Free Press, 1980), 234–35. "Parent corporations or their subsidiaries also affect local communities through philanthropic contributions. These gifts of course benefit the corporate donors, as they can reduce federal, state and local taxes, thereby limiting public revenue. Control over the disbursement of these funds may even be retained by the donor, thus indirectly promoting corporate policies and reaping invaluable publicity for the 'community concern' the firm has shown."

38. Dana Polan, *Power and Paranoia: History, Narrative, and the American Cinema, 1940–1950* (New York: Columbia University Press, 1986), 75.

39. Galbraith, *Affluent Society,* 127. Galbraith speaks of "a declining urgency of need" or "diminishing urgency of consumption" to distinguish the fulfillment of basic needs from more frivolous pursuits that create a consumer "dependency effect" (122–23).

40. Hartmann, 370.

41. Mainstream Hollywood cinema of the 1950s, with both feet firmly planted in corporate capitalism, was hardly willing to promote stories that suggested reductions in career ambition and consumer desire without considerable qualification. The drive to get ahead and be "successful" is at the heart of the American Dream and of classical Hollywood narratives. See Richard Weiss, *The American Myth of Success* (New York: Basic Books, 1969).

42. Elizabeth Traube, *Dreaming Identities: Class, Gender and Generation in 1980s Hollywood Movies* (Boulder, Colo.: Westview Press, 1992), 140–41.

43. Nancy Chodorow, *The Reproduction of Mothering: Psychoanalysis and the Sociology of Gender* (Berkeley: University of California Press, 1978), 106.

44. Quoted in *The Observer* (London), January 15, 1950.

45. Christopher Anderson, "Hollywood in the Home: TV and the End of the Studio System," in *Modernity and Mass Culture,* ed. James Naremore and Patrick Brantlinger (Bloomington: Indiana University Press, 1991), 89. Anderson points out that even after the film studios began to embrace TV programming, they "still hoped to construct a different exchange value for their theatrical and television product."

46. Another film from 1957, *A Face in the Crowd,* does begin to make clear how the electronic imaging system in the family living room was rapidly breaking down long-held assumptions regarding family autonomy and its social influence. See Chapter 5.

47. Godden, 42.

48. Herman, 244. "The relationship between government and business has been obscured by a tendency to exaggerate both the degree of conflict between business and government and the scope and impact of government regulation."

49. Jean-Francois Lyotard's controversial work *The Postmodern Condition: A Report on Knowledge* (Minneapolis: University of Minnesota Press, 1997) was originally published in French in 1979 (Les Editions de Minuit). In it Lyotard periodizes the postmodern moment as the end of the 1950s. He also notes capitalism's "crisis of legitimation, centered in science," where "the desire for wealth replaces the desire for knowledge. The university becomes a site where capitalism directs and controls research, directly through grants from large corporations (IBM, Du Pont and so on), and indirectly through the state (for example Defense contracts funneled through private corporations)" (36–37).

50. Dugger, xvii.

51. Mills, *Power Elite,* 131.

CHAPTER 2

1. Juliet Mitchell, *Psychoanalysis and Feminism* (London: Lane, 1974), 290.

2. Susan Van Horn, *Women, Work, and Fertility, 1900–1986* (New York: New York University Press, 1988), 145.

3. Ibid. Women represented fully 37 percent of the paid workforce by 1970.

4. Ibid.

5. Molly Haskell, *From Reverence to Rape* (Baltimore: Penguin Books, 1973), 172.

6. Van Horn, 195.

7. This version of *So Big* is the liberal answer to Ayn Rand's *The Fountainhead* (adapted to film in 1949), which insists that an entrepreneurial spirit of creativity is the best measure for social rank and capitalist progress.

8. In *All That Heaven Allows* the single mother (Jane Wyman) has an empty nest, which in her mind allows the freedom to accept a socially controversial relationship with a man of her own choosing. But it does not also include the necessity for her to work.

9. Haskell, 172.

10. The deep cultural resistance to unmarried working mothers in the classical film era is further attested to by the fact that these two films represent such an extreme generic diversity of film noir and of family melodrama (particularly as to style).

11. Michael Rogin, "Kiss Me Deadly: Communism, Motherhood, and Cold War Movies," *Representations* 6 (spring 1984): 17.

12. Jeanine Basinger, *A Woman's View* (Hanover, N.H.: Wesleyan University Press, 1993), 257.

13. John Kenneth Galbraith, *The Affluent Society* (Boston: Houghton Mifflin, 1958), 146–47.

14. Nancy Chodorow, *The Reproduction of Mothering: Psychoanalysis and the Sociology of Gender* (Berkeley: University of California Press, 1978), 106.

15. U.S. census figures, reported in the *Atlanta Constitution,* October 16, 1995, A6.

16. It is important to note that mothers from the working class—in *Norma Rae* (1979) or *Matewan* (1987), for example—enjoy no such luxury and face even more stringent blue-collar attitudes toward the gainful employment of women, if they must work outside the home at all.

17. In *Sybil* (a made-for-TV film from 1976 that explicitly recounts a true event), significantly, it is the surrogate mother figure as psychiatrist (Joanne Woodward) who breaks the patriarchal (and textual) restrictions on what can be seen of the bad mother's barbarism. Her investigation forces male authority figures, such as the local town doctor, to take the blame along with Sybil's religiously fundamentalist father and psychotic mother. As a TV movie, *Sybil* is a cry for the prompt recognition and exposure of child abuse, but its painful revelations stop short of tracing such abuse to the society beyond the mother's particular psychic dysfunction. See also *I Never Promised You a Rose Garden* (1977).

18. For an expanded discussion on corporate audacity and the technological/human identity crisis, see my "*Blade Runner:* Crashing the Gates of Insight," in *Retrofitting Blade Runner,* ed. Judith Kerman (Bowling Green, Ohio: Popular Press, 1991).

19. Marcia Landy, *Imitations of Life* (Detroit: Wayne State University Press, 1991), 536.

20. This case refers to the real-life experience of Sherri Finkbine, who was forced to give up the children's TV show that she hosted, and to fly all the way to Japan to rid herself of the unwanted fetus. No American or European hospital was willing to accept her because of the antiabortion hysteria.

21. Mary Desjardin, "*Baby Boom:* The Comedy of Surrogacy in Film and Television," *Velvet Light Trap* 29 (spring 1992): 25.

22. See Marshall B. Clinard and Peter C. Yeager's *Corporate Crime* (New York: Free Press, 1980), 260. "The production and sale of Ford's subcompact Pinto represents a classic case of safety versus profits. In 1978 government pressures forced Ford to recall 1.5 million Pinto sedans made between 1971 and 1976, after National Highway Safety Administration tests had determined that they leaked large amounts of fuel and were prone to explode in moderate-speed rear-end collisions. As of 1977 it had been conservatively estimated that the Pinto's fire-prone gas tank had been responsible for 500 burn deaths of persons who would not have been seriously injured had their cars not burst into flames" (Dowie, 1977, p. 24).

Clinard and Yeager make the point that individuals working in competitive corporate situations to make money for the company and to advance their careers tend at times toward socially irresponsible decisions in groups under the legal umbrella of the company that they would never make as individuals (273).

23. This is another film based on a true story of a mother who tried to contract for the murder of her daughter's competitor for the school cheerleading squad. She was eventually convicted for conspiracy and spent a few years in prison before being released.

24. See E. Ann Kaplan, *Motherhood and Representation* (New York: Routledge, 1992). Among other things, Kaplan notes the "phallic" mother paradigm in *Now Voyager* (1942) and *Marnie* (1964). She also provides a worthy description of the "Super-Mom," who "worries about getting the child into the best schools before the baby is born, takes the baby to swimming classes at 3 months, plies the baby with all the latest learning devices in hopes of increasing intelligence, strives for the healthiest diet for the baby to insure a trim body later on, and so on" (189).

25. Albert J. LaValley, *Mildred Pierce* (Madison: University of Wisconsin Press, 1980), 19–20.

26. Ibid.

27. See the chapter on "Children's Desires/Mothers' Dilemmas" in Ellen Seiter's *Sold Separately* (New Brunswick, N.J.: Rutgers University Press, 1993).

28. Barbara Creed, "Horror and the Monstrous-Feminine—An Imaginary Abjection," *Screen* 27, 1 (January–February 1986).

29. Chodorow.

30. Rebecca Bailin, "Feminist Readership, Violence, and *Marnie,*" *Film Reader* 5 (Northwestern University, 1982), 27. Bailin's reading of this film appears to contrast with Juliet Mitchell's rather blanket statement quoted at the beginning of this chapter. Bailin notes that screenwriter Allen is quite sympathetic to Marnie's troubled psychological history and its knowability even within sexist economic contexts.

31. Julia Lesage, "The Hegemonic Female Fantasy in *An Unmarried Woman* and *Craig's Wife,*" *Film Reader* 5 (1982), 92.

32. Michelle Piso, "Mark's Marnie," in *A Hitchcock Reader,* ed. Marshall Deutelbaum and Leland Poague (Ames: Iowa State University Press, 1986), 289.

33. *Chinatown* is a neonoir text made 10 years after *Marnie.* It too features a woman's unfortunate family history, but even more fully elaborates her relationship to a business and family elite. Evelyn Mulwray's demise results from her inability to control her fate, to free herself from the perverse personal and insidious business methods of her tycoon paterfamilias. It is the daughter Evelyn conflated with her maternal role to her father's incestuous child that establishes the collapse or implosion of the woman's position. This is also a metaphor for Barbara Creed's notion of the maternal conduit for patriarchy into a specific political economic context. The combination of personal/family seduction with the perquisites of wealth and power suggest the difficulty of locating any family or business alternative to a new sign-dominant commercial hegemony.

34. Andreas Huyssen, *After the Great Divide* (Bloomington: Indiana University Press, 1986), 23.

35. Ibid., 21.

36. Stephen Frosh, *The Politics of Psychoanalysis* (New Haven: Yale University Press, 1987), 169.

37. Ibid., 171.

38. Ibid., 172.

39. Ibid.

CHAPTER 3

1. In this regard, Robert Stam has introduced the term "polycentric multiculturalism" as an ideal for economic and cultural activity. "The emphasis in polycentrism is not on point of origin but on fields of power, energy, and struggle. The 'poly' does not refer to a finite list of centers of power but rather introduces a systematic principle of differentiation, rationality, and linkage. No single community or part of the world, whatever its economic or political power, is epistemologically privileged." *Film Theory: An Introduction* (Malden, Mass.: Blackwell Publishers, 2000), 271.

2. In his autobiography, *The Name above the Title,* Capra explains his own extended nightmare when he was accused of being a communist because he was photographed in front of the Russian embassy. Had the charges stuck, his considerable reputation at the time would surely have been tarnished to the point that he may not have been able any longer to direct major films.

3. See Larry Clark's "*Tucker: The Man and His Dream;* A Look behind the Scenes," at <www.tuckerclub.org/tuckmov.html> (p. 2 of 6).

4. Ibid., 3.

5. Ibid., 6.

6. *Doctor Detroit* and *Trading Places* (both 1983) also reflect very similar business plot patterns and themes, where a shy college professor in the former and a Wall Street outcast in the latter find success via the friendly support of prostitutes. Another comic example of this solicitous form of business is Paul Bartel's *Eating Raoul* (1982), in which a couple anxious to raise money to open a restaurant advertise for sexual "swingers" whom they promptly knock off and sell for dog food.

7. Reagan's "anything goes" capitalism as a Cold War tool reached its peak in the Iran-Contra "Enterprise" debacle, where a secret for-profit business was established inside the National Security Council that made money from foreign weapon sales and from marked-up goods designated for the Contras. These secret government procedures were revealed in Senate hearings by testimony of Reagan functionaries such as Oliver North and National Security Adviser John Poindexter. Runaway capitalist enterprise became a characteristic theme of 1980s history.

8. Feature documentaries have recently proven as effective in identifying middle-class career issues as they have in identifying working-class crises. In this case, a pair of computer business types form a company based on a parking ticket payoff software concept. They also manage to get on TV with President Clinton and appear on *Late Night* to promote their "product." The slightest apparent or real advantages in new technology and public relations are exploited for the momentary benefits. Fiction film could hardly tell the story better.

9. Gina Marchetti, "Ethnicity, the Cinema, and Cultural Studies," in *Unspeakable Images: Ethnicity and the American Cinema,* ed. Lester Friedman (Urbana: University of Illinois Press, 1991), 278.

10. Stam, 271.

11. See Ana Lopez, "Are All Latins from Manhattan? Hollywood, Ethnography, and Cultural Colonialism," in *Unspeakable Images: Ethnicity and the American Cinema,* ed. Lester Friedman (Urbana: University of Illinois Press, 1991).

The Hollywood film industry, of course, is heavily indebted in its early history to the contributions of minority ethnic groups, and immigrant film producers, directors, and actors have had a massive influence on Hollywood filmmaking over the years.

12. According to David A. Cook, her film life is easily traced to the femme fatale of the "modishly decadent melodramas" in the French and Italian cinemas, which provided a model for the vamp of early American films, first made famous by actress Theda Bara. See *A History of Narrative Film* (New York: W. W. Norton, 1996), 55. Also see Mary Ann Doane, *Femmes Fatales* (New York: Routledge, 1991), 1. She dates the recent historical significance of this figure to the Industrial Revolution—a time that saw "the confluence of modernity, urbanization, Freudian psychoanalysis and new technologies of production and reproduction

(photography, the cinema)." Doane believes that at the historical moment when the male working body was being "confiscated" and thus alienated by machines, the woman's body took on added significance.

13. Molly Haskell, *From Reverence to Rape* (Baltimore: Penguin Books, 1973), 197.

14. *Postnoir* is merely a convenient term to denote the period following Hollywood's transitional, or neonoir, era, but it is not meant to suggest specific stylistic changes. While postclassic noir films in general have moved away from strict expressionistic stylization, they have not foregone this film form's emphasis on doom, including both its themes of transgression and its character perspectives of anguish and disorientation. Such formal elements in relation to visual style have always been part of the debate about classic noir as a genre. And similar considerations relating to the greater noir tradition only complicate the issue.

15. Thomas Schatz, *Hollywood Genres* (New York: McGraw-Hill, 1981), 113–14.

16. Susan Van Horn, *Women, Work, and Fertility, 1900–1986* (New York: New York University Press, 1988), 140–45.

17. Janey Place, "Women in Film Noir," in *Women in Film Noir,* ed. E. Ann Kaplan (London: British Film Institute, 1978), 54. This observation was disproved by the femme fatale of the 1980s and 1990s.

18. Laura Mulvey, "Visual Pleasure and Narrative Cinema," in *Film Theory and Criticism,* ed. Gerald Mast, Marshall Cohen, and Leo Braudy, 4th ed. (New York: Oxford University Press, 1992).

19. Michele Piso, "Mark's Marnie," in *A Hitchcock Reader,* ed. Marshall Deutelbaum and Leland Poague (Ames: Iowa State University Press, 1986), 289.

20. See John Cawelti's much anthologized article "*Chinatown* and Generic Transformation in Recent American Films," in *Film Theory and Criticism,* ed. Mast, Cohen, and Braudy. He explains the hard-boiled detective myth and how it is transformed to suggest impotency for both the detective and the putative femme fatale in Roman Polanski's film. Cawelti defines this in terms of the exhaustion of genres and cultural myths.

21. For the nonlethal femme fatale — and none of these Hollywood Renaissance–era examples are — the possibility of nurturing relationships is made nearly impossible because of their constant objectification. Christine Gledhill writes not only of the woman's marginal place in the labor market represented by Bree, but of "a moral, existential alienation of the psyche which is to be resolved in personal relationships, if at all." "*Klute* 2: Feminism and *Klute,*" in Kaplan's *Women in Film Noir,* 122.

22. See Garry Wills, *Reagan's America* (Garden City, N.Y.: Doubleday, 1987), 367–70.

23. See the "Director's Cut" version of *Fatal Attraction,* which also provides the original ending. This version features director Lyne proudly playing an audiotape he recorded of a live audience's screaming reactions to this film.

24. The new fear of AIDS has highlighted the dangers of casual sex, and in some ways Alex may embody that. The audience sympathizes with the way Dan and his family must pay and pay for his unfortunate one-night stand.

25. "Realistically," the film attributes Alex's obsession to the early loss of her father and her resulting anxiety over male commitment (perhaps fed by her claims of pregnancy). But postmodernists would find metaphoric significance in these plot patterns. See, for example, Louis Althusser's "Ideology and Ideological State Apparatuses," in *Lenin and Philosophy,* trans. Ben Brewster (New York: Monthly Review Press, 1971); Guy Debord's *Society of the Spectacle* (Detroit: Black and Red, 1983); and Jean Baudrillard's *Selected Writings,* ed. Mark Poster (Stanford: Stanford University Press, 1988).

26. *Pacific Heights* (1990), *Cape Fear* (1991), *The Hand That Rocks the Cradle* (1992), and *The Firm* (1993) all follow this same theme of the violation of bourgeois family security in relation to career issues.

27. *The Temp* (1993) is a corporate thriller, and *To Die For* (1995), concerning a woman who has her husband killed to advance her floundering TV career, is based on a true story featured in a book by Joyce Maynard.

28. Nick's police sidekick Gus (George Dzundza) is a dedicated worker and voice of reason, but unlike the stoic observers in prior noir texts, this standard-bearer is killed in the process of the investigation.

29. For an extended consideration of the sexual controversies surrounding the film, see also Chris Holmlund, "Cruisin' for a Bruisin': Hollywood's Deadly (Lesbian) Dolls," *Cinema Journal* 34, no. 1 (1994). Ms. Holmlund provides a good account of the different, mostly gay protest groups and their mixed viewpoints.

30. In their choice of a female sex abuser, Crichton and Levinson were no doubt commercially motivated, but they also demonstrate how phallocentric behavior is encouraged in contemporary corporate commerce whatever one's sex, class, race, or nationality. The novel's motto includes a character quote: "Power is neither male nor female." Crichton's "Afterword" notes that the harassment episode is based on a true story but is "not intended to deny the fact that the great majority of harassment claims are brought by women against men. . . . [T]he advantage of a role-reversal story is that it may enable us to examine aspects concealed by traditional responses and conventional rhetoric." *Disclosure* (New York: Ballantine Books, 1993), 497.

31. This and the other recent film roles of Michael Douglas as the put-upon male careerist also suggest just how precarious the man's road to success has apparently become by the mid-1990s. He serves as the protagonist victim not only in *Fatal Attraction, Basic Instinct,* and *Disclosure,* but also in *Falling Down* (1993). The defensive white-collar male figure is obviously a fact and symptom of the times.

32. The front page of the Business section of the *Atlanta Journal-Constitution* (April 15, 1998) reports on a two-year study by the Families and Work Institute covering American workers over the last 20 years: "Most Americans are working longer and feeling more insecure about their jobs compared with sentiment two decades ago." See also Barbara Ehrenreich's comments on the middle class in *Fear of Falling* (New York: Pantheon Books, 1989), 15.

33. This is not new for men in cinema, of course, since leading males as private eyes or cops have often been sexually involved with the killer/temptress without compromising their search for truth, from *The Maltese Falcon* (1941) to *Basic*

Instinct. But blame for such acting out by a woman administrator highlights the perpetuation of a double standard that initially attracted attention to the problem of sexual harassment.

34. Elizabeth G. Traube, *Dreaming Identities: Class, Gender and Generation in 1980s Hollywood Movies* (Boulder, Colo.: Westview Press, 1992), 121.

35. Fred Pfeil, *White Guys: Studies in Postmodern Domination and Difference* (New York: Verso, 1995). See also the most recent popular account by Susan Faludi, *Stiffed: The Betrayal of the American Man* (New York: Morrow, 1999). Faludi blames the masculinity crisis on a celebrity-worshiping consumer culture.

36. M. J. Anderson, "'Survivor' Skills Prevail in Workplace," *Atlanta Journal-Constitution,* September 12, 2000, A21. Anderson cites sociologist Richard Sennett's recent book, *The Corrosion of Character: The Personal Consequences of Work in the New Capitalism* (New York: W. W. Norton, 1998), noting that "Sennet's provocative thesis is that the terms of employment have so changed as to make the habits of good character a liability. Hence, character steadily erodes. . . . [H]e argues that the sheer unpredictability of employment in today's world makes old virtues such as loyalty, trust and commitment irrelevant. People feel upset about having to sacrifice these virtues."

CHAPTER 4

1. Sut Jhally, *The Codes of Advertising: Fetishism and the Political Economy of Meaning in the Consumer Society* (New York: St. Martin's Press, 1987), 23. Jhally quotes from S. Kline and W. Leiss, "Advertising, Needs, and Commodity Fetishism," *Canadian Journal of Political and Social Theory* 2, no. 1 (1978): 18.

2. Sut Jhally, *Advertising and the End of the World,* an educational video from the Media Education Foundation, 1996.

3. Jhally, 200. Sut Jhally cites Martin Esslin in his belief that advertising is the new religion of modern life: "We may not be conscious of it, but this *is* the religion by which most of us actually live, whatever our more consciously and explicitly held beliefs and religious persuasions may be. This is the actual religion that is being absorbed by our children from almost the day of their birth." "Aristotle and the Advertisers: The Television Commercial Considered as a Form of Drama," in *Television: The Critical View,* ed. H. Newcomb (New York: Oxford University Press, 1976), 271.

4. The likely basis for the "27 Varieties" is obviously Heinz's "57 Varieties," a trademark gimmick developed in 1896.

5. The public relations industry was born on a negative note. Bad press followed the slaughter of striking mine workers and their families in the Ludlow Colorado Massacre of 1914, and attention became focused on the combine owner, John Rockefeller Jr. He located a man, Ivy Lee, who found ways to turn Rockefeller's tainted image around in the press. Lee's experience was picked up in the theory and practice of a follower, Edward Bernays, who elaborated a full discipline of press agency and became the American father of public relations. Bernays catered to the special interests of his moneyed clients, whether it was en-

couraging women to smoke in public or defending a client's reputation in the press. In the Jeremy Kirk novel *The Build-up Boys* (1951), which is the basis for the interesting film *Madison Avenue* (1962) to be discussed later in this chapter, advertising and public relations are declared to be like two wings of the same airplane.

6. Stuart Chase and F. J. Schlink, *Your Money's Worth* (New York: Macmillan, 1927), 260.

7. Ibid.

8. Tracing the exact cultural impact of an entire movie is more difficult than deconstructing a film's content. This is especially true where assertions about the primacy of one medium over another in the circulation of meanings are concerned. Certainly films have the potential to flesh out influential character types and situations and themes more thoroughly than shorter and more narrowly focused advertising and publicity messages can hope to do.

9. Stuart Ewen, *Captains of Consciousness: Advertising and the Social Roots of the Consumer Culture* (New York: McGraw-Hill, 1976), 80. Ewen also identifies early one-to-five-reel entertainment films that were produced by the ad industry. *"Blowout Bill's Busted Romance,* an advertising comedy, portrayed a particular brand of tires as the solution to the insecurities of love. Other films, such as *Sole-Mates,* a shoe comedy; *Candy Courtship* (for Lowney Candy Co.), and *Brushing the Clouds Away* (Fuller Brush), were produced in 1920 and 1921. Here, mass-produced commodities were located securely in daily life and shown to captive audiences in movie theaters along with the regular features" (73).

10. Ibid., 79–80.

11. Janet Staiger, "Announcing Wares, Winning Patrons, Voicing Ideals: Thinking about the History and Theory of Film Advertising," *Cinema Journal* 29, no. 3 (spring 1990): 6.
She goes on to describe the growing institutional power of the International Motion Picture Advertising Association (IMPAA), which established a code. "The passing of the advertising code in June 1930 exists within the larger context of pressure groups and threats of national censorship. This code followed the March 1930 reformation of the industry's production code for film content" (15). But these codes lasted only a decade and were eventually replaced in the 1950s with the spread of statistical marketing analysis and more narrow audience targeting and specific strategy for any one particular film.

12. John Sinclair, *Images Incorporated: Advertising as Industry and Ideology* (London: Croom Helm, 1987), 2.

13. Richard Fox and T. J. Lears, *Culture of Consumption* (New York: Pantheon Books, 1983), xii.

14. Ibid.

15. Judith Williamson, *Decoding Advertising: Ideology and Meaning in Advertising* (New York: Marion Boyars, 1988), 13.

16. The national and international propaganda battles of that war, however, also demonstrated the power of promotional media, particularly when joined with the entertainment potential of sound film, whether documentary or fiction.

17. William Manchester, *The Glory and the Dream* (Boston: Little, Brown, 1974), 593.

18. Ibid.

19. John Kenneth Galbraith, *The Affluent Society* (Boston: Houghton Mifflin, 1958), 127.

20. Vic's rescue from the coarseness of American enterprise by a British woman also goes against the grain of the times, since America was inclined to see itself as the primary military-industrial savior of Western Europe.

21. David Potter, *People of Plenty: Economic Abundance and the American Character* (Chicago: University of Chicago Press, 1954), 167.

22. Ibid., 125.

23. Raymond Williams, *Problems in Materialism and Culture* (London: Verso, 1980), 191.

24. Ibid.

25. William Leiss, S. Kline, and S. Jhally, *Social Communication in Advertising* (New York: Methuen, 1986), 124.

26. Ewen, 171.

27. Jhally, 135.

28. Williams, *Problems in Materialism and Culture,* 190.

29. Christopher Lasch, *The Culture of Narcissism* (New York: W. W. Norton, 1978), 72.

30. Ibid.

31. Hitchcock's *Vertigo* (1958) could also be included here, since its protagonist's (Scotty's) construction of the desired female image is almost the exact opposite of Thornhill's own deconstruction by the forces associated initially with Eve Kendall.

32. Stanley Cavell, "*North by Northwest,*" in *A Hitchcock Reader,* ed. Marshall Deutelbaum and Leland Poague (Ames: Iowa State University Press, 1986), 253.

33. Washington, Jefferson, and Lincoln are prominently featured on Mount Rushmore, with Teddy Roosevelt appearing almost as an afterthought.

34. Advertising becomes a form of romantic or marital competition in *Lover Come Back* and *The Thrill of It All,* which furthers the sense of promotions as a game.

35. Leiss, Kline, and Jhally, 304–5.

36. Richard Schickel, *Intimate Strangers* (New York: Doubleday, 1985), 288.

37. Ewen, 220.

38. Paul du Gay, "Organizing Identity," in *Questions of Cultural Identity,* ed. Stuart Hall and Paul du Gay (London: Sage, 1996), 154.

39. See also Paul du Gay, *Consumption and Identity at Work* (London: Sage, 1996), 60–61.

40. Ibid., 163. A dark comic version of this ethical split is also provided in the British film *How to Get Ahead in Advertising* (1989). This is a very talky doppelgänger story where the exploitative advertiser who began as a large boil on the reluctant advertiser's neck grows to take him over except for the little boil of a reluctant advertiser that is left on the exploiter's neck. The commercial disease of moral (commodity) absolutism, then, has become dominant.

41. Ron Howard's *Gung Ho* (1986) also plays on the theme of renewal through a recovery of a ground of past indentity and meaning. The setting is America's dying Rust Belt auto industry. In response to a car assembly plant's closing, the former assembly-line manager (Michael Keaton) manages to recruit Japanese owner investment and the plant is reopened. But the experiment is a failure until the American workers adjust to the culture of their new administration and relearn their lost commitment to teamwork and pride in their joint effort.

42. This theme is taken up by Randy Martin (ed.) in *Chalk Lines: The Politics of Work in the Managed University* (Durham, N.C.: Duke University Press, 1998). He finds what he calls "the onslaught of managerialism" continuing to gain ground in higher education. He notes the demise of a common dedication to a cause of social uplift in conjunction with the increased pressure for profitability placed on individuals within universities, whose traditional charge once had a very different intent: "The sense of a life-enhancing project beyond sheer employment used to be captured by the term 'career'. Displacement and downsizing give a cynical cast to such claims. All the more reason, then, to think of education as a kind of ongoing surplus, a sense of what's left over when the demand for production has been met" (12–13).

43. *Independence Day* (1996), for example, had a production cost of $76 million and a promotional cost of $76 million.

44. Stuart Ewen and Elizabeth Ewen, *Channels of Desire: Mass Images and the Shaping of American Consciousness* (Minneapolis: University of Minnesota Press, 1992), 190, 193.

45. John Tomlinson, *Cultural Imperialism* (Baltimore: Johns Hopkins University Press, 1991), 106.

46. In professional sports, team profits are dependent on television market exposure, which also helps create individual stars and inflated athlete contracts garnered by hard-bargaining agents. TV exposure continues to inflate the cost of entertainment and alter the nature of the sports experience for athletes and fans alike. The pressures in such a world where the media reign both off and on the field direct attention to commercial rather than purely athletic priorities.

47. Jhally, 203.

CHAPTER 5

1. See Margaret Morse, *Virtualities* (Bloomington: Indiana University Press, 1998), 4. Morse notes the process currently under way of television's integration into computer-based electronic networks representing "the far greater complexities of a post-industrial and post-national sociopolitical information economy. The economy is now the excuse or the occasion for a wrenching restructuring of the workforce that both displaces some people and brings others together electronically—but only as they are separated from each other in physical space."

See also John Caldwell's *Televisuality: Style, Crisis, and Authority in American Television* (New Brunswick, N.J.: Rutgers University Press, 1995). Caldwell notes mainstream television's excessive electronic stylization as a response in the 1980s to the threat of video and cable encroachment.

2. Sherry Turkle, *Life on the Screen: Identity in the Age of the Internet* (New York: Simon and Schuster, 1995), 268.

3. Ellen Seiter, "Television and the Internet," in *Electronic Media and Techno-culture,* ed. John Thornton Caldwell (New Brunswick, N.J.: Rutgers University Press, 2000), 228.

4. Ibid., 229.

5. Ibid. Seiter also references here a 1997 article in French by D. Schiller.

6. M. Carnoy et al., *The New Global Economy in the Information Age* (University Park: Pennsylvania State University Press, 1993), 5.

7. Robert D. Putnam, *Bowling Alone* (New York: Simon and Schuster, 2000), 411. Putnam also expresses the hope that new technology might somehow reinforce new possibilities for active social engagement, particularly at the grassroots community level.

8. Douglas Kellner, *Media Culture* (New York: Routledge, 1995), 18.

9. These new data have just been published by the Annenberg Public Policy Center of the University of Pennsylvania. The original title of one of the four reports for the annual Conference on Children and Television was changed from "Television in the Home" to "Media in the Home," given the fact that the number of computer homes with Internet access has doubled since 1996. The report is based on a national random television survey in April–May, 1999 of parents of children aged 2 to 17 and a random sample of their 10- to 17-year-old children in homes with TVs. See Bob Dart, "U.S. Kids Clock 4½ Hours Daily Screen Time," *Atlanta Constitution,* June 28, 1999, A1.

At the production end of the high-tech revolution is the job picture. The Information Technology Association of America reports that high-tech companies have more than 842,328 unfilled jobs nationally against a national unemployment rate of only 4 percent. See Peralte C. Paul, "Firms Offer Stock Options to Lure Interns Back," *Atlanta Constitution,* August 1, 2000.

10. In addition to hours logged in front of the TV, the *Atlanta Constitution* (June 28, 2000) reports a Gallup poll finding that the average American worker receives 202 messages each day. This seems exaggerated, but the number is reached through the following combination: 52 telephone calls; 36 e-mails; 23 voice-mails; 18 pieces of interoffice mail; 18 pieces of U.S. mail; and 14 faxes.

Along with these trends is the coming of HDTV and the replacement of celluloid motion picture film with digital formats and projectors, which will alter movie exhibition in the next few years. These developments, including cell phone and other wireless transmissions, all point to the complete integration and sophistication of a digital domain of electronic simulation.

11. Hollywood cinema, of course—a grandparent to precocious television and almost 50 years ahead of it in time—initially reacted to TV in a defensive, competitive way. But this attitude did not persist because of TV's similar entertainment function and lucrative cash potential. In addition to the film industry's rapid mergers with TV in the areas of studio production, distribution, and sales,

television has in turn advertised, reviewed, and broadcast Hollywood films, and provided an outlet for videotaping and display. A fine example of Hollywood's competitive reaction to TV is apparent in the opening section of *Will Success Spoil Rock Hunter?* (1957).

12. See Chapter 1.

13. McLuhan is mainly remembered for popularizing the phrase "The medium is the message" in his widely read *Understanding Media* (1964). The academic work of TV media scholars soon to follow such as Raymond Williams is more astute and significant. Both expanded the public's appreciation of television's growing impact on culture. Williams's work falls into the larger Frankfurt school tradition of culture critique, even as he sought to modify some of its high culture/low culture perspective. See Williams's *Television: Technology and Cultural Form* (New York: Schocken Books, 1975).

14. Perhaps taking their cue from Judy Holliday's role as a dizzy self-promoter in *It Should Happen to You* (1954), consider the Doris Day vehicles *Lover Come Back* (1961) and *The Thrill of It All* (1963). In all of these texts, including Jack Lemmon's *Good Neighbor Sam* (1964), TV and advertising are collapsed together as a kind of joke tied to sexual and romantic confusion.

15. The real Dan Enright was forced to leave TV for a while, but according to the closing film titles, NBC eventually brought him back as a producer. It is far more difficult to pin down corporations for crimes than individuals. See Marshall B. Clinard and Peter C. Yeager, *Corporate Crime* (New York: Free Press, 1980). Considering the commercial bias of TV, Douglas Kellner notes in *Media Culture* (New York: Routledge, 1995) that "only in the United States is television so free from accountability to the public and government."

16. See Williams, *Television: Technology and Cultural Form*. See also the work of Stuart Hall et al., *Culture, Media, Language* (London: Hutchinson, 1980), and Todd Gitlin, particularly the latter's *Inside Prime Time* (New York: Pantheon Books, 1983).

17. Herbert Marcuse, *One-Dimensional Man* (Boston: Beacon Press, 1964), 57.

18. Guy Debord, *Society of the Spectacle* (Detroit: Black and Red, 1983), item #1 in Chapter 1.

19. Jean Baudrillard, *Simulations* (New York: Semiotext[e], 1983).

20. Stephen R. Granbard's comment appears in his book, *Mr. Bush's War: Adventures in the Politics of Illusion* (New York: Hill and Wang, 1992). His claims are supported by another article cited by Larry Beinhart in the *Nation* (May 11, 1992) and entitled "Pentagon-Media Presents—The Gulf War as Total Television." Beinhart also cites the wide gap in the military forces of the United States. compared to Iraq, which assured a brief conflict with minimal American casualties and victory important for political popularity. President Bush's approval ratings soared during and immediately after the nation's videowar experience, but they did not hold up through his reelection bid 20 months later, perhaps indicating more of a problem with his timing of the war than with its planned political efficacy. Bush's failure to gain reelection is widely believed to be due in large part to the incontrovertible evidence of a troubled, debt-ridden economy.

21. Something like this apparently happened to a U.S. soldier in Bosnia, who ate bugs to survive before he was discovered and returned home.

22. Stuart Ewen and Elizabeth Ewen, *Channels of Desire: Mass Images and the Shaping of American Consciousness* (Minneapolis: University of Minnesota Press, 1992), 215–16.

23. Neil Postman, *Amusing Ourselves to Death: Public Discourse in the Age of Show Business* (New York: Penguin Books, 1985), 126.

24. Recent data suggest that candidates for president in the year 2000 required a minimum of $22 million just to carry out a serious campaign for a major-party nomination. See article by Andrew Mollison in *The Atlanta Journal-Constitution,* December 27, 1998, A12.

Another article in the same paper a day later is taken from Jonathan D. Salant of the Associated Press: "At least 94 House candidates in 76 districts broke the $1 million spending barrier, according to the latest Federal Election Commission reports covering January 1, 1997, through this past November 23. . . . Big spending . . . scored a winning record. Seventy-eight percent of those who reported spending $1 million on their campaign ended up winning the race."

25. Lumet's plot emphasizes the gradual transformation of a ruthless spin doctor (Richard Gere) into one who begins actually to care about the ethics of the candidates he chooses to represent. While everyone may have some level of corruptibility where so much money and image control are being waged, the film asserts that the spin doctor can still locate his own professional ethics and thus his choice of causes. *Power* suggests rather optimistically in its romantic conclusion that good ethics are still maintainable in the vortex of political spin, and can still mean victory for the best candidate in the ongoing culture wars fought out on television.

26. In his review of this contemporary film, popular journalist Roger Ebert simply concludes that it "is about how we've all become stooges of the media, and about the lack of privacy in the U.S." His review of *Wag the Dog* appears in the *Chicago Sun-Times,* July 8, 1998, accessible online at <www.suntimes.com/ebert/ebertser.html>.

27. It has been convincingly shown that television not only disorients its viewers' sense of reality but inhibits personal and political interaction. In his review of an exhaustive survey on TV viewing, Michael Morgan concluded that it promotes alienation, complacency, and passivity while reducing social as well as political participation, including voting. Television "bombards audiences with images of the 'good life' and the benefits of consumption [which] is more conducive to depoliticization than to activism." Michael Morgan, "Television and Democracy," in *Cultural Politics in Contemporary America,* ed. Ian Angus and Sut Jhally (New York: Routledge, 1980).

28. Democratic political figures such as Jack and Bobby Kennedy and Martin Luther King Jr. have been the victims of assassination in America rather than the perpetrators of it. But this is a minor historical inaccuracy in a film that otherwise highlights some of the ways American politics has embraced the powers of commercial popular entertainment and made it a tool of image and influence.

29. Kellner, 237.

30. Carnoy et al., 6.

31. Dean Alger, *Megamedia: How Giant Corporations Dominate Mass Media, Distort Competition, and Endanger Democracy* (Lanham, Md.: Rowan and Littlefield, 1998), 219–20. Alger includes a quote from *New York Times* editor Gene Roberts, which he also applies to the broadcast news media: "It is time, high time, that newspaper corporations become subjects of debate and be held accountable for covering the communities they serve. Meanwhile, many are managing their newspapers like chain shoe stores, with no sense of being important community institutions with highly important responsibilities to the public." Gene Roberts, "Corporate Journalism and Community Service," *Media Studies Journal* 10, no. 2–3 (spring–summer 1996): 107.

32. See Henri Lefebvre, "Space: Social Product and Use Value," in *Critical Sociology: European Perspectives,* ed. J. W. Feinberg (New York: Irvington, 1979).

33. In this sense Truman mimics most fictional main characters on prime-time TV programs, who are meant to be appealing. Program sponsors of dramatic as opposed to comic material generally avoid characters and situations that might prove too controversial and thereby create problematic associations for their products (as with the *Twenty-One* program in *Quiz Show*). Hal Himmelstein has noted that commercial broadcast network television prefers to "avoid the overtly threatening." *Television Myth and the American Mind* (Westport, Conn.; Praeger, 1994), 159.

34. Mark Crispin Miller, *Boxed In: The Culture of TV* (Evanston, Ill.: Northwestern University Press, 1988), 327.

35. Ibid.

36. Arthur Kroker and David Cook, *The Postmodern Scene* (New York: St. Martin's Press, 1988), 268. See also Fredric Jameson, "Post-modernism: The Cultural Logic of Capitalism," *New Left Review,* no. 146 (July–August, 1984).

37. Anthony Giddens, *Modernity and Self-Identity* (Stanford: Stanford University Press, 1991), 198.

38. See, for example, John Fiske, *Television Culture* (New York: Methuen, 1987); Stuart Hall, *Representation* (London: Sage/The Open University, 1997); and Paul du Gay, ed., *Production of Culture/Cultures of Production* (London: Sage/The Open University, 1997).

39. George Gerbner, *Invisible Crisis: What Conglomerate Control of Media Means for America* (Boulder, Colo.: Westview Press, 1996. See Dean Alger on the U.S. Telecommunications Act of 1996 in *Megamedia,* 103: "Thus, an extraordinary amount of the scarce broadcast spectrum—which has long been recognized as public airwaves—was given away to existing TV station owners, most of whom are huge national corporations, allowing them to use multiple channels for electronic business in addition to their TV broadcasts." Commercial television therefore has only the slightest accountability to the American electorate at large, and the only alternative to it is the grossly underfunded and increasingly commercial and politicized sector of public television.

40. See Vincent Mosco, *The Political Economy of Communication* (London: Sage,

1996): "It remains the case that the largest transnational media firms retain a base in one generally identified nation. Nevertheless, they are increasingly able to use the genuine multinational dimensions of their product, marketing, labor, and financing to transcend the legal, regulatory, cultural, and financial constraints of their home base" (179).

41. For more on this overall tendency, see Paul du Gay, *Production of Culture/Cultures of Production* (London: Sage/The Open University, 1997).

42. Stuart Hall and Paul du Gay, *Questions of Cultural Identity* (London: Sage, 1996), 99.

Roger Ebert's online review for the *Chicago Sun-Times* mentions the following: "If you think "The Truman Show" is an exaggeration, reflect that Princess Diana lived under similar conditions from the day she became engaged to Charles." Diana's circumstance reflects the condition of celebrity fixation and the public's need for live media heroes, which is only a part of the much larger and seductive condition of televirtuality. Ebert's comment about Princess Diana's experience actually seems more directly relevant to Ed's in *Ed TV.*

43. Paul du Gay, *Consumption and Identity at Work* (London: Sage, 1996), 79.

44. Marcuse, 72.

45. Julia Kristeva, *New Maladies of the Soul* (New York: Columbia University Press, 1996).

46. See Arthur Kroker and Michael A. Weinstein, *Data Trash: The Theory of the Virtual Class* (New York: St. Martin's Press, 1994). Historically, it is also interesting to look back on psychological theorist William James. Living at the height of the industrial age at the turn of the twentieth century, he saw the extension of the human body into mechanization as harming the individual psychically and physically with specialized, repetitively overused body functions. He stressed the need for balanced body and body-and-mind usage for a healthy sense of reality. William James, *Principles of Psychology* (Cambridge: Harvard University Press, [1890] 1996); see Chapter 10.

Even more significantly today, as the narrow sensory input of the eyes and ears common to electronic media experience becomes more dominant over time, the psychic mechanism may also become less astute at distinguishing projected, mediated experience from actual direct real-world interactivity. Evidence of this is already increasingly plentiful, and some of the consequences have been deadly, as in auto accidents resulting from cell phone use. See also Thomas Elsaesser's "TV through the Looking Glass" in *American Television,* ed. Nick Browne (Langhorne, Penn.: Harwood Academic Publishers, 1994), 116. See also Giddens's *Modernity and Self-Identity.*

47. See note 19. Because Truman Burbank is born without any possibility of forming a "coherent subject position," he exemplifies the forced quality of televirtuality more than its seductive side. Baudrillard would insist on simulacra seduction as the dominant characteristic.

48. This is the closing sentence in Bill Nichols's much anthologized "The Work of Culture in the Age of Cybernetic Systems," which originally appeared in *Screen* 29, no. 1 (winter 1988).

CONCLUSION

1. See Tamar Lewin, "Working Moms Push Dual-Income Families to Majority," *Atlanta Constitution,* November 6, 2000.

2. Rick Altman, *Film/Genre* (London: British Film Institute, 1999), 194.

3. An example of the lack of political resolve regarding the drawing down of natural resources and environmental degradation is the perennial refusal in Congress to require that the cars on which so many Americans depend in their working life be made more fuel-efficient and cleaner operating.

BIBLIOGRAPHY

Adorno, Theodor, and Max Horkheimer. *Dialectics of Enlightenment*. London: Verso, reprinted 1979.

Alger, Dean. *Megamedia: How Giant Corporations Dominate Mass Media, Distort Competition, and Endanger Democracy*. Lanham, Md.: Rowan and Littlefield, 1998.

Althusser, Louis. "Ideology and Ideological State Apparatuses." In *Lenin and Philosophy*, translated by Ben Brewster. New York: Monthly Review Press, 1971.

Altman, Rick. *Film/Genre*. London: British Film Institute, 1999.

Anderson, Christopher. "Hollywood in the Home: TV and the End of the Studio System." In *Modernity and Mass Culture*, edited by James Naremore and Patrick Brantlinger. Bloomington: Indiana University Press, 1991.

Bailin, Rebecca. "Feminist Readership, Violence, and *Marnie*." *Film Reader* 5. Northwestern University, 1982.

Basinger, Jeanine. *A Woman's View*. Hanover, N.H.: Wesleyan University Press, 1993.

Baudrillard, Jean. *Selected Writings*. Edited by Mark Poster. Stanford: Stanford University Press, 1988.

———. *Simulations*. New York: Semiotext[e], 1983.

Beinhart, Larry. *American Hero*. New York: Ballantine Books, 1993.

Biskind, Peter. *Seeing Is Believing*. New York: Pantheon Books, 1983.

Boozer, Jack. "*Blade Runner:* Crashing the Gates of Insight." In *Retrofitting Blade Runner*, edited by Judith Kerman. Bowling Green, Ohio: Popular Press, 1991.

———. "*Wall Street:* The Commodification of Perception." *Journal of Popular Film and Television* 17, no. 3 (fall 1989).

Bordwell, David, Janet Staiger, and Kristin Thompson. *The Classical Hollywood Cinema: Film Style & Mode of Production to 1960*. New York: Columbia University Press, 1985.

Browne, Nick, ed. *Refiguring American Film Genres.* Berkeley: University of California Press, 1998.

Byars, Jackie. *All That Hollywood Allows.* Chapel Hill: University of North Carolina Press, 1991.

Caldwell, John. *Televisuality: Style, Crisis, and Authority in American Television.* New Brunswick, N.J.: Rutgers University Press, 1995.

Capra, Frank. *The Name above the Title.* New York: Macmillan, 1971.

Carnoy, M., et al. *The New Global Economy in the Information Age.* University Park: Pennsylvania State University Press, 1993.

Cavell, Stanley. "North by Northwest." In *A Hitchcock Reader,* edited by Marshall Deutelbaum and Leland Poague. Ames: Iowa State University Press, 1986.

Cawelti, John. "*Chinatown* and Generic Transformation in Recent American Films." In *Film Theory and Criticism,* edited by Gerald Mast, Marshall Cohen, and Leo Braudy. 4th ed. New York: Oxford University Press, 1992.

Chase, Stuart, and F. J. Schlink. *Your Money's Worth.* New York: Macmillan, 1927.

Chodorow, Nancy. *The Reproduction of Mothering: Psychoanalysis and the Sociology of Gender.* Berkeley: University of California Press, 1978.

Clark, Larry. "*Tucker: The Man and His Dream:* A Look behind the Scenes." <www.tuckerclub.org/tuckmov.html>.

Clinard, Marshall B., and Peter C. Yeager. *Corporate Crime.* New York: Free Press, 1980.

Cook, David A. *A History of Narrative Film.* New York: W. W. Norton, 1996.

Creed, Barbara. "Horror and the Monstrous-Feminine—An Imaginary Abjection." *Screen* 27, no. 1 (January–February 1986).

Crichton, Michael. *Disclosure.* New York: Ballantine Books, 1993.

Dart, Bob. "U.S. Kids Clock 4½ Hours Daily Screen Time." *Atlanta Constitution,* June 28, 1999, A1.

Debord, Guy. *Society of the Spectacle.* Detroit: Black and Red, 1983.

Desjardin, Mary. "*Baby Boom:* The Comedy of Surrogacy in Film and Television." *Velvet Light Trap* 29. (spring 1992).

Doane, Mary Ann. *Femmes Fatales.* New York: Routledge, 1991.

du Gay, Paul. *Consumption and Identity at Work.* London: Sage, 1996.

———, ed. *Production of Culture/Cultures of Production.* London: Sage/The Open University, 1997.

Dugger, William M. *Corporate Hegemony.* New York: Greenwood Press, 1989.

Ebert, Roger. Review of *Wag the Dog. Chicago Sun-Times,* July 8, 1998.

Ehrenreich, Barbara, and Deirdre English. *For Her Own Good: 150 Years of the Experts' Advice to Women.* New York: Anchor Press, 1978.

Ehrenreich, Barbara. *Fear of Falling.* New York: Pantheon Books, 1989.

Elsaesser, Thomas. "Tales of Sound and Fury: Observations on the Family Melodrama." In *Film Theory and Criticism,* edited by Gerald Mast, Marshall Cohen, and Leo Braudy. 4th ed. New York: Oxford University Press, 1992.

———. "TV through the Looking Glass." In *American Television,* edited by Nick Browne. Langhorne, Penn.: Harwood Academic Publishers, 1994.

Esslin, Martin. "Aristotle and the Advertisers: The Television Commercial Considered as a Form of Drama." In *Television: The Critical View,* edited by H. Newcomb. New York: Oxford University Press, 1976.

Ewen, Stuart. *Captains of Consciousness: Advertising and the Social Roots of the Consumer Culture.* New York: McGraw-Hill, 1976.

Ewen, Stuart, and Elizabeth Ewen. *Channels of Desire: Mass Images and the Shaping of American Consciousness.* Minneapolis: University of Minnesota Press, 1992.

Faludi, Susan. *Stiffed: The Betrayal of the American Man.* New York: Morrow, 1999.

Fiske, John. *Television Culture.* New York: Methuen, 1987.

Fox, Richard, and T. J. Lears. *Culture of Consumption.* New York: Pantheon Books, 1983.

Frosh, Stephen. *The Politics of Psychoanalysis.* New Haven: Yale University Press, 1987.

Galbraith, John Kenneth. *The Affluent Society.* Boston: Houghton Mifflin, 1958.

———. *The New Industrial State.* Boston: Houghton Mifflin, 1971.

Gerbner, George. *Invisible Crisis: What Conglomerate Control of Media Means for America.* Boulder, Colo.: Westview Press, 1996.

Giddens, Anthony. *Modernity and Self-Identity.* Stanford: Stanford University Press, 1991.

Gitlin, Todd. *Inside Prime Time.* New York: Pantheon Books, 1983.

Gledhill, Christine. "*Klute* 2: Feminism and *Klute.*" In *Women in Film Noir,* edited by E. Ann Kaplan. London: British Film Institute, 1978.

Godden, Richard. *Fictions of Capital.* New York: Cambridge University Press, 1990.

Granbard, Stephen R. *Mr. Bush's War: Adventures in the Politics of Illusion.* New York: Hill and Wang, 1992.

Hall, Stuart. *Representation.* London: Sage/The Open University, 1997.

Hall, Stuart, et al. *Culture, Media, Language.* London: Hutchinson, 1980.

Hall, Stuart, and Paul du Gay. *Questions of Cultural Identity.* London: Sage, 1996.

Hartmann, Heidi. "The Family as the Locus of Gender, Class, and Political Struggle: The Example of Housework." *Signs* 6, no. 3 (spring 1981).

Haskell, Molly. *From Reverence to Rape.* Baltimore: Penguin Books, 1973.

Herman, Edward S. *Corporate Control, Corporate Power.* Cambridge: Cambridge University Press, 1981.

Himmelstein, Hal. *Television Myth and the American Mind.* Westport, Conn.: Praeger, 1994.

Holmlund, Chris. "Cruisin' for a Bruisin': Hollywood's Deadly (Lesbian) Dolls." *Cinema Journal* 34, no. 1 (1994).

Huyssen, Andreas. *After the Great Divide.* Bloomington: Indiana University Press, 1986.

James, William. *Principles of Psychology.* 1890. Reprint, Cambridge: Harvard University Press, 1996.

Jameson, Fredric. "Post-Modernism and Consumer Society." In *The Anti-Aesthetic,* edited by Hal Foster. Port Townsen, Wash.: Bay Press, 1983.

———. "Post-Modernism: The Cultural Logic of Capitalism." *New Left Review,* no. 146 (July–August 1984).

Jhally, Sut. *The Codes of Advertising: Fetishism and the Political Economy of Meaning in the Consumer Society.* New York: St. Martin's Press, 1987.

Kaplan, E. Ann. *Motherhood and Representation.* New York: Routledge, 1992.

Kellner, Douglas. *Media Culture.* New York: Routledge, 1995.

Kristeva, Julia. *New Maladies of the Soul.* New York: Columbia University Press, 1996.

Kroker, Arthur, and David Cook. *The Postmodern Scene.* New York: St. Martin's Press, 1988.

Kroker, Arthur, and Michael A. Weinstein. *Data Trash: The Theory of the Virtual Class.* New York: St. Martin's Press, 1994.

Landy, Marcia. *Imitations of Life.* Detroit: Wayne State University Press, 1991.

Lasch, Christopher. *The Culture of Narcissism.* New York: W. W. Norton, 1978.

LaValley, Albert J. *Mildred Pierce.* Madison: University of Wisconsin Press, 1980.

Lefebvre, Henri. "Space: Social Product and Use Value." In *Critical Sociology: European Perspectives,* edited by J. W. Feinberg. New York: Irvington, 1979.

Leiss, William, S. Kline, and S. Jhally. *Social Communication in Advertising.* New York: Methuen, 1986.

Lesage, Julia. "The Hegemonic Female Fantasy in *An Unmarried Woman* and *Craig's Wife.*" *Film Reader* 5. 1982.

Lopez, Ana. "Are All Latins from Manhattan? Hollywood, Ethnography, and Cultural Colonialism." In *Unspeakable Images: Ethnicity and the American Cinema,* edited by Lester Friedman. Urbana: University of Illinois Press, 1991.

Lyotard, Jean-Francois. *The Postmodern Condition: A Report on Knowledge.* Minneapolis: University of Minnesota Press, 1987.

Maccoby, Michael. *The Leader: A New Face for American Management.* New York: Ballantine Books, 1981.

McLuhan, Marshall. *Understanding Media.* New York: McGraw-Hill, 1964.

McVeagh, John. *Tradeful Merchants.* Boston: Routledge and Kegan Paul, 1981.

Manchester, William. *The Glory and the Dream.* Boston: Little, Brown, 1974.

Marchetti, Gina. "Ethnicity, the Cinema, and Cultural Studies." In *Unspeakable Images: Ethnicity and the American Cinema,* edited by Lester Friedman. Urbana: University of Illinois Press, 1991.

Marcuse, Herbert. *One-Dimensional Man.* Boston: Beacon Press, 1964.

Martin, Randy, ed. *Chalk Lines: The Politics of Work in the Managed University.* Durham, N.C.: Duke University Press, 1998.

Mason, Edward S., ed. *The Corporation in Modern America.* Cambridge: Harvard University Press, 1959.

Miller, Mark Crispin. *Boxed In: The Culture of TV.* Evanston, Ill.: Northwestern University Press, 1988.

Mills, C. Wright. *The Power Elite.* New York: Oxford University Press, 1956.

———. *White Collar.* New York: Oxford University Press, 1953.

Mitchell, Juliet. *Psychoanalysis and Feminism.* London: Lane, 1974.

Morgan, Michael. "Television and Democracy." In *Cultural Politics in Contemporary America,* edited by Ian Angus and Sut Jhally. New York: Routledge, 1980.

Morse, Margaret. *Virtualities.* Bloomington: Indiana University Press, 1988.

Mosco, Vincent. *The Political Economy of Communication.* London: Sage, 1996.

Mulvey, Laura. "Visual Pleasure and Narrative Cinema." In *Film Theory and Criticism,* edited by Gerald Mast, Marshall Cohen, and Leo Braudy. 4th ed. New York: Oxford University Press, 1992.

Nowell-Smith, Geoffrey. "Minnelli and Melodrama." In *Imitations of Life,* edited by Marcia Landy. Detroit: Wayne State University Press, 1991.

Packard, Vance. *The Pyramid Climbers.* New York: McGraw-Hill, 1962.

Palmer, R. Barton. *Hollywood's Dark Cinema: The American Film Noir.* New York: Twayne Publishers, 1994.

Paul, Peralte C. "Firms Offer Stock Options to Lure Interns Back." *Atlanta Constitution,* August 1, 2000.

Pells, Richard H. *The Liberal Mind in a Conservative Age.* New York: Harper and Row, 1985.

Pfeil, Fred. *White Guys: Studies in Postmodern Domination and Difference.* New York: Verso, 1995.

Piso, Michelle. "Mark's Marnie." In *A Hitchcock Reader,* edited by Marshall Deutelbaum and Leland Poague. Ames: Iowa State University Press, 1986.

Place, Janey. "Women in Film Noir." In *Women in Film Noir,* edited by E. Ann Kaplan. London: British Film Institute, 1978.

Polan, Dana. *Power and Paranoia: History, Narrative, and the American Cinema, 1940–1950.* New York: Columbia University Press, 1986.

Postman, Neil. *Amusing Ourselves to Death: Public Discourse in the Age of Show Business.* New York: Penguin Books, 1985.

Potter, David. *People of Plenty: Economic Abundance and the American Character.* Chicago: University of Chicago Press, 1954.

Putnam, Robert D. *Bowling Alone.* New York: Simon and Schuster, 2000.

Riesman, David. *The Lonely Crowd.* New Haven: Yale University Press, 1950.

Roberts, Gene. "Corporate Journalism and Community Service." *Media Studies Journal* 10, no. 2–3 (spring–summer 1996).

Rodowick, David N. *The New Industrial State.* Boston: Houghton Mifflin, 1971.

———. "Madness, Authority, and Ideology: The Domestic Melodrama of the 1950s." In *Home Is Where the Heart Is,* edited by Christine Gledhill. London: British Film Institute, 1987.

Rogin, Michael. "Kiss Me Deadly: Communism, Motherhood, and Cold War Movies." *Representations* 6 (spring 1984).

Schatz, Thomas. *Hollywood Genres.* New York: McGraw-Hill, 1981.

Schickel, Richard. *Intimate Strangers.* New York: Doubleday, 1985.

Seiter, Ellen. *Sold Separately.* New Brunswick, N.J.: Rutgers University Press, 1993.

———. *Television and New Media Audiences.* London: Oxford University Press, 1999.

———. "Television and the Internet." In *Electronic Media and Technoculture,* edited by John Thornton Caldwell. New Brunswick, N.J.: Rutgers University Press, 2000.

Sennett, Richard. *The Corrosion of Character: The Personal Consequences of Work in the New Capitalism.* New York: W. W. Norton, 1998.

Sinclair, John. *Images Incorporated: Advertising as Industry and Ideology*. London: Croom Helm, 1987.

Staiger, Janet. "Announcing Wares, Winning Patrons, Voicing Ideals: Thinking about the History and Theory of Film Advertising." *Cinema Journal* 29, no. 3 (spring 1990).

Stam, Robert. *Film Theory: An Introduction*. Malden, Mass.: Blackwell Publishers, 2000.

Tomlinson, John. *Cultural Imperialism*. Baltimore: Johns Hopkins University Press, 1991.

Traube, Elizabeth. *Dreaming Identities: Class, Gender and Generation in 1980s Hollywood Movies*. Boulder, Colo.: Westview Press, 1992.

Turkle, Sherry. *Life on the Screen: Identity in the Age of the Internet*. New York: Simon and Schuster, 1995.

Van Horn, Susan. *Women, Work, and Fertility, 1900–1986*. New York: New York University Press, 1988.

Weiss, Richard. *The American Myth of Success*. New York: Basic Books, 1969.

Whyte, William. *The Organization Man*. New York: Simon and Schuster, 1956.

Williams, Raymond. *Problems in Materialism and Culture*. London: Verso, 1980.

———. *Television: Technology and Cultural Form*. New York: Schocken Books, 1975.

Williamson, Judith. *Decoding Advertising: Ideology and Meaning in Advertising*. New York: Marion Boyars, 1988.

Wills, Garry. *Reagan's America*. Garden City, N.Y.: Doubleday, 1987.

Wood, Robin. *Hollywood from Vietnam to Reagan*. New York: Columbia University Press, 1986.

Zaniello, Tom. *Working Stiffs, Union Maids, Reds, and Riffraff*. Ithaca, N.Y.: ILR Press, 1996.

INDEX

57, 60, 64–65, 69, 71, 79, 81, 83,
  87, 89, 101, 108, 133, 135
differences, 123, 141
division, 117
executive, 20, 22, 41, 45, 47
middle, 27–28, 31–32, 36–37, 39, 42–
  44, 51–53, 60, 63, 65, 69, 73–74,
  76–77, 88, 106, 112, 124, 132, 140
mobility, 126, 129, 134
stability, 140
working class, 44, 71, 73, 107, 133
Class Action (Apted), 48, 78
Classical Corporate executive film, v,
  18–49
and family, 21
mythological model of culture, 22,
  146
Coal Miner's Daughter (Apted), 70
Cold War, 35, 37, 58, 69, 124, 175–176
Commercialism, 9, 44, 54, 79, 84,
  92–93, 108, 134, 141, 143–144, 180
Commercial Objectification, 44, 54, 84,
  137, 141, 143–144
Commodity Fetishism, 148, 152, 172
and power, 180
Commodity Reification, 30, 124
Consumerism, 1, 5, 7–9, 16–19, 31–32,
  37, 39–40, 43, 45–47, 49, 52–53, 63–
  64, 74, 77, 80, 86–87, 92–93, 102, 115,
  123, 134, 140, 144
as codependent pathology, 185
confers prestige, 171
contradictions in ideals, 165
culture of, 15
as democratic ideal, 153
dependent on media signification, 156
as discourse, 11
as expression of identity, 164
ideology, 137
promotional, 5
trends, 16, 63–64
Coppola, Francis Ford, 6, 91, 104–106
Corporate Business Film, 14, 22, 50, 108
Corporate Culture, 1, 35–36, 38, 41, 45,
  49
Corporate Executive Film, 18, 21–23,
  43–44, 46–49

career quest paradigm, 49
Corporate Family Equation, 45
Corporate Hierarchy, 37, 48
and family, 48
corporate liberal films, 38
narrative, 22, 43
Corporate Managerial Ethos, 48
Corporate Nationalism, 34
Corporate Raider, 107
Corporate Successorship Films, 18–19
Crawford, Christina, 58
Crawford, Joan, 58, 62, 68, 81
Creed, Barbara, 84
CrissCross (Menges), 55, 72–73
Cross Creek (Ritt), 70
"Culture Industry," 166
Curtiz, Michael, 54, 80, 89

Damien — Omen II (Taylor), 69
Damned Don't Cry, The (Sherman), 135
Darwinian Business Success, 2, 4, 137,
  141
Darwinian Economics, 46
Day, Doris, 62–64, 109
Death of a Salesman, 7, 12, 106
  1951 film (Benedek), 7–8
  1985 film (Schlorndorff), 7
  play (Miller), 7–8
Decoding Advertising (Williamson), 157, 173
Democratic Idealism, 6
Demon Seed (Cammell), 69
Desk Set (Lang), 45
Digital Age, 110
Disclosure (Levinson), 48, 135, 137–140,
  144–145, 189
  novel (Crighton), 137
Discrimination
  ethnic, 6, 8
  gender, 6, 85–86
Doane, Mary Ann, 123
Do the Right Thing (Lee), 112, 116–118
Domestic melodrama, 21–22, 27, 47
  defined, 21
"double bind," 55–56
  history, 55
Double Indemnity (Wilder), 52, 80, 123,
  125–128

novel (Cain), 80–81, 125
Du Gay, Paul, 10, 187–188, 190, 235
Dugger, William, 37, 49

Einstein, Albert, 45
Eisenhower, Dwight, 35–36, 175
Electric Horseman, The (Pollack), 180, 182
"Engineers and the Price System,"
  (Veblen), 152
Enron Corporation, 5
Entrepreneurial business film, 1, 12,
  14–15, 81, 95–96, 99, 106, 108, 110–111
  comedies, 14, 75, 97, 106
  dramas, 15
  ethnic minorities in, 15, 97, 111–112,
    117–120
  families in, 97, 100–102, 111–114, 116,
    118–120
  immigrants in, 15, 97, 111–120
  women using sex to get ahead, 15,
    61–62, 90, 98, 107–108
Entrepreneurial Femmes Fatales, vi, 15,
  123–134
Entrepreneurialism, 5–6, 11, 14, 19, 23,
  37, 59, 81, 95–96, 102, 105, 112, 188
  ethics, 37
  immigrants and minorities, 97, 111–
    112, 114–115, 118, 122
  small business, 14, 95–96, 100, 102–
    104, 106–107, 111–112, 116–118
  women and, 15, 59, 62, 81, 96, 108,
    129, 131–132, 135–37, 140–141
Entrepreneurialization of Employment,
  183
"Entrepreneurial Organizational Governance," 187
  company devotion as substitute
    meaning, 188
  private moral absolutism, 188
  pseudo-individuality, 194
  self-promotional extremes, 192
Ephron, Nora, 97, 108–109
Erin Brockovich (Soderbergh), 55, 78–79
Ethics
  business, 115
  corporate success, 6, 27, 37, 39, 67,
    139

entrepreneurial, 37, 101, 107, 114
family-based, 23, 25, 78, 122
government, 67
media, 67
personal, 96
professional, 77–78, 81
Ethnicity, 15, 111. *See also* Family, Entrepreneurialism
Ewen, Stuart, 153, 167, 183
  and Elizabeth Ewen, 183
Executive Promotion, 23
Executive Suite (Wise), 19, 22–26, 28, 31,
  34, 36, 38
  novel (Hawley), 21
Executive Wife, 31
  expectations of, 31–32
Exorcist, The (Friedkin), 68

Face in the Crowd, A (Kazan), 165
Fairbanks, Douglas, 149–150, 156
Family, 21, 23–28, 30, 37–39, 41, 43–45,
  47–49, 55, 57, 63–64, 75, 81, 84, 89,
  95, 99–100, 102, 128
  absence of, 27, 54, 75, 88, 134
  abuse, 129–131
  allegiance, 23, 48, 78, 120
  concerns, 39–40, 75, 98, 129
  corporate advancement and, 45,
    47–48, 50
  decline, 93, 98, 114, 130, 135, 138,
    143
  dependency on the male, 27, 124, 126,
    129
  domestic maternal role, 40, 51–52,
    54–55, 58, 63–64, 66, 129
  domestic paternal role, 40, 42, 51–52,
    54–55, 60, 64, 66, 72, 75, 78, 124,
    129
  ethics, 23, 25
  ethnicity, 112
  ideal nuclear, 52, 56, 61, 64, 85, 90,
    133–34
  immigrant, 113–114
  materialism, 40, 44, 63
  national divorce rate, 43, 50, 66, 70,
    72
  needs, 39, 76